SCRIPTA HIEROSOLYMITANA / VOLUME XXIV

SCRIPTA HIEROSOLYMITANA

PUBLICATIONS OF THE HEBREW UNIVERSITY, JERUSALEM

VOLUME XXIV

STUDIES IN ART

EDITED ON BEHALF OF

THE FACULTY OF HUMANITIES

BY

MOSHE BARASCH

JERUSALEM, 1972

AT THE MAGNES PRESS, THE HEBREW UNIVERSITY

*Distributed in Great Britain, the British Commonwealth
and Europe by the Oxford University Press
P.O.Box 156, London, W. 1 England*

Printed in Israel
At Goldberg Press, Jerusalem

CONTENTS

EDITOR'S FOREWORD

The present volume is a first attempt to present the comparatively young Department of Art History at the Hebrew University as a group. As in the building up and developing of the department no attempt has been made to artificially create a Jerusalem "school" of art history, so in preparing this volume we have not tried to unify the variety of interests, styles and critical approaches of the contributors. Even in the form of references and other particulars of presentation a certain latitude, perhaps not altogether usual in periodicals, has been allowed the authors.

The papers collected in this volume are written by members of the department. Professor Otto Kurz of the Warburg Institute of the University of London has several times been visiting professor at the art history department of the Hebrew University. Professor Moshe Lazar, although a scholar of Romance languages and literatures, took some part in the working of the department, especially in "inter-disciplinary" seminars.

I wish to thank Mrs. Mira Reich who carefully reviewed the style of the English contributions. Mr. Gustav Kühnel shouldered the thankless task of seeing the book through the press.

MOSHE BARASCH

Jerusalem, Oct. 1972

THE LEDA SARCOPHAGUS FROM BETH SHE'ARIM *

M. AVI-YONAH
Hebrew University, Jerusalem

In the late second and early third centuries A.D., Beth-She'arim was the seat of the Jewish patriarch Judah I, who was also buried there. In the following centuries a necropolis grew up around the sepulchre of the sainted patriarch, in which Jews were interred from as far afield as Syria and Arabia. The site of the necropolis was excavated in 1936 and onwards under the direction of Prof. B. Mazar.[1] In the 1938/9 season fragments of a marble sarcophagus, ornamented with reliefs, were found in the debris below the mausoleum built on top of catacomb No. 11.[2] The fragments were transferred to the Palestine Archaeological Museum (the Rockefeller Museum) in 1941; they were put together and displayed in the North Cloister, where they still are. The sarcophagus was registered in the Museum inventory under No. 41.525. The one short side of the coffin which has been fairly well preserved has been published by E. R. Goodenough.[3] The fragmentary long sides have remained unpublished.

The length of the sarcophagus is 92 cms., its width 31 cms. and its height 87.5.[4] The following description is quoted from the Museum catalogue :

"It was covered by a gabled lid with an acroterion at each corner; of the whole lid only one corner piece survives. On the top of the

* This paper is a revised version of one published in Hebrew in *Eretz Israel* 8 (1966), pp. 143–148.
1 I have to thank Prof. B. Mazar for permission to publish this sarcophagus, and the authorities of the Israel Museum for permission to photograph it.
2 B. Maisler: *The Excavations of Beth She'arim (Sheikh Ibreik)*, Jerusalem, 1940, p. 16; id., *Bull. Jew. Palest. Explor. Soc.*, 9 (1942), p. 17; (both in Hebrew); id., *Quart. Dept. Antiq. Palest.* 9 (1941), p. 215. The number of the object in the excavations register is 303.
3 E. R. Goodenough: *Jewish Symbols in the Greco-Roman Period*, New York 1953, Vol. I, pp. 102, 138 f.; Vol. III, No. 456. Copied in B. Kanael: *Die Kunst der antiken Synagoge*, München, 1961, p. 35, Fig. 36.
4 I have to thank the Israel Museum and the Department of Antiquities for placing the details of the catalogue card of the Rockefeller Museum at my disposal.

trough a ridge runs along the inner ledge to take the lid . . . Near the upper edge runs a profiled ornamental double band consisting of a Lesbian cymation and an egg-and-tongue pattern; these bands are partly covered by the main decoration in high relief. Along the lower edge is a small secondary frieze; the only one preserved part of which, below the right edge of the Leda relief, shows a goat nibbling at a plant."

The reliefs have been preserved, more or less completely, on one short side; the second short side is missing except for the left ledge. The upper part of one of the long sides has been preserved; of the other long side only a few fragments have been found, some of which cannot be placed with certainty. The fact that the profiled ornamental double band and the secondary frieze were not continued on the second long side, taken together with its rough execution, indicate that this side was considered less important.

(A)

The well-conserved short side shows a representation of the familiar Greek myth of Leda and Zeus who took the shape of a swan (Fig. 1).

This subject is to be found in Greek art at least from the end of the fifth century onwards, possibly as a result of Euripides' drama "Helena".[5] In the earlier sources, a slightly differing version is given: [6] Zeus, metamorphosed into a swan, pursues the goddess Nemesis. The goddess then gives birth to an egg, from which issue the Dioscuri and Helena; according to this account Leda is only Helena's foster-mother. This variant of the myth was followed by Phidias who, according to Pausanias,[7] carved the frieze of the Temple of Nemesis at Rhamnos in Attica where Leda was shown presenting Helena to Nemesis, her mother. However, in the middle of the fifth century the myth took the more familiar form of Zeus the swan and Leda. According to the usual version Zeus pretended to be fleeing from an eagle (the eagle of Zeus, of course, acting in collusion with his master who had adopted the guise of a swan). The god approached Leda while she was protecting the "swan" from the bird-of-prey. The event was located on the banks of the river Eurotas, in the vicinity of Sparta.

Three different versions of the myth appear in Greek art: (a) The earliest version, which we can trace to the end of the fifth century B.C.,[8] is connected in particular with the name of the sculptor Timo-

5   Euripides: *Helena,* lines 17 ff.
6   Athenaeus VII, 334 c.
7   Pausanias, I, 33, 7.
8   On a fragment of sculpture now in Boston (A. Giuliano in *Enciclopedia dell'Arte*

theus, who made a figure of Leda with the swan about 360 B.C.[9] The best example of the type of representation derived from this statue is to be found in the Capitoline Museum in Rome (Fig. 2). Leda holds the swan, represented in its natural size, with her right hand; while she calms the frightened bird, she lifts her cloak with her left hand to fend off the eagle. Her head is turned upwards and to the left, in the direction of the presumed attack. This statue, which represents the mythical event as something natural, with no metaphysical overtones, is found in numerous copies. It represents the euhemeristic approach to the ancient myths, derived from the sophistic rationalization of the legend.

(b) The absence of the divine element seems to have been felt in subsequent periods. In particular, the lack of proportion between the body of the bird and that of the woman led to many difficulties; in some representations it seems as if the bird were only holding on to the body of Leda while remaining suspended in the air.[10] To obviate this difficulty, the swan was sometimes placed upon an altar [11] or even upon the head of Eros.[12] The best solution to this difficulty was, however, to increase the proportions of the swan to human size, thus indicating that this was no ordinary bird, but a god in disguise.

The artists who followed this pattern adopted three different subvariants of the general scheme:

1. The first possibility is represented on the Beth-She'arim coffin, and also on other examples (Fig. 3). Here the god, in the shape of a gigantic swan, advances with lifted wings towards a surprised Leda, who tries to push the bird away with her right hand, placed against its neck.[13] The swan's beak moves forward as if to kiss Leda's lips. The heroine stands slightly raised on her toes, her legs pressed together. Her left hand

---

antica, IV, Roma, 1961, p. 525, Fig. 617).

9 Ch. Picard: *Manuel d'archéologie grecque — La sculpture*, Paris, 1948, III, 1, pp. 365 ff.

10 Pompeian painting, H. Roux–M. L. Barré: *Herculanum et Pompéi, Recueil général*, VIII, Paris, 1876, Pl. 3; S. Reinach: *Répertoire des reliefs grecs et romains*, Paris, 1912, II, p. 219 (Relief at Champlieu).

11 A relief from Greece, now in the Berlin State Museum, No. 923 (O. Jahn, *Sächsische Berichte*, 4 [1852], Pl. 2) and on a relief from Budapest (*Archäologisch-epigraphische Mitteilungen aus Oesterreich-Ungarn* 14 [1891], p. 43.

12 Silver ewer from Moldavia, now in the Hermitage, Leningrad (S. Reinach, *Répertoire des réliefs*, III, p. 384).

13 Cf. the Kophissa sarcophagus, now in Athens (C. Robert: *Die antiken Sarkophag-Reliefs*, Berlin, 1890, II, pp. 3, 9) and, of course, the sarcophagus discussed here.

holds a cloak, which is bunched in front of the lower part of her body; part of it is also visible behind her. A shield is seen behind Leda; it has no special connection with the myth, and might have been placed here as a reminder of the Trojan war, one of the consequences of the scene before us. An overturned basket with figs can be seen between the legs of the advancing bird; behind the swan stands a fig tree. It seems that according to one version of the myth Leda was busy picking figs (a fertility symbol) when surprised by Zeus.

2. In the second version Leda does not defend herself against the swan, but seems to waver between pushing the neck of the bird away and drawing it near.[14] The swan is gripping her tightly. In one of the representations of this version, a relief found at Cnidus and now in Rome, Eros is seen pushing the swan towards Leda; elsewhere, as in a relief from Enns, Eros is standing at the side holding the sceptre and the thunderbolt, symbols of Zeus. The well-known sculpture now in Venice (Fig. 4) belongs to this type of representation, although Eros is not included.

3. The third version is more sensual: the swan seizes Leda and bites her in the neck. The artist who invented this version knew how to take advantage of the sinuous neck of the bird, and gave it an arched form.[15] This was the definitive version of the standing type; most of the extant copies follow it. It should be noted, however, that except for the bowed head of Leda and her invisible right arm, the body of the heroine is represented as in the first version: here too she rises on her toes and her cloak flows down in front.[16]

---

14 Terracotta tablet from Cnidus, now in the British Museum, (W. H. Roscher: *Lexikon der griechischen und römischen Mythologie*, II, Leipzig, 1894–1897, p. 1927, Fig. 2); relief in Berlin (see above, note 11); relief now in Rome (G. Lippold: Leda und Ganymedes, *Sitzungsberichte der Bayerischen Akademie der Wissenschaften*, Phil.-hist. Klasse, 1954, Heft 3, Pls. 3, 5; E. Maronica: *Archäologisch-epigraphische Mitteilungen aus Oesterreich-Ungarn*, II [1878], pp. 164–165, Pl. IX.

15 Argos relief, now the British Museum (Roscher, *op. cit.* [above, n. 14], p. 1930, Fig. 3); relief from Medinacoeli, now in Madrid (O. Jahn *Archäologische Zeitung*, 22 [1865], Pl. 198; A. Baumeister: *Denkmäler des klassischen Altertums*, München, 1887, II, p. 813; S. Reinach; *Répertoire des reliefs*, II, p. 354, No. 5 — relief now in Athens).

16 In addition to the examples quoted, there are many representations of the Leda myth on gems (A. Fürtwangler: *Die antiken Gemmen*, Leipzig 1900, Pls. 28: 27; 42: 21–22; 45: 75; 46: 68; Gisela M. Richter: *Catalogue of engraved gems*, Metropolitan Museum, New York, 1956: No. 424), on mosaics in Palermo (A. B. Cook: *Zeus*, III, Cambridge, 1940, Pl. XXXIX), Antioch (D. Levi: *Antioch Mosaic Pavements*, Princeton, 1947, pp. 208–209 Pl. XLIV a),

G. Lippold has tried to connect this type of the Leda myth with the school of Lysippos,[17] mainly because of the resemblance between the body of Leda and that of the Capuan Aphrodite, the Roman copy of an original attributed to Lysippos, and a further resemblance with the body of Kairos in the well-known relief copied from Lysippos' original. This theory does not, however, seem plausible for several reasons: Lysippos was not famous for his statues of women and the Capuan Aphrodite is attributed to him on stylistic grounds which do not seem convincing. In the long list of his works there is no mention of a female statue, except for that of a drunken flute-player. It is true, of course, that the elongated body and small head of the Venice Leda correspond to the Lysippean canon, but this form had become standard in the Hellenistic period. It is known that Lysippos worked exclusively in bronze. But the theory advanced by Lippold that Leda and the swan were originally cast in bronze does not seem likely. It seems much more probable because of the one-sided nature of the representations even if they are three-dimensional, that the origin of the type was a relief or a painting. Furthermore, the whole sensuous representation of the myth is far removed from the Lysippean outlook; Lysippos was a Peloponnesian sculptor, throughout whose work the athletic male spirit of the Dorians predominates. If, then, we do not attribute the invention of this Leda type to Praxiteles, we must seek its origin in some unknown Hellenistic sculptor from Asia Minor.

(c) The third type of representation of this myth is still more sensual: Leda is lying on the ground, with the upper part of her body propped up on one hand, while the other encircles the swan. The bird is more or less attached to her body.[18] The artist who conceived this type was skilful enough to hide the difference in size between the woman and the bird. This type is also found in many examples, one of the best being a group found at Kef in Tunisia.[19] A recent find in Caesarea (Fig. 5)

Beirut (M. Chehab ap. *La mosaïque greco-romaine*, Paris, 1965, p. 334, Fig. 3); in frescoes, especially in Pompeii (S. Reinach: *Répértoire des peintures gréco-romaines*, Paris, 1922, p. 16, No. 8; p. 17, No. 1), as well as on many lamps.

17 Lippold, *op. cit.* (above, n. 14); A. Giuliano, *op. cit.* (above, n. 8).

18 S. Reinach: *Répértoire des reliefs*, I, p. 231, Fig. (Rheims); II, p. 213, No. 2 (Arles); III, p. 222, No. 5, p. 422, No. 5 (Tortona). Some other representations are based on drawings made in the Renaissance period; the originals seem to be lost. The subject was still represented in Coptic art (K. Wessel: *Koptische Kunst*, Recklinghausen 1963, pp. 44, 51, 155, Fig. 37; E. Riefenstahl: New Sculpture from Christian Egypt, *Brooklyn Museum Bulletin*, 16 [1956], pp. 16–18.

19 Ch. Picard, *Revue archéologique*, 35 (1950), p. 191 f.; A. Merlin and L. Poins-

belongs to the same group.[20] In the lower left-hand corner of the front
side of a sarcophagus we find a representation of Leda, her right arm
resting on a reversed fig basket; figs are falling from the basket. The
left arm appears lifted above the head, giving Leda the aspect of a
nymph or of Ariadne sleeping. In this detail the relief differs from the
common type. The lower part of Leda's body is covered by a cloak
which is also visible below her right elbow; obviously the artist intended
to show a mantle falling open while the heroine was sleeping. Her left
leg is extended towards a Cupid. The hair is parted into two curled
strands which fall on the shoulders. The whole attitude of the head, inclined backwards, and the expression of mouth and face seem to express submission to fate. The eyes appear to be without expression, but
were once probably painted. The mouth is well shaped, the face is full
and the forehead broad. The head is small and the body elongated; the
modelling, with all the surface folds, is naturalistic and not stereotyped;
it seems quite likely that the sculptor worked from a living model, copying faithfully the forms of the body. The pensive expression, the deeply
cut eyes and the down-curving melancholy mouth — all these details
recall the Scopaic style. To the right of Leda stands a fig tree, its trunk
rising diagonally in front of the swan. The swan itself has its wings
lifted, and it is apparently advancing; the neck and head are broken
and missing, and therefore we cannot define them any further. The pat-
terning of the wings and body of the bird are somewhat schematic. The
Cupid behind the swan seems to be riding on a dolphin; it is represented
between the legs of a large figure, part of the main decoration of the
sarcophagus, which does not concern us here.

Among the many examples of a recumbent Leda we should mention
the mirror-handle now in Madrid.[21] There Leda is represented with the
wings of Nemesis, thus returning syncretically to the earlier form of the
myth.

sot, *Bulletin archéologique du comité des travaux historiques* 51 (1941/2),
pp. 58–61 with a very full bibliography of the subject. I am greatly obliged
to M. Cl. Poinssot for an offprint of this article.

20 I am most obliged to Dr. A. Biran, Director, Department of Antiquities, for
permission to publish this object and to Mr. S. Levi, Inspector of Antiquities,
who discovered it and who gave me all possible assistance in studying it.

21 R. Thouvenot: *Catalogue des figurines et objets d'art du Musée archéol. de
Madrid,* I, p. 16, No. 31, Pl. V (Bibl. de l'Ecole des Hautes Etudes hispa-
niques, XII, 1, 1927); P. Pâris: *Le Musée archéol. de Madrid,* p. 107, Pl. XLII,
No. 5; S. Reinach, *Revue archéologique* 1929, II, p. 88.

(B)

The better-preserved of the two long sides of the Beth She'arim sarcophagus is nevertheless also fragmentary, only the upper part being extant. The surviving fragments form a more or less consistent picture (Figs. 6 and 7). We shall describe the visible remains before attempting to interpret the representation. We see the façade of a palace in the background, with the event depicted taking place in the court — taking into account the presence of the horses in the two corners. Two gates are to be seen at the two extremities, flanked by pillars with Attic bases; the gateways are arched over. The representation shows nine persons visible in front of the façade; a tenth can be presumed.

1. On the extreme left an athletic youth is seen in front of the gate. His himation is visible behind his back, exposing the front of the body, with folds covering the lower left arm and flowing down from the right arm behind the wide apart legs. The figure is moving energetically to the left; its right knee is bent, as we can see from the position of the thigh and the foot, the knee itself being lost. The left leg is kept straight and is extended to the right. The right arm, which appears in front of the left gate column at the utmost extremity of the relief, is holding a sheathed sword, with the handle below and the curved end of the sheath pointing upwards. The left hand is extended towards the neck of the horse visible in the interval between this and the next figure; it was probably holding the reins. The head of the horse is visible to the right of the gateway, its body being presumably outside the gate.

2. A bearded figure is sitting to the right of the horse; he wears a diadem. His right hand is extended forwards.

3. Behind the sitting man stands a bearded person, wearing a short chlamys which is fastened by a fibula, or stitched together on his left shoulder, leaving his right breast bare. He is wearing a pointed cap (pileus) on his head.

4. In front of the man wearing the chlamys stood a woman, to judge from the traces of a coiffure gathered behind the head; this figure is, however, almost entirely destroyed. She was extending her left hand.

5. Almost in the centre of the relief a young man is to be seen, facing right. His long hair descends upon his shoulders. His right arm is bent at the elbow, and is extended forwards. His left hand is holding some round object (a shield?). A belt descends from his right shoulder, and crosses the chest diagonally. Remains of a cloak covering the left shoulder are also visible. In contrast to all the other figures hitherto discussed, which — with the exception of the first one — are seen from the side and

face to the right, this central personage is facing frontally, with a slight inclination of the head to the right.

6. Turning her face towards this youth stands a woman, whose head is turned slightly to the right. She is dressed in a belted peplos. Her hair is bunched together in a sakkos, and descends on her left shoulder.

7. Beyond her we notice the head of a young woman, facing left. The head is thrown backwards in an attitude of astonishment or surprise. The outstretched hand is visible behind the head of the woman in front of her.

8. Further to the right can be seen the head of a man, who also faces left and bends his head slightly backwards. He is blowing an ornamented trumpet, which curves upwards. The wide end of the trumpet can be seen behind the head of the young woman (No. 7), further left. The cheeks of the trumpeter are blown up as a result of the effort he is making, his mouth is contracted. He is wearing on his head a cap resembling that of No. 3.

9. In the left gate, beyond the trumpeter, we see the helmeted head of a man; the helmet is crested. This man seems to be holding the reins of a horse, the head of which is visible to his right.

10. For reasons of symmetry we may assume another sitting figure on the right, to balance the figure No. 2 on the left.

We can now proceed to interpret the representation. The editors of the catalogue of the Palestine Archaeological Museum assumed the two flanking figures to be the Dioscuri, and interpreted the central event as either the rape of the daughters of Leucippus or as Achilles on Scyrus. It seems from the mythological data and parallels that only the latter suggestion is acceptable, and that we see here the famous scene of the discovery of Achilles among the daughters of King Lycomedes.[22] This is evident from the presence of the hero with a pileus (Odysseus), the trumpeter, the seated king (Lycomedes), the youthful hero in the centre (Achilles), the surprised daughters of the king, etc. A comparison with parallel representations, in particular the Borghese sarcophagus now in the Louvre[23] (Fig. 8) show that this sarcophagus and the Leda sarcophagus from Beth She'arim are derived from the same prototype, al-

22 For the sources of this myth see R. Graves: *The Greek Myths,* London, 1955, II, p. 285, notes 10–22.

23 C. Robert: *Die antiken Sarkophagreliefs,* Berlin, 1890, II, p. 26; for other examples of the same general type see *ibid.*, pp. 6, 11–12, 14–15, 19–20, 23, 25–27, 33, 38–39, 54. For another sarcophagus, now in Cambridge, see L. Budde and R. Nicholls: *A Catalogue of Greek and Roman Sculpture in the Fitzwilliam Museum,* Cambridge, 1964, pp. 102–103, No. 162, Pl. 56. The sarcophagus is from the second half of the second century A.D. The catalogue

though in each case the artists introduced variants of their own. The number of figures in the Borghese sarcophagus is thirteen as compared with ten (at the utmost) in the Leda sarcophagus. There are three horses there as compared with two here. Nevertheless the general arrangement and the repetition of some of the types indicate their relationship. In particular we find in the Borghese coffin the hero with the reversed sword, holding a horse at the left extremity, the seated figure, the standing figure with the pileus, the youthful hero with baldric and shield in the centre; in one detail the Beth She'arim coffin represents a truer version of the myth, for in the Louvre sarcophagus the figure standing for the trumpeter is disjointed, lifting his hand too high and holding no instrument. The helmeted figure at the extreme right appears in both reliefs.

(C)

The second long side of the coffin has been less well preserved. The extant two fragments, which could be joined together, show in the centre a huntress dressed in a short tunic and high boots, who is hurrying to the right. She is accompanied by a male figure, of which only a bare leg has been left. The other fragment shows a man on a horse, striking downwards with his spear. The clue to the whole scene is to be found below the belly of the horse — a clear indication of the back bristles of a boar. The scene therefore represented the Calydonian hunt, with the two central figures standing for Atalanta and Meleagros (Fig. 9).

The Leda sarcophagus is a work of art of Hellenistic inspiration, executed by a mediocre craftsman of the Roman period. In spite of certain well-made details, such as the back and legs of Leda, there are quite a number of technical mistakes, some frankly puzzling. Note for example the right hand of Leda, who is pushing back the swan with her stronger arm while covering herself with the other. The right hand is visible (as a fragment) against the neck of the swan; the rest of the arm disappears behind the stylized wing feathers, reappearing only at the two extremities. Still more puzzling is the curious feature of the horse's leg shown at the left extremity of the long side, where the (broken) shank should pass between the knee set against the pillar and the foot visible on the ground. The technical difficulties in carving the horse's leg behind the detached shank seem to have been almost insuperable.

quoted contains a full discussion of this type of sarcophagus and a bibliography. The elements enumerated above occur on all the coffins listed above in various combinations, and are almost invariably all present.

Various details indicate the relatively late date of the coffin : the crowding of the figures and the generous use of the drill being the most evident. Nevertheless the artist still had a feeling for the shape of the human body and he followed the rich trend of drapery depiction as evolved in the Late Classical period. The date suggested by the Museum authorities : second half of the second century A.D., appears quite plausible.

* * *

In conclusion, two questions should be answered, one general in nature, the other connected with the peculiar circumstances of this discovery. Why were these particular mythological scenes selected for the ornamentation of a coffin? And what is this frankly pagan sarcophagus doing in, Beth She'arim the central Jewish necropolis of the third to fourth centuries.

Roman funeral symbolism [24] is based on two principles, both of which were intended to afford a measure of consolation to the relatives of the deceased.

One element consisted of representations of the happy after-life. These representations are connected with the mystical teachings related to the "saving gods" who would take care of their mystae in this and the other world. To this class we may assign the representation connected with solar and astral subjects, with the Dioscuri and the Dionysiac and Orphic mysteries. The choice lay between the ascension of the departed among the celestial bodies, or his share in the eternal banquet in the Elysian fields. In both cases, consolation flowed from the presumed happiness of men after their death.

The second thematic approach, which was indeed sometimes combined with the first one, was based on the idea that death was merely part of the eternal order of nature, immutable and impervious to human will. From this idea stem the representations on sarcophagi of the Four Seasons, of Aeon etc. The connection between the two orders of ideas rests upon the assumption that the seasons in nature are eternally renewed, and that as the flourishing spring follows the deathlike winter, thus the individual or the whole human race will witness a rebirth, whether in this or in another world, whether by way of metempsychosis or eschatological consummation and renewal.

Another way of thinking assumed that the Moira (Fate) determines that death is inescapable, and that even the best of mankind must sub-

---

24 F. Cumont: *Le symbolisme funéraire des Romains,* Paris, 1942.

mit to it. If even the heroes were doomed to die, why mourn the similar fate of a simple mortal? Moreover, the heroes proved their mettle by choosing a short but glorious life, instead of a long and inglorious one. This was the choice before Achilles [25] and — even if his after-life in Hades was not a happy one [26] — he was nevertheless considered to have made the right choice.

The subjects of the Beth She'arim sarcophagus are based on this last assumption. The myth of Leda and the Swan was the first link in the chain of events which ended in the Trojan war and the death of Achilles and many other heroes. As we have seen, the goddess of divine vengeance, Nemesis, was connected in the early myth with the birth of Helena — a divine vengeance which was provoked by the overbearing behaviour of mortals.[27] The idea that the wrath of the gods was provoked by the hybris of human beings is one of the basic axioms of the Greek cosmic conception.

We can thus understand the selection of the other representations chosen for this coffin. Achilles is forced by fate (aided by the cunning of Odysseus, the archetypal Greek) to embark on the course which can only end in death with glory, in spite of all the efforts of his mother to save him from his destiny. The myth of Meleagros similarly deals with the untimely death of a young hero, saved from death as a newborn child, only to perish under the same curse while in the full vigour of his youth.

* * *

So far we have dealt with the Beth She'arim sarcophagus as if it were an object entirely contained within the Greco-Roman world of myth and art. But in fact it was, as we know, found in a Jewish necropolis. The use (or — more likely — re-use) of a pagan coffin in a burial place which included the tombs of Jewish patriarchs and sages, originally caused much astonishment. Of course we know from the Galilean synagogues that — compared with the opinions held in the time of the Second Temple down to the end of the Bar-Kochba War — the last generations of the Tannaites and the early Amoraim (at least in Palestine) were liberal in their approach to figurative art. We notice figures

25   Ilias, IX, 410–416.
26   Odyssey, XI, 489–491.
27   D. Mustilli: Leda e il uovo di Nemesis, *Annuario Scuola Atene*, n.s. 8/10 (1946–48), pp. 123–131, 2 Figs.; F. Chapouthier, *Bulletin de correspondance héllenique*, 66/67 (1942–1943) pp. 1–21; Ch. Picard: *Manuel d'archéologie grecque — La sculpture*, III, 1, Paris, 1948, pp. 365 ff.

taken from the Greek myths, such as Centaurs, Medusa, Heracles, Nike etc. on some of the synagogue friezes (in particular at Chorozain). There is, however, a great deal of difference between these representations and that of Leda and the Swan.

The case of the Leda coffin ceased, however, to be unique in 1955. In that year N. Avigad cleared catacomb No. 20 at Beth She'arim which included — together with tombs of "saints" and members of the patriarchal family — also many fragments of coffins with mythological subjects, such as the Amazonomachy, Eros, goddesses etc.[28] We have here not an isolated case, but another expression of the generally tolerant attitude of the talmudic sages in the second to early fourth centuries,[29] which of course did not apply in cases where idolatry was suspected. This general tolerance allowed the re-use of coffins brought from abroad. Obviously the Leda sarcophagus belongs to this class, together with the Amazon sarcophagus from Caesarea and the fragments of marble coffins found in catacomb No. 20. At that period the Jews did not regard the mythological subjects as pagan cult objects, but only as literary or artistic expressions of "modern" culture, which they were unwilling to leave to the "gentiles."

In the case of the Leda sarcophagus we might recall that it was found within the debris of Mausoleum 11, above the catacomb of that number. Among the other remains of that building was a Greek inscription, commemorating in the form of a hexametric epigram one Justus of Besara (= Beth She'arim in Greek).[30] In this epigram there is a mention of "going down to Hades" ($\dot{\varepsilon}\lambda\theta\acute{\omega}\nu$ $\varepsilon\dot{\iota}\varsigma$ $^{c}A\delta\eta\nu$) and the "mighty Moira" ($Mo\tilde{\iota}\varrho\alpha$ $\varkappa\varrho\alpha\tau\alpha\acute{\iota}\eta$). The concluding words of the funerary epigram: "Be comforted, Justus, no one is immortal" ($\Theta\acute{\alpha}\varrho\sigma\varepsilon\iota$ $'Io\tilde{\upsilon}\sigma\tau\varepsilon$ $o\dot{\upsilon}\delta\varepsilon\dot{\iota}\varsigma$ $\dot{\alpha}\theta\acute{\alpha}\nu\alpha\tau o\varsigma$) are identical with those found in thousands of pagan tombs.

Not a few of the basic conceptions of the epigram appear in visual form on the sides of the coffin which stood in the same mausoleum although we cannot tell whether it contained the mortal remains of Justus or of another member of his family. "The mighty Moira" caused Zeus and Leda to beget Helena; Achilles and Meleagros, the great hero and the great hunter, were not immortal.

It seems likely, however, that the courtship of Zeus and Leda as represented here was beyond what was permitted even in a period when

28   N. Avigad, *Israel Explor. Journal*, 7 (1957), pp. 90–92; id., *Beth She'arim* III, Jerusalem, 1971, pp. 120–127, Pls. LII–LVII.

29   E. E. Urbach, *Israel Explor. Journ.*, 9 (1959), pp. 149 ff., 229 ff.

30   M. Schwabe and B. Lifshitz: *Beth She'arim*, Vol. II: *The Greek Inscriptions*, Jerusalem, 1967, No. 127, pp. 45–51, Pl. IV, 3 (Hebrew).

the stringent regulations against figurative art were much relaxed. We might well ask whether the coffin was fully visible when re-used in the mausoleum. It might possibly be assumed that it was placed within a narrow niche in such a way that only the long side with the Achilles relief was visible (the Meleagros relief was from the beginning meant as the rear-side, if only because of its rougher execution). In this way the Leda relief and the other short side (the subject of which is unknown) would be hidden from the eye of the beholder. When the mausoleum fell into ruin the sarcophagus was damaged, apparently by Moslem iconoclasts, as harm was caused principally to the faces of the figures, and was carried out crudely — quite differently from the careful hammering away of the offending parts in the Galilean synagogue reliefs.

As has been stated, the coffin was made about A.D. 200, one generation before the beginning of the Beth She'arim necropolis, in which it was re-used. There is some similarity between its ornament and that of the architectural details of the mausoleum.[31]

The use of this sarcophagus in the Beth She'arim necropolis is more evidence of the fact that as far as the visual arts are concerned, Judaism was integrated (within certain limits) into the Greco-Roman world from the death of Rabbi Judah I to the completion of the Palestinian Gemara (third to fourth centuries A.D.).

31 M. Avi-Yonah: *Oriental Art in Roman Palestine*, Roma, 1961, pp. 40 f., Pl. VI: 1.

LION-MASKS WITH RINGS IN THE
WEST AND IN THE EAST

By OTTO KURZ

The lay visitor to an archaeological collection is apt to look at the explanatory labels with a curious mixture of surprise, profound admiration and good-natured scepticism when he is told by the experts that a figure without head or limbs represents a certain god or goddess, or a badly battered fragment some recondite scene from Greek mythology. But even the most ignorant museum visitor will have no difficulty in mentally completing a Roman bronze mask of a lion like the one shown in Figure 1.[1] Without hesitation he will say that what is missing must be the circular ring which was once suspended between the teeth of the lion. He has seen such door-handles or door-knockers hundreds of times simply in walking through the streets of any city on any continent.

The mere fact that such a modest art form as the combination of a lion's head with a ring is as much alive to-day as it was in ancient Greece is an invitation to look at least cursorily at its long and — as we shall see — continuous history which covers some 2,500 years.[2]

We do not know how this odd and far from obvious association of a lion's head with a swinging ring came into existence. We know, however, that in the eighth and seventh centuries B.C. bronze vessels from Anatolia were often decorated with the *protomai* of bulls, gryphons or lions, and that these same vessels were also furnished with swinging rings for carrying. It was not particularly far-fetched to combine the two and indeed in some vessels from Urartu and Phrygia we see that the head of the animal and the suspension were physically, if not organically, united by the loop for the ring being fixed between the horns of the bull.[3]

1   I am very grateful to the authorities of the Israel Museum for permission to reproduce the bronze even before its official publication. It was found in a mansion from the Byzantine period at Beit She'an. Mr. Nehemia Tsori will discuss it in his forthcoming excavation report.

2   In the following notes some examples have been put together. To aim at completeness would be foolish and futile.

3   P. Amandry, Chaudrons à protomes de taureau en Orient et en Grèce, in: *The Aegean and the Near East, Studies presented to Hetty Goldman*, 1956,

It would be attractive to state that at first artists showed a bull with a ring through the septum of his nose, as they must have observed in their native villages, and that later generations replaced the bull by the other powerful and even more majestic animal, the lion. Unfortunately, there exists not a shred of evidence to support such a reconstruction on paper and, what is more, the history of art has seldom or never followed such a logical sequence. It is, however, a fact that artists did try out various solutions, and at least in one case the head of the lion was allowed to grow out of the circular ring.[4]

ANTIQUITY

The oldest surviving example of such a door handle was excavated at Olynthus.[5] Olynthus was destroyed in 348 B.C., and by then this bronze lion's head must have been fairly old. Its style points to the fifth century B.C. The severely stylised head of the lion is surrounded by tufts of hair which have been aptly compared to a "flame palmette". A large, heavy ring in the mouth of the beast served as a handle.[6]

Innumerable such door handles must have existed in antiquity; indeed the association "Door and Lion Head" became so fixed that when artists had to represent the street door of a building they took care to show the lion-masks to make their meaning perfectly clear. In the frescoes with architectural scenes from a Roman villa in Boscoreale (now in the Metropolitan Museum in New York) the painter was careful to provide the doors with the customary ringed lion heads enabling one to open or close the leaves.[7]

Even on the minute scale of a coin reverse the die-engraver managed somehow to bring in this essential detail. When Nero proudly announced

pl. 28. E. Akurgal, *Die Kunst Anatoliens von Homer bis Alexander*, 1961, p. 54 f., pl. III b. B. B. Piotrovskij, *Iskusstvo Urartu*, 1962, p. 61. R. S. Young, in *Art Treasures of Turkey*, Smithsonian Institution, Washington 1966, pp. 23, 26.

4   Urartian handle from Toprak Kale, near Van (British Museum): R. D. Barneth, *Iraq* XVI, 1954, pl. II; H. Gabelmann, *Marburger Winckelmann-Programm* 1964, pl. 7.

5   D. M. Robinson, *Excavations at Olynthus. X. Metal and minor miscellaneous finds*, 1941, No. 989, pls. 66–67. E. Meyer, Antike Türzieher, in *Festschrift Eugen von Mercklin*, 1964, p. 81, pl. 39, 1.

6   The excavation report speaks of a "door-ring or knocker", but as R. E. Wycherley says rightly in his review, it can only have been a handle, "if one considers the position of the ring" (*Journal of Hellenic Studies* LXII, 1943, p. 104).

7   G. M. A. Richter, *Greek painting* (Metropolitan Museum of Art), 1944, p. 21. Ph. Williams Lehmann, *Roman wall paintings from Boscoreale*, 1953, p. 193, pls. XII, XV.

on his coins that at last peace reigned in his Empire and that the *belli portae* of the temple of Janus had been shut, the artist showed this by depicting the indispensable lion handles on the door leaves.[8] And again, when an early Christian artist had to represent the miracle of Christ's resurrection, the obvious way was to show the half-open gates of the Holy Sepulchre with their handles consisting of the mask of a lion (Fig. 2).[9]

With the "Holy Sepulchre" we pass from the "House of the Living" to the "House of the Dead". It is only natural that the door which gave the mourners access to the tomb should look like any other door, and possess a usable handle conforming to the current fashion.[10]

In other cases the door was a sham entrance, the leaves of the door, the heads of the lions and even the rings being carved out of the rock.[11] It would be over-rationalistic to divide such stone doors into the two categories of real and simulated ones. A marble door with lions and rings in low relief in Palmyra could still be opened to allow access to a corridor which lead to the actual tombs, although the rings were only make-believe.[12]

The "Doors of Hades" which we find on cinerary urns, funeral altars, stelae and sarcophagi represent the entrance to the Underworld in the guise of a house door, often with its traditional fittings.[13]. That lions

8 M. Bernhart, *Handbuch zur Münzkunde der römischen Kaiserzeit*, 1926, pl. 91, 3–4. *A guide to the exhibition of Roman coins in the British Museum*, 1927, pl. VI, 2. H. Mattingly, *Coins of the Roman Empire in the B.M.*, I, 1923, p. 215, No. 111, pl. 41, 1; p. 239, No. 203, pl. 49, 9; p. 263, No. 320, pl. 46, 2.

9 Early Christian ivory in the British Museum: W. F. Volbach, *Elfenbeinarbeiten*, 2. Aufl. 1952, No. 116, pl. 35. C. Gurlitt, Das Grab Christi in der Grabeskirche in Jerusalem, *Festschrift zum 70. Geburtstag von P. Clemen*, 1926, p. 195, fig. 9.

10 Tomb at Langaza (Macedonia) dating from the fourth century B.C. Th. Macridy, *Jahrbuch d. K. D. Arch. Inst.* XXVI, 1911, p. 203, fig. 19; Meyer, *l.c.*, p. 81, pl. 39, 2. The bronze decoration of the door consists of a Medusa and a lion. We shall find the same combination of the two powerful guardians on the ships from Lake Nemi and on the sarcophagus with Muses in the Vatican (see below). It is always the lion which serves as a handle.

11 The so-called Bellerophon Tomb at Tlos in Lycia: Ch. Fellows, *An account of discoveries in Lycia*, 1841, pl. facing p. 136. Reinach, *Rép. Rel.* II, 112. *Tituli Asiae Minoris* II, p. 205.

12 R. Amy and H. Seyrig, Recherches dans la nécropole de Palmyre, *Syria* XVII, 1936, p. 232, pl. 28.

13 On the "Doors of Hades" see W. Altmann, *Die römischen Grabaltäre*, 1905, pp. 14 ff.; F. Eichler, Griechische Grabmäler in Wien, *Jahrbuch der kunsthistor. Sammlungen in Wien*, N. F. XIII, 1944, p. 32 f.; and now especially A. Garcia y Bellido, El sarcófago romano de Córdoba, *Archivo español de arqueologia*

had often served as funerary monuments may have been a contributory factor,[14] but without doubt it was the identification with the house of the living which made lion handles so popular. On a Roman tomb altar from the first century in the Belvedere of the Vatican, two Victories with their hands on the rings are shown in the act of opening the gates.[15]

These Hades doors with heads of lions appear both on Roman stelae [16] and sarcophagi.[17] But in most instances the doors leading to the Underworld were not shown, or rather they were reduced to what was thought to be their essential element: the heads of lions with handles in their jaws. They occur frequently on sarcophagi of various classes and materials, and not only on pagan ones.

A widespread type are the "strigilated" sarcophagi of tub shape with their strigil-shaped grooves. They usually show two very large heads of lions with the make-believe handle-rings; in most cases these heads are the only décor of these sarcophagi,[18] but sometimes they appear together with scenes from the Dionysiac cycle,[19] or combined with the hanging garlands of another well-known type of sarcophagus.[20]

The majority of these sarcophagi are undoubtedly of pagan origin, but the Jews of Rome had no objection to using them as their eternal

XXXII, 1959, pp. 3 ff., on the Gates of Hades p. 13 ff.

14 H. Usener, *Kleine Schriften*, III, 1914, pp. 423 ff. See also the references put together by E. von Mercklin, in *Scritti in onore di B. Nogara*, 1937, p. 284.

15 Altmann, l.c., fig 85. W. Amelung, *Die Sculpturen des Vatican. Museums*, II, 1908, p. 216, pl. 21. A drawing for a tomb monument by Rubens is inspired by this tomb altar; see J. S. Held, *Rubens, Selected drawings*, vol. 1, 1959, p. 164, fig. 36–37.

16 Stele of Rameius, Museo Nazionale, Aquileia: G. A. Mansuelli, in *Studi in onore di A. Calderini e R. Paribeni*, III, 1956, p. 371; *Storia di Venezia*, I, 1957, p. 462, fig. 139.

17 Sarcophagus with Muses in the Vatican (Belvedere 48): Amelung, l.c., p. 117 ff., pl. 13; E. A. Voretzsch, *Röm. Mitteil.* 64, 1957, p. 24; M. Wegner, *Die Musensarkophage*, 1966, No. 134, pl. 56. Sarcophagus from Cordoba: see above note 13. Sarcophagus in the Palazzo Riccardi in Florence: Ch. R. Morey, *The sarcophagus of Claudia Antonia Sabina*, 1924, fig. 99; G. Rodenwaldt, *Röm. Mitteil.* 38/39, 1923/24, p. 18, fig. 8.

18 Sarcophagus in the Belvedere 102: Amelung, l.c., pl. 29. R. T. Günther, *Pausilypon. The Imperial Villa near Naples*, 1913, p. 267, fig. 167. G. Rodenwaldt, Römische Löwen, *La Critica d'arte* I, 1935–36, p. 226, pl. 157. U. Scerrato, Su alcuni sarcofagi con leoni, *Archeologia classica* IV, 1952, p. 263, pl. LXI.

19 D. Strong, Some unknown classical sculpture . . . at Hever Castle, *The Connoisseur* CLVIII, 1965, p. 224, fig. 24.

20 G. Mendel, *Musées Imperiaux Ottomans, Catalogue des sculptures*, I, 1912, No. 12; III, 1914, No. 1167.

resting place. In the Jewish catacomb of the Villa Torlonia such a sarcophagus appears painted on the wall, while the fragment of a marble original, the prototype of the painting, was found in another corner of the catacomb.[21]

Other religious communities were not slow in adopting this type of sarcophagus. This happened in Palmyra in the second century, when a vigorous school of sculpture flourished there, at precisely the time when the Greek stone doors with lion-masks were taken over.[22]

An early Christian sarcophagus with the figure of the Good Shepherd between leonine masks can be seen in the church of S. Trinita in Florence, where it was used a second time in the fifteenth century as the tomb monument of Giuliano Davanzati (d. 1444).[23] We can even watch an early Christian sculptor in the very act of producing such a sarcophagus. A certain Eutropos had himself depicted on his tomb slab at the moment of putting the finishing touches to the lion's head with the help of a drill (Fig. 3).[24]

While such stone sarcophagi can be found all over the Roman Empire, the use of leaden ones was more or less restricted to Syria. They were occasionally provided with lion-mask handles, but the rings are not, as one would expect, movable; like the rest of the decoration they are executed in low relief.[25]

Wooden sarcophagi with metal fittings, this time with real movable rings, were a speciality of the Roman provinces of Palestine and Syria. Most of the ancient lion-heads with rings come from this part of the world, like the one which was our starting point (Fig. 1).[26] The wood itself has disintegrated, but the bronze parts survived, often together with the rusty iron nails with which the handles had been fixed to the

21 H. W. Beyer and H. Lietzmann, *Die Jüdischen Katakombe der Villa Torlonia*, 1930, p. 11, pl. 24.

22 Fragment from a Palmyrene sarcophagus in the Museum at Geneva: *Guides illustrés 6, Antiquités orientales*, 1958, p. 22. The high pointed ears of the lion are like horns. W. Deonna thought the animal was a dog (Portes et heurtoirs genevois, *Les Musées de Genève*, VII, No. 6, 1950, p. 2, fig. 1).

23 P. Fontana, *Filippo Brunelleschi*, 1929, pl. 28. G. Bovini, *Monumenti figurati paleocristiani conservati a Firenze*, 1950, pp. 2–4. W. and E. Paatz, *Die Kirchen von Florenz*, V, 1953, p. 302.

24 Originally in the catacomb of SS. Marcellino e Pietro in Rome. Cabrol-Leclercq, *Dict. d'archéol. chrét.*, XV, 781. P. Testini, *Le catacombe a gli antichi cimiteri cristiani in Roma*, 1966, p. 313, fig. 199.

25 E. von Mercklin, *Archäol. Anzeiger* 51, 1936, p. 259.

26 Typical examples can be seen in the Rockefeller Museum in Jerusalem (Nos. 1380–1381, 1383–1385; 1382 never had a ring).

wooden coffins.[27] Although their origin has long been known, they are often loosely described as door handles or knockers. They are, however, the descendants, and not as one might imagine the prototypes, of the corresponding handles on stone sarcophagi.

Goodenough managed to discover in them a hidden Jewish symbolism — what was not a Jewish symbol for him? — but as M. Avi-Yonah pointed out when reviewing Goodenough's book, these lion-masks and rings "served throughout the ancient world as coffin handles".[28] If they were a religious symbol, it would have to be one equally acceptable to pagans, Jews and Christians, not to mention those who worshipped the *dii minorum gentium* of Palmyra. Equally unconvincing but neverthe-less delightful is the explanation given in the *Hieroglyphica* of Hora-pollo (I 19), the only one found in ancient literature. According to Ho-rapollo the lion-heads on temples are a symbol of watchfulness, "be-cause the lion, when awake, closes his eyes, but when asleep keeps them open." [29]

The most famous of all the lion-masks with rings which have come down to us from antiquity are, of course, those which decorated the ships of Caligula on Lake Nemi (Fig. 4). In 1895, divers discovered a group of such bronze heads of superb craftsmanship consisting of three lions and two wolves. And when in 1929 the lake was drained and the ships could be salvaged (alas, only for a short period) the number of

27 E. von Mercklin, Ein Grabfund aus Sidon im Hamburger Museum für Kunst und Gewerbe, *Archäol. Anzeiger* 41, 1926, col. 291 ff., figs. 2–8. On the style and chronology of these bronzes see an excellent and very thorough mono-graph by E. Meyer, Antike Türzieher, *Festschrift Eugen von Mercklin,* 1964, pp. 80–89, pls. 39–43. On the lion-masks in the Museum in Hamburg see also *Jahrbuch der Hamburger Kunstsammlungen* III, 1958, p. 221, figs. 4–6; VI, 1961, p. 242, fig.; *Archäol. Anzeiger* 75, 1960, p. 121, fig. 57. On a similar mask in Boston see C. C. Vermeule, Additions to the Greek, Etruscan and Roman collections in Boston, *The Classical Journal* 58, 1962, pp. 13–15, fig. 18.
28 E. R. Goodenough, *Jewish symbols in the Greco-Roman period,* I, 1953, p. 87; VII, 1958, pp. 63–68, figs 62–63; review by M. Avi-Yonah, *Israel Explora-tion Journal* VI, 1956, p. 196.
29 Horapollo, *The Hieroglyphics,* ed. and transl. A. T. Cory, 1840, p. 40. It has been suggested that Horapollo had in mind the late Egyptian door bolts with the figure of a lion (F. W. von Bissing, Ägyptische Löwenriegel, *Orientalistische Literaturzeitung* 27, 1924, col. 118–119; O. Koenigsberger, *Die Konstruktion der ägyptischen Tür,* 1936, pp. 53–58). Bissing's interpretation is incorrect as these bolts show a lion couchant, while the Greek text of Horapollo refers to "heads of lions". Temple doors in Syria in the first century were — accord-ing to inscriptions — decorated with "little lions" (λεοντάρια; *CIG* 4558; Ditten-berger, *OGIS* 426; Drexel, *Röm. Mitteil.* 36/37, 1921/22, p. 49). Whether these were masks with rings it is, of course, impossible to say, but seems likely.

these bronzes increased to altogether five lions, one panther and four wolves. Here for the first time we are confronted not with mass-produced fittings but with the works of a real artist who refused to repeat himself and modelled each head separately, and even avoided the monotony of leonine heads only.[30] The fascination exercised by the lions from Lake Nemi is not easy to put into words. They lack the awe-inspiring majesty of archaic lions and they are not really what one would call "realistic". Their expression seems more human than leonine. The artist was evidently fascinated by the bulges and cavities of the head, the loose furry skin, and especially by the powerful, protruding eyebrows. One is reminded of a somewhat later text, a passage in the *Thoughts of the Emperor Marcus Aurelius* (III 2) where he remarks how something which is not beautiful in itself can be attractive, and quotes as examples ripe ears of corn which are hanging down, the foam dripping from the mouth of a wild boar, or — of particular interest in our context — "the wrinkled skin of the brow (ἐπισκύνιον) of a lion."

The luxurious decoration of a ship must always have been an exception.[31] That the masks of lions, and occasionally of other animals, appear as the handles of bronze vessels is not surprising; it is perhaps surprising that we do not encounter them more often.[32]

The thrones of rulers were decorated with lions, the old symbol of majesty, since Solomon, and it was only in late antiquity that the guardian lions were replaced by masks with rings on the *sella* of the consul on the long series of consular diptychs (Fig. 5).[33]

It would have been strange if an art form of such irresistible attraction had not been copied by the "Barbarians" on the frontiers of Roman civilisation. Among the finds from a tomb dating from the first century of our era at Harpenden (Hertfordshire) was a wooden bucket. In its

30 G. Ucelli, *Le navi di Nemi*, 1950, pp. 205 ff., 396 f.; cf. *ibid.* p. 202 on the suggestion of P. Perali that similar heads from these ships were found at an earlier date and were known to artists in the sixteenth century.

31 A Roman lion-mask of unusual size (ca. 114 cm.) has convincingly been claimed to have come from a ship; cf. *The Burlington Magazine*, June 1966, supplement "Notable works of art now on the market", pl. XX.

32 Brazier in Naples: F. B. Tarbell, *Catalogue of bronzes, etc., in Field Museum of Natural History reproduced from originals in the National Museum of Naples*, 1909, fig. 94a. There is a bronze kettle with rams' heads and rings in the Museum in Heraklion, Crete. On Coptic bronze *paterae* in London and Cairo see J. Strzygowski, *Koptische Kunst*, 1904, pl. 31; O. M. Dalton, *Cat. of Early Christian antiquities*, 1901, No. 534. For further references s. E. Meyer, *l.c.*, p. 83.

33 R. Delbrueck, *Die Consulardiptychen*, 1929, pls. 9 ff., 16–25, 32. W. F. Volbach, *Elfenbeinarbeiten*, 2. Aufl., 1952, pls. 4–6.

outline its bronze handle follows Roman prototypes, but it is heavy and very large and thus more practical, and the head of the lion has been replaced by an animal more familiar to the Celtic artist, a horse. He decorated the nostrils of the horse with inlay of coral, the favourite material of late La Tène art.[34]

MIDDLE AGES

The Celtic tradition represented by our last example lived on in Ireland. A small bronze disk found there shows the head of an animal belonging to no particular zoological species, but apparently intended to be a lion, holding in his jaws a ring to which a short chain and another and larger ring have been fixed. The eyes of the beast are inlaid with red enamel. The object, the original purpose of which is unknown, has been dated as "late ninth or early tenth century"; [35] it obviously belongs to a world which was no longer pagan. Engraved on the muzzle of the animal is a human face, an obvious allusion to the words of the psalmist (XXI, 22): *Salva me ex ore leonis.*

The long series of lion heads on mediaeval church doors starts with the famous ones on Charlemagne's Palatine Chapel in Aix-la-Chapelle.[36] Here as in everything else Carolingian artists took up the classical tradition. From then onwards the lion-masks appear as an integral part of mediaeval church doors, and we encounter them even more often than the stone lions which guard the entrance of so many Romanesque cathedrals.[37] On the door in Novgorod there are human figures in the

---

34   Th. W. Bagshawe, Early Iron Age objects from Harpenden, *The Antiquaries Journal* VIII, 1928, pp. 520–522, pl. LXXXII f. J. M. C. Toynbee, *Art in Britain under the Romans*, 1964, p. 22. There has been some uncertainty about the identity of the animal. The first report and Miss Toynbee speak of a ram, Bagshawe calls it a horse. I think he is right.

35   E. C. R. Armstrong, Some Irish antiquities of unknown use, *The Antiquaries Journal* II, 1922, pp. 6–12. N. Aberg, *The Occident and the Orient in the art of the seventh century*, I, 1943, p. 38, fig. 18. Both authors reproduce the object from a line drawing. The photographic reproduction in A. Mahr, *Christian art in ancient Ireland*, I, 1932, pl. 33 shows the human head, but not the lion.

36   P. E. Schramm and Fl. Mütherich, *Denkmale der deutschen Könige und Kaiser*, 1962, p. 115, pls. 206–209. See also the next note.

37   Such mediaeval door knockers are very numerous; some from Germany and Italy can be seen in H. Leisinger, *Romanesque bronzes-Church portals in mediaeval Europe*, 1956. On English examples see M. Christy and O. M. Dalton, Notes on an early medieval latten door knocker, *Proceedings of the Society of Antiquaries of London*, second series, XXII, 1907–09, pp. 380–391. *Die frühmittelalterlichen Bronzetüren*, herausgeg. von R. Hamann, 1926 ff., vol. I (Aix, Mainz, Hildesheim, Augsburg), II (Novgorod, Gnesen), III (Verona), IV

jaws of the lion. A Russian inscription explains the lion as a symbol of
"Hell (Russian *Ad* from Greek *Hades*) devouring the sinners".[38] While
this bronze door is an import from Germany, the later (13th century)
doors at Susdal are of native Russian workmanship. They, too, show the
lions with rings.[39]

In the majority of cases the handle is of leonine shape, but occasionally a human head replaces that of the animal.[40] In some places, the door
handle of the church signified the right of asylum; whoever touched
the ring was granted protection.[41]

With the classical heritage, the Middle Ages took over the use of lions'
heads both as door handles and for the decoration of various implements.[42] In his *Schedula diversarum artium* the monk Theophilus gives
not only technical instructions, but often makes suggestions of how to
decorate an object. Thus a colander ought to show a "caput leonis, in
cuius ore pendebit anulus, per quem inserto digito portari possit." [43]
We learn from this not only the mediaeval terminology, but also that
no symbolic meaning was implied.

(Ravello, Trani). *Geschichte des Kunstgewerbes,* herausgeg. von H. T. Bossert,
vol. V, 1932, pp. 233, 237, 410. *Die Sammlung Albert Figdor,* vol. 5, 1930,
Nos. 456–457. A *corpus of* mediaeval door knockers has been announced by
E. Meyer.

38 *Die frühmittelalterlichen Bronzetüren* II, p. 12 (A. Goldschmidt). V. P. Darke-
vič, *Proizvedenija zapadnogo chudozhestvennogo remesla v Vostočnoj Evrope,*
1966, p. 29 f., pl. 1. R. Hamann, Türkopf und Löwendarstellung, *Pantheon* X
1932, pp. 358–361. The human head in the mouth of the lion is a not uncommon motif; cf. E. Meyer, Deutschordenskunst im mittelalterlichen England,
Anzeiger des Germanischen Nationalmuseums 1963, pp. 28–34, figs. 1–2.

39 *Istorija russkogo iskusstva* I, 1953, p. 480, fig. German edition: *Geschichte der
russischen Kunst* I, 1957, p. 306, fig. 282.

40 *Die frühmittelalterlichen Bronzetüren* III, p. 14 (A. Böckler). *Die Sammlung
Albert Figdor,* vol. 5, 1930, No. 446.

41 H. R. Hahnloser, Urkunden zur Bedeutung des Türrings, *Festschrift für Erich
Meyer,* 1959, pp. 125–146. Jews had to touch the door ring of a synagogue
when taking an oath; cf. H. Voltelini, Der Wiener und Kremser Judeneid,
Mitteilungen des Vereines für Geschichte der Stadt Wien XII, 1932, pp. 65, 69,
70. Nothing, of course, is known about the shape of these rings.

42 Late Gothic brazier with the heads of grotesque animals, North German, A.D.
1493: *Reallexikon zur deutschen* Kunstgeschichte II, 1948, p. 162, fig. 9. Corn
measure of 1463, Musée Communal, Brussels: H. Michel, *Scientific instruments,* 1966, pl. 3. Here the ring is suspended behind the head of the lion
as on the Islamic mortars.

43 Theophilus Presbyter, *Schedula diversarum artium,* ed. Ilg, 1874, p. 243; *ibid.,*
p. 249 on a richly decorated censer where the chains were hinged in the hair
of lions and men.

The sham lion-handles in stone which so often decorated classical sarcophagi were not copied in the Middle Ages. The exception which confirms this rule is the porphyry sarcophagus of Frederick II in Palermo where the classical inspiration is particularly obvious.[44]

ISLAM

"Lions bite the rings of the door knockers", says Ibn Hamdis when describing the beauties of a palace in Bejaia (Bougie) in Algeria. His *qasida* dates from the last years of the eleventh or the very first years of the twelfth century.[45]

How widespread the use of these "lions which bite the rings of the door knockers" was, becomes apparent from a miniature which brings us to the extreme east of the Islamic world. Here we need no longer be satisfied with a verbal description. The picture (Fig. 6) helps us to visualize the two massive heads of lions which adorned a fortified gate. The miniature comes from the Istanbul manuscript of Rashid ad-Din's *History of the World* and dates from the year 717 H. (1317 A.D.).[46] Later, the use of lion-shaped door knockers seems to have become rather rare, and ornaments of various kind replaced the objectionable animal forms. It seems, however, that on Jewish houses in the Yemen they survived almost to our own days.[47]

In the minor arts such handles have always been an exception, and in the rare instances where we encounter them, they are of a rather unorthodox shape. A Seljuq bronze lamp from A.H. 679 (A.D. 1280–81) in the Etnografya Müzesi in Ankara shows three projecting heads of bulls with their foreheads pierced so that the lamp can be suspended by chains.[48]

44 A good reproduction in *Attraverso l'Italia. Sicilia,* 1961, fig. 18. J. Deér, *The dynastic porphyry tombs of the Norman period in Sicily,* 1959, p. 47, fig. 21; cf. also the review by K. Wessel, *Byzantinische Zeitschrift* LIII, 1960, p. 158 and Schramm and Mütherich, *l.c.,* p. 197.

45 F. Gabrieli, Il palazzo ḥammādita di Biǧāya descritto da Ibn Ḥamdis, in *Aus der Welt der islamischen Kunst. Festschrift für E. Kühnel,* 1959, p. 56. I abstain from quoting the next verse as the text is not certain. Gabrieli quotes an emendation suggested by Massé, but not an earlier one by A. F. von Schack (*Poesie und Kunst der Araber in Spanien und Sicilien,* 2. Aufl., 1877, I, p. XI n. 1; II, p. 27).

46 M. Aga-Oglu, *Ars Islamica I,* 1934, p. 183 f. fig. 3.

47 My only source of information is a passing reference in C. Rathjens, *Jewish domestic architecture in San'a, Yemen,* 1957, p. 21.

48 D. S. Rice, Studies in Islamic metalwork V, *BSOAS* XVII, 1955, pp. 207–212, pls. 1–7. *Art Treasures of Turkey,* Washington 1966, No. 164. E. Akurgal,

The only group of Islamic works of art which almost always shows lion handles are the decorated polygonal bronze mortars of Persian workmanship, which can be seen in many collections and which date from the twelfth and thirteenth centuries.[49] Even here the handles differ slightly from the traditional pattern as the ring is, strictly speaking, fixed behind the head of the lion. In a few instances we find a second loop beneath the head.[50]

We have already observed the same phenomenon in the art of classical antiquity and of the Western Middle Ages: while lion handles were used freely on doors, there was a certain reluctance to put them on vessels and implements. The king of the beasts was an appropriate guardian of a monumental building, but his use on a minor object seemed incongruous. This attitude changed with the coming of the Renaissance.

RENAISSANCE AND MODERN TIMES

It is probably rarely noticed that the traditional heads of lions with rings decorate Ghiberti's first bronze door of the Baptistery in Florence.[51] That the tradition of the mediaeval church door was already dying out can be seen from the fact that the lions have now been relegated from their place of honour to a modest position on the inside of the door, but that they appear there at all shows that they were still regarded as indispensable for a church door. Ghiberti certainly did not regard them as of secondary importance. His grandiose beasts (Fig. 7) are worthy companions of Donatello's *Marzocco* and of the lions on Luca della Robbia's Orpheus relief on the Campanile.

But we do not want to discuss lions in art, only the king of the animals in his servile position of offering a metal ring to the human hand. Here the mediaeval tradition might have died out had artists not discovered that the motif could be found everywhere among the ven-

C. Mango and R. Ettinghausen, *Treaures of Turkey,* 1966, pp. 154 (reprod.), 156.

49 They have been studied by E. Kühnel, Ein persischer Bronzemörser, *Festschrift für Erich Meyer,* 1959, pp. 32–34. See also M. Aga-Oglu, Some Islamic bronzes of the Middle Ages, *Bulletin of the Detroit Institute of Arts* XII, 1930–31, p. 92. *Survey of Persian Art,* vol. VI, pl. 1280 f. H. Kocabaş, Une collection de cuivres seldjoukides, *Atti del secondo Congresso internazionale di arte turca,* 1965, p. 178, figs. 2–7.

50 G. Migeon, *Les cuivres arabes,* 1900, p. 17. Sale catalogue, Sotheby's, November 27, 1967, No. 63 (now the property of the L. A. Mayer Memorial, Jerusalem).

51 R. and T. Krautheimer, *Lorenzo Ghiberti,* 1956, p. 113, pl. 68a.

erated relics of classical antiquity. In the sketchbooks which artists of the Renaissance filled with drawings of classical monuments, the lions with rings were not forgotten.[52]

In general one might speak of a democratization of the old motif. What was once restricted to monumental church buildings could now be found on innumerable private houses. Before long, it was brought from the Old to the New World.[53]

No implement was deemed unsuitable, no material too cheap or too costly to be decorated with these handles. Nobody could stem the flood. One Renaissance craftsman thought that a ring held by a clenched human fist would look more original and make better sense.[54] He found no followers. The power of the tradition was too strong. A ring handle at once suggested the head of a lion.

So the two appear together wherever we look. We find them not only in their traditional place on doors,[55] but even on stoves [56] and on water fountains.[57] On a porphyry vase the classical inspiration could be taken for granted,[58] less so on a globe or a clock.[59] We find them on furniture from every period and country.[60] Nobody asked whether these rings

52   Chr. Hülsen and H. Egger, *Die römischen Skizzenbücher des Martin van Heemskerck*, 1913, I, fol. 38r. The so-called "Peruzzi Sketchbook", Biblioteca Comunale, Siena, fol. 58 (H. Egger, *Jahrbuch der kunsthistorischen Sammlungen* XXIII, 1902, p. 43). The strange container with a lion-mask which appears in a codex of Francesco di Giorgio Martini (Trattati di architettura, a cura di C. Maltese, 1967, pl. 180; *Festschrift U. Middeldorf*, 1968, pl. 101) is, however, a pseudo-classical creation of the Quattrocento.

53   *Documentos de Arte Argentino*, Cuaderno XVII, 1945, pl. XIII. M. Toussaint, *Colonial art in Mexico*, 1967, p. 370.

54   Bronze mortar at Los Angeles: J. Pope-Hennessy, *Renaissance bronzes from the S. H. Kress collection*, 1265, No. 564.

55   Entrance door to Raphael's Logge: A. Pedrini, *L'ambiente, il mobilio e le decorazioni del Rinascimento*, 1925, fig. 461. Flemish interior, late 15th century: engraving by Israel van Meckenem, *The Art Quarterly* XXX, 1967, p. 218, fig. 9. There is no point in quoting any of the innumerable later examples.

56   Swiss Renaissance tile under Italian influence: *Anzeiger für schweizerische Altertumskunde* N. F. II, 1900, pl. II.

57   Relief by Alfonso Lombardi: A. Venturi, *Storia dell'arte italiana*, XI, p. 594.

58   F. J. B. Watson, Wallace Collection Cat., Furniture, 1956, No. 356, pl. 111.

59   Woodcut (by Dürer?) of a terrestrial globe in J. Schöner, *Luculentissima quaedam terrae totius descriptio*, Nürnberg 1515 (reprod. W. H. Schab, *Catalogue 27*, 1960, pl. 98). Clock: *The Burlington Magazine* 1961, p. 345.

60   F. Schottmüller, *Wohnungskultur und Möbel der italienischen Renaissance*, 2. Aufl., 1928, fig. 222. Here one might refer also to the architectural decoration on the Altar of the Holy Kinship by Quentin Massys in the Museum in Brussels. An interesting example of a later addition in Watson, *l.c.*, No. 405, pl. 38.

served any practical purpose. Often enough they are merely *trompe l'oeil*.

It might be thought too trivial to add Dutch armchairs from the seventeenth century to this already overlong catalogue, were it not that Rembrandt was once fascinated by their lions with rings. In his etched portrait of Jan Lutma he concentrated the light on the two fierce-looking animals on the uprights of the back of the chair (Fig. 8).[61]

Gold and silversmiths put lion-masks on their vessels.[62] On art objects made by or for Jews the lion with its biblical associations was always deemed permissible when all other imagery was avoided. So there could be no objection, even by the strictest standards, to the heads of lions on a Hevrah Kadisha cup.[63]

For arms and armour a ferocious lion was a most appropriate decoration. But to put a ring in its mouth was the triumph of an artistic formula over common sense. Only in a few instances, as on a sword pommel, could it be justified as serving a useful purpose.[64] The power of an art form once coined manifests itself in the lion-masks with rings which we find on harnesses,[65] baldrics,[66] helmets,[67] shields,[68] and even

61   The chair with the lions is not a fanciful invention by Rembrandt. Such chairs were then in fashion. They can be seen in Dutch interior paintings (Pieter de Hooch, etc.) and in contemporary portraits, like the one of Samuel Coster by Sandrart (*Münchner Jahrbuch der bild. Kunst*, N. F. II, 1935, 134). Even some originals still exist (J. Lauweriks, *Alt-Holland*, 3 Aufl., 1924, pl. 127).

62   The two English silver flagons in the Kremlin in Moscow have often been reproduced. They show the London hall-mark of 1600–01. Ch. Oman, *The English silver in the Kremlin*, 1961, frontispiece and p. 57; the same, *The Burlington Magazine* 1967, p. 183, fig. 103. The flagons are shaped like leopards. From their shoulders sprout two lion-masks with rings to which the chains of the movable lids are attached. This is a typical mannerist absurdity, but it may be wrong to blame the original silversmith for it as the flagons were evidently altered after having been sold to Russia. The shields originally contained a coat-of-arms. The lion-masks look like an afterthought.

63   Cup at Worms from 1608: *Monumenta Judaica. 2000 Jahre Geschichte und Kultur der Juden am Rhein, Katalog*, 1963, No. E 210.

64   Sword of Hector on Burgkmair's woodcut in the Genealogy of the Emperor Maximilian I: *Jahrbuch der kunsthistorischen Sammlungen* I, 1888, pl. I; L. Baldass, *Der Künstlerkreis Kaiser Maximilians*, 1923, pl. 72.

65   Both on actual examples and on the always more fanciful pictorial representations. For the former see the armour of Caspar von Frundsberg at Vienna, described in the inventory of 1583 as "Ain Harnisch hat vornen auf der Brust ein Lewenkopf mit einem Ring im Maul" (L. Luchner, *Denkmal eines Renaissancefürsten*, 1958, p. 74). Typical examples of the latter can be seen on Gerard David's wing from a Crucifixion triptych in the Museum in Antwerp (wrongly called "The Just Judges"); on the figure of Agamemnon in the "War

on horse armour and saddles.[69]

Our survey would not be complete without a passing reference to sarcophagi. Here, as in the Middle Ages, the imitation of classical models is manifest.[70]

CHINA

In a Chinese fairy-tale we hear about a house with a "high gateway, ornamented with bosses and a ring in a lion's mouth, as is the custom in the dwellings of those of high estate".[71] Such "rings in the mouth of lions" are as common in China as they are in Europe. Indeed, they belong to the items of material culture which Mongolians and Manchus received from the Chinese.[72]

When we study the appearance of such animal masks with rings in ancient Chinese art, we find that they occur quite frequently and served three different purposes:

(1) as handles of bronze (and later of other) vessels
(2) as door handles

of Troy" tapestry, Tournay, late 15th century, Victoria and Albert Museum; and on a statue from the tomb of Maximilian I (V. Oberhammer, *Die Bronzestandbilder des Maximiliangrabmales in der Hofkirche zu Innsbruck,* 1935, figs. 56, 103).

66 Oberhammer, *l.c.,* figs. 67, 224, 226.

67 Sixteenth century morion of the Trabanten Guard of the Electors of Saxony, Fitzwilliam Museum, Cambridge. Bashford Dean, *Handbook of arms and armor,* 4th ed., 1930, g. 99.

68 *Ehrenpforte des Kaisers Maximilian I.* (in the facsimile edition 1885–86, pl. 14).

69 B. Thomas, Der Prunkharnisch Kaiser Friedrichs III, *Belvedere* XIII, 1938/ 43, p. 198, fig. 184. Thomas has pointed out that the lion-masks with rings on the saddle are "possibly a fraudulent addition dating from a later epoch". Horse armour decorated in this way did, however, exist in the fifteenth century as can be seen on miniatures by Fouquet (J. Alazard, *Jean Fouquet,* 1952, pls. 14, 52). There exists a possible parallel from the Islamic world. A woodcut in a German travelbook from 1589 shows a cavalcade of Mohammedans with many details evidently observed on the spot; whether this applies also to the leonine masks on the horse trappings it is impossible to say. The book in question is Johann Helffrich, *Kurtzer und warhafftiger Bericht von der Reyss,* Leipzig 1589; a detached and unidentified copy of the woodcut was item 3293 in the exhibition of Islamic art in Munich 1919.

70 K. Ginhart, *Die Kaisergruft bei den PP. Kapuzinern in Wien,* 1925.

71 R. Wilhelm, *Chinesische Volksmärchen,* 1917, p. 77; *The Chinese Fairy Book,* translated by F. H. Martens, 1922, p. 85.

72 F. W. K. Müller, *Uigurica III, Abhandlungen der Preussischen Akademie der Wissenschaften,* 1920, p. 92. F. D. Lessing, *Mongolian–English Dictionary,* 1960, p. 530 ("Animal heads made of copper or iron with rings in their mouths attached to doors in lieu of knockers").

(3) for the decoration of coffins.

We notice, not without surprise, that these are exactly the functions for which the lions with rings in the Greco-Roman world were produced.

Nobody will deny that the Chinese learned the art of casting bronze vessels and implements from Western Asia, but at the same time their artistic decoration is clearly highly original and owes very little or nothing to foreign influences. When we find animal heads on the handles of early Chinese bronze vessels, it would be wrong to assume that this idea must have come from abroad. As in so many styles all over the world, there always existed, here also, a tendency towards a zoomorphic interpretation of abstract shapes. The upper half of the handle of some early Chinese bronze vessels received protruding eyes with eyebrows, nose and ears, and was thus transformed into a living being which seems to hold the handle in its mouth.[73] Or the handles by which the vessel was carried could appear as issuing from the jaws of two such beasts, one above and the other below.[74] This applies to fixed handles. In the case of swinging handles, it is either the handle itself which undergoes the metamorphosis into an animal, or the knob around which the handle moves becomes the head of an animal in its own right.[75]

These transformations are typical of the earlier phase of Chinese bronze art. Later, at a date which the still fluctuating chronology of early Chinese art prevents us from fixing precisely but which must fall within the period of the "Warring States" (480–221 B.C.), proper animal masks with rings appear everywhere.[76] In the Han period (202 B.C.– 220 A.D.) they are one of the most common motifs of decoration. If we try to tabulate their most striking characteristics, we might say that

(a) unlike the earlier zoomorphic handles, they do not form an integral part of the vessel; they were cast separately and soldered on;

(b) they are of comparatively small size and decorate the body of the vessel;

(c) the animal is a fantastic creature of the type which we call, traditionally but with little justification, a t'ao-t'ieh (glutton);

(d) while the Western lions hold the ring in their jaws, the Chinese beast holds it in its protruding beak or nose.

Derivations from this standard type are rare among the early bronzes,

---

73 For typical examples see W. Willets, *Chinese art,* 1958, I, p. 134, pl. 14a; W. Watson, *Ancient Chinese bronzes,* 1962, pl. 42b, 43b.

74 J. L. Davidson, The bird-in-the-animal-mouth on Chinese bronzes, *Gazette des Beaux-Arts,* 1945/I, p. 6, fig. 3.

75 Willets, l.c., pl. 11a; Watson, l.c., pls. 16, 24, 33b, etc.

76 For examples see Watson, l.c., pls. 58, 75a, 77b, etc.

but at least in one case we find in addition to the masks also complete, three-dimensional animals with rings sitting on the lid of the vessel.[77]

In our museums there are many such bronze t'ao-t'ieh masks with rings which are now detached fragments. It is not always possible to state what their original purpose was. Some have obviously been found separated from the bronze vessels which they once decorated.[78] Others, however, were found in tomb chambers, occasionally still attached to fragments of wooden boards. They were evidently used as handles for wooden coffins, a striking parallel to the identical usage in the Greco-Roman world at exactly the same time.[79]

Our knowledge of Han art comes mainly from tombs which at that period tended to be small-scale replicas of dwelling houses. These tomb chambers were often provided with "make-believe" doors where the engravings on the flat surface of the stone show the head of an animal or, sometimes, of a demon, always with a ring between the teeth (Fig. 9).[80] The same arrangement can be seen on bricks from the Han period, which also come from tombs.[81] On the doors and bricks the ring

77 Watson, l.c., pl. 60a (British Museum).
78 Several have been published by O. Karlbeck, Selected objects from ancient Shou-Chou, *Bulletin of the Museum of Far Eastern Antiquities*, Stockholm XXVII, 1955, pls. 35–38.
79 It has been suggested that these bronzes were fixed not only to the coffins, but also to the doors and beams of the tombs. O. Karlback, Notes on a Hui Hsien tomb, *Röhsska Konstslöjdmuseet Göteborg Arstryck* 1952, pp. 40–47. The masks there discussed and reproduced, one of which is still attached to the fragment of a beam, show the typical spirals of the Huai style (according to Karlgren ca. 650–200 B.C.). See also in the same yearbook (of the Röhss Museum of Arts and Crafts in Göteborg) 1951, p. 10 two such handles, one in Chou, the other in Han style. Practically identical with the "Huai" handle in Göteborg is one in the Kunstindustri Museum in Copenhagen (reproduced in W. Watson, *China before the Han dynasty*, 1961, pl. 55 as "5–4th c. B.C.") and another in a private collection (reprod. W. Watson, *Ancient Chinese bronzes*, 1962, pl. 88a, as "3rd–2nd c. B.C."). A mask still fixed to the wood, now in the British Museum, corresponds to Karlbeck, *l.c.*, fig. p. 47. Cf. W. P. Yetts, *The Eumorfopoulos Collection, Cat. of Chinese and Corean bronzes*, vol. 2, 1930, B 242–247, pl. LVII; the same, *The Cull Chinese bronzes*, 1939, p. 75 f.
80 The demons support the ring with their mouths, and also with arms which grow out of their heads. R. C. Rudoph and Wen Yu, *Han tomb art of West China. A collection of first and second-century reliefs*, 1951, fig. 5, pls. 60–63, 68–71. W. Willets, *Chinese art*, I, 1958, p. 288. A. Salmony, Le mascaron et l'anneau sur les pendentifs et appliqués dans l'art chinois, *Revue des arts asiatiques* VIII, 1934, p. 183, pl. 58b.
81 O. Jansé, *Briques et objets céramiques funeraires de l'époque des Han appartenant à C. T. Loo*, 1936, pl. IV, 3; cf. the review by P. Pelliot, *T'oung Pao* XXXII, 1936, p. 385.

handles are only simulated, and this applies also to a very common type of Han pottery vessels where the clay rings in relief have rightly been interpreted as imitations of metal prototypes.[82] In the same way, the lacquered wooden vessels from the Han period were provided with painted imitations of the metal t'ao-t'ieh masks and rings.[83]

The question which will be asked is whether this surprising spread of the mask with rings in late Chou and Han art was an indigenous Chinese development, a gradual transformation of the zoomorphic handles, or whether it was due to impulses received from the West. As in practically all such cases, any answer has to be tentative and cautiously worded, but it seems that we can say "yes" to both questions, or, to make our answer sound less paradoxical, we might say that the long tradition of zoomorphic handles enabled the Chinese craftsmen to accept whole-heartedly a Western art form, to regard it as something congenial, and to incorporate it into their artistic repertory.

During the latest phase of the Chou period and even more during the reign of the Han dynasty, China was widely open to foreign influences. Ideas and goods travelled in both directions. But, some might object, metal fittings hardly belong to the category of goods which would travel across the continent of Asia like silk from East to West, or glass beads or glass ware in the opposite direction.

Late Hellenistic lions with rings in their jaws did, however, undertake the long transcontinental journey. In excavations at Begram, Afghanistan, the French archaeological expedition under Joseph Hackin came across a trading post where Indian ivories, Chinese lacquer ware and Hellenistic glasses and bronzes had been stored, all dating from the first century of our era. Among the Western bronzes which were found there and which were presumably intended to be exported to the Far East, there were two which their discoverer described as "Masque de lion en bronze ayant tenu dans la gueule un anneau (anse de vase)." [84] We can safely assume that this was neither the first nor the last occasion that traders took such handles across the continent of Asia.

82 B. Laufer, Kunst und Kultur Chinas im Zeitalter der Han, Globus XCVI, 1909, p. 22; the same, Chinese pottery of the Han dynasty, 1909 (photographic reprint 1962), pp. 130, 133, 138–141, 145, 162, 201, 207, 210 f. Several of the reproductions in Laufer's book show bronze vessels. Some Chinese antiquarians speak of "animal rings", others call them "tiger heads"; see the discussion in Laufer p. 140. B. Gray, Early Chinese pottery and porcelain, 1953, p. 5, pl. 12.

83 Wiener Beiträge zur Kunst- und Kulturgeschichte Asiens VII, 1933, plate facing p. 60, fig. 5; and the remarks by O. Mänchen-Helfen, ibid., XI, 1937, p. 61.

84 Listed, but unfortunately not reproduced, in J. Hackin, Recherches archéologiques à Begram, 1939, p. 39, No. 198.

The West-East route was not the only one these bronzes travelled. At practically the same time the Chinese brought what they had received from the West to the North, to the nomads of Southern Siberia. At Abakan on the Yenisei a Russian expedition discovered a tomb with two bronze door handles of a most unusual kind.[85] They consist of heads of demons with bovine horns, who wear rings in their pierced noses.[86] The tomb can be dated with the help of a Chinese disc found there which shows an inscription in typical Han characters. The two heads of demons are of Chinese workmanship and character, but in their realistic modelling seem to show traces of Western influence.

The Han period was the golden age of the "animal rings". We find them everywhere. This does not mean that they disappeared later. It would be easy to quote examples from every century of Chinese art right up to modern times, but these are more or less exceptions or came into existence as conscious imitations in various materials of the early bronze vessels.[87]

In the art of the Han period, the animals are sometimes comparatively realistic and no longer the traditional t'ao-t'ieh types. A doe-like animal might be found with the suspension-ring in the jaw (the method of fixing the ring which was used in the Western world),[88] or a beast which although not a lion shows unmistakable feline characteristics, but carries the ring in the traditional Chinese way in its nose.[89] It is only later, on a bronze stand which is believed to date from the period of the Six Dynasties (220–589), that we find on one and the same bronze the head of a lion (or at least an animal intended to be a lion) together with the Western method of hinging the ring between the teeths of the beast.[90]

The lion does not occur in China, and for the Chinese it was always a foreign animal which few artists had ever seen.[91] The animals on the

85 L. A. Evtjuchova, Drevnekitajskoe zdanie na srednem Enisee, *Vestnik drevnej istorii* 1946, 1, pp. 107–111. S. V. Kiselev, *Drevnaja istorija Juzhnoi Sibirii*, 1951, p. 482, pl. XLI.

86 For modern instances of the use of nose rings see B. Laufer, Anneaux nasaux en Chine, *T'oung Pao*, 2e ser., VI, 1905, pp. 321–323.

87 The Han pottery vessels are copies of contemporary metal models. Archaizing pottery inspired by ancient bronzes occurs for the first time in the Sung period (960–1279); a typical example with mask and ring can be seen in R. L. Hobson, *Handbook of the pottery and porcelain of the Far East*, 1937, fig. 50.

88 V. Elisséeff, La hache et quelques bronzes de la récente donation de D. David-Weill, *Arts asiatiques* 1, 1954, p. 14, fig. 15.

89 O. Karlbeck, *Bulletin of the Museum of Far Eastern Antiquities* XXVII, 1955, p. 101, pl. 37, 3.

90 O. Sirén, *Histoire des arts anciens de la Chine*, II, 1929, p. 94, pl. 113.

91 P. Pelliot (*La Haute Asie*, 1931, p. 8) says: "Les Chinois, chez qui le lion n'a

large Chinese storage vessels, which were made for export and which are now found in large numbers in the Philippines and elsewhere, were apparently intended to be lions.[92] Their muzzles are pierced in the Western manner, so that the jars could be carried by ropes; a utilitarian ware as distinct from the artistic show-pieces with their make-believe rings.

We must not think that the Western lion with ring was taken over only once. In the course of time foreign models must have reached the Far East on many occasions. The handles on K'ang-hsi porcelain (1662–1722) look as if they had been inspired by contemporary European models.[93] On the other hand, the lion could also become completely sinicized and assume the familiar benign features of the Chinese horned dragon, as on a ceramic mask from the T'ang period [94] (Fig. 10) or, to quote an example roughly a thousand years later, on the wine container depicted on a porcelain dish from the Yung-cheng period (1723–35) [95] (Fig. 11).

To sum up: at some time during the last centuries B.C. the Greek lion-masks with rings reached China where they were imitated on bronze vessels. From the first they fitted extremely well into a style where zoomorphic handles had a long history. Such Western bronze fittings must have reached the Far East on many occasions. During the Han period they appear innumerable times in Chinese art, now also in their Western functions as door handles and door knockers. From then on the motif of the "animal ring" never disappeared from Chinese art; usually it was sinicized but sometimes, under the impact of fresh imports from the West, is appeared as a more or less faithful copy of European models.

When in the late eighteenth century a French designer incorporated

jamais existé, ont connu l'animal au 1er siècle de notre ère par la Perse et l'ont alors appelé de son nom iranien; mais ils l'avaient connu une première fois au IVe siècle avant notre ère, et cette fois sous son nom indien." Henning has shown that the Indian and the Iranian words for "lion" are etymologically related, and has moreover tentatively suggested that the earlier Chinese loanword might be of Iranian origin too; cf. W. B. Henning, A Grain of Mustard, *Annali dell'Istituto Orientale di Napoli* VI, 1965, p. 45 f. Naturally, the linguistic relationship of the two words does not effect Pelliot's statement; it would have to be modified if the Iranian origin of both loans could be proved.

92 F.-C. Cole, *Chinese pottery in the Philippines,* 1912, p. 23, pls. 6–8.
93 Reproduced in the catalogue of a sale at Christie's, London, June 19, 1967, item 33.
94 Fitzwilliam Museum, Cambridge (L. C. G. Clarke Bequest, C 101–1961).
95 From the W. J. Holt collection (sale Christie's, May 15, 1964). A very similar dish belongs to the Percival David Foundation, London (Lady David, *Illustr. Cat. of Ch'ing enamelled wares,* 1958, No. 861).

such a vessel into his *Chinoiserie* arrangement, he regarded as exotic something which had originally come from the West.[96]

SOME FINAL REMARKS

Some 2,500 years ago a Greek artist conceived the strange idea of putting a movable ring into the mouth of a lion, or rather of combining two traditional elements, an artistic and a utilitarian one, by uniting a lion *protome* with a swinging handle. The new art form, once created, lived on everywhere and became almost immortal.

It would never have been so successful if its appeal were so simple that it could be expressed in a short formula. As in every "success story", there were many contributary factors and ambiguity played a considerable part. The figure of a lion was the traditional guardian of the dwellings and belongings of the living and of the dead. Human pride could find immense satisfaction in imposing on the fiercest of beasts a most menial task. And in addition, a playful element slipped in. The *homo ludens* made the lion into a performing animal, frightened by it and at the same time showing his superiority over it.

Almost from the beginning, the lion-masks with rings belonged, although by no means exclusively, to the sphere of tomb art with its traditionalism and fear of innovations. This was one of the reasons why the masks were copied so often. They are frequently very difficult to date, as the range of artistic possibilities was necessarily limited, and as many of them were the work of artisans who handed on traditional forms, often in provincial backwaters. This applies also to those destined for secular use. And yet this conservatism often provided artists with a stimulus to re-create a form which had become stale.

It would be wrong to say that a form which once served a practical purpose late became a mere decoration. The two intentions existed side by side from the beginning and helped each other to achieve their world-wide acceptance.

Not the least of the contributing factors was that both in ancient Greece and in ancient China these door handles were used so much in a phase of art which for posterity became the "classical" one. Whenever later generations took their inspiration from works of the past, they came across the masks with rings.

The name of the artist who was the first to combine the two is unknown, but posterity has honoured him with many monuments. Some will say, far too many.

96 Block-printed cotton, French (Jouy), c. 1780, Victoria and Albert Museum, London (T. 320–1919).

FONTAINES MYSTIQUES ET FONTAINES PROFANES
dans l'art du 15ème siècle

par

LOLA SLEPTZOFF

Les représentations de fontaines symboliques sont fréquentes au 15ème siècle dans l'art des Pays-Bas, de la France, de la Rhénanie et même de l'Italie du nord. Nous nous proposons d'en considérer quelques variétés, de caractère religieux aussi bien que non-religieux, et d'analyser leur signification.

Le motif, certes, n'était pas nouveau; il avait un long passé dans l'art chrétien, et son origine remontait beaucoup plus haut encore.

Le concept de la Fontaine de Vie avait existé dans les antiques religions de l'Inde et de l'Iran. Dans l'Ancien Testament se rencontrent souvent des métaphores telles que l'"eau de la vie" et la "fontaine de vie" évoquant la vie spirituelle et l'inépuisable bénédiction de Dieu. Ces images sont reprises maintes fois dans le Nouveau Testament. Le paganisme grec et romain établissait de son côté un rapport entre l'eau de fontaines sacrées et l'immortalité.[1]

Des représentations du *Fons Vitae* apparurent dans les catacombes chrétiennes, parfois en parallèle avec Moïse faisant jaillir l'eau du rocher;[2] elles symbolisaient évidemment la résurrection spirituelle et la béatitude apportées par la doctrine du Christ et, dans un sens plus général, l'Eglise. A partir du 6ème siècle, l'idée plus précise du baptême se surajouta à ces notions.[3] Dans les manuscrits carolingiens, le *Fons Vitae* reproduisit la forme d'un baptistère. Enfin, l'idée de l'Incarnation et de la Maternité Virginale s'associa à celle du baptême; Marie fut

---

1 Cf. Franz Cumont, *After Life in Roman Paganism* (Yale Univ. Press, New Haven, 1922), p. 110 sq.

2 Oskar Wulff, *Altchristliche und Byzantinische Kunst* (Handbuch der Kunstwissenschaft, Potsdam, 1924), pp. 75 et 88.

3 Paul Underwood, *The Fountain of Life in MSS of the Gospels* (Dumbarton Oaks Papers No 5, 1950), p. 51, rappelle que St Jérôme, commentant l'image du Psaume XLII ("Comme une biche soupire après les courants d'eau...") lui associait déjà l'idée du baptême. Il signale qu'une fresque du cubiculum d'Abdon et Sennen (catacombes romaines de Pontianus, 6ème siècle) représentait le baptême du Christ dans le Jourdain avec, dans le coin inférieur à gauche, un cerf s'abreuvant.

assimilée à l'Eglise, ayant été comme elle fécondée par le Saint-Esprit. Le baptême étant l'équivalent d'une naissance (ou plutôt d'une résurrection ou re-naissance) la fontaine fut acceptée comme symbole de la Vierge, mère du Rédempteur, aussi bien que comme symbole de l'Eglise, à travers qui l'humanité renaît à la vie spirituelle.

Pendant un millénaire, le *Fons Vitae* avait gardé une signification très homogène, quoique nuancée. Pour la forme, il se réduisait à quelques types principaux : amphore, cratère, vasque ronde ou polygonale ou rotonde.[4]

A la fin du Moyen-Age, le motif se morcela; sa forme se diversifia et il s'enrichit d'implications nouvelles qui reflétaient les tendances de la pensée chrétienne de l'époque — son mysticisme tendre ou tragique, sa foi sereine et candide ou, au contraire, sourdement tourmentée par une mauvaise conscience résultant de circonstances historiques et culturelles.

Pour commencer, nous examinerons un genre de fontaines qui illustre le côté sensible, poétique et familier de la pensée religieuse : le *Fons Hortorum*.[5]

Le Fons Hortorum

Hortus conclusus soror mea sponsa,
hortus conclusus, fons signatus.
Fons hortorum, puteus aquarum viventium
(Cantique des Cantiques, IV, 12, 15)

Une fontaine scellée dans un jardin fermé : nulle image ne pouvait mieux convenir à la Vierge. Il y avait d'ailleurs plusieurs siècles que les commentateurs avaient reconnu dans la Sulamite une préfigure de Marie.

Le *Fons Hortorum* fut une métaphore également chère aux artistes, qui ne la séparèrent pas de celle de l'*Hortus Conclusus*. Jardin et fontaine devinrent les principaux attributs de la *Vierge à l'Enfant* — de la Vierge toute jeune et qui n'as pas encore connu la douleur. Ils figurent souvent aussi dans les *Annonciations* et même, parfois, dans les *Nativités*. D'autres images provenant du *Cantique des Cantiques*, tels le Lys de la Vallée et la Rose de Sharon, s'y incorporèrent.

4 Lars-Ivar Ringbom, *Paradisus Terrestris* (Acta Societatis Scientiarum Fennicae, Helsingfors, 1958), *passim*.
5 Certains auteurs (Cf. Evelyn Underhill, *The Fountain of Life: an iconographical study*, Burlington Magazine, Vol. XVII, 1910) veulent séparer nettement du *Fons Vitae* cet attribut de Marie. Nous pensons qu'une telle distinction n'est pas justifiée et que l'image du *Cantique des Cantiques* s'est superposée à celle suggérée par l'équation Mater-Ecclesia/Marie/Fontaine de Vie, déjà apparente dans les Evangéliaires carolingiens (Cf. Underwood, *art. cit.*).

Dans la peinture, le motif apparaît vers 1400. Un tableau anonyme du premier quart du siècle montre Marie entourée de ces symboles [6] (Fig. 1). On y voit notamment une servante qui puise de l'eau dans un simple bassin de pierre de forme rectangulaire. Une louche est fixée au bout d'une chaîne, et l'eau se déverse par un conduit de bois faiblement incliné où un oiseau est perché. Le caractère symbolique de l'oeuvre est estompé; le peintre veut exprimer la grâce divine en s'adressant aux sens du spectateur, en faisant ressortir la jeunesse et la douceur des personnages, le charme du ciel, de la verdure, des fleurs; il suggère l'harmonie par la présence d'oiseaux et d'instruments de musique et flatte même le sens du goût en mettant des pommes rouges et un gobelet sur la table. Mais cette sensualité est évidemment toute pure et innocente. La fontaine s'accorde à cette atmosphère rustique, car sa forme est celle des auges dans lesquelles on fait boire le bétail. Elle évoque l'humble origine de la Vierge et sa modestie.[7]

D'autres artistes imaginaient la Vierge moins familière, plus isolée

6 Musée de Francfort-sur-le-Main. Oeuvre couramment désignée sous le nom de *Paradiesgärtlein*.

7 Des fontaines semblables existaient dans d'autres oeuvres d'artistes du nord, par exemple dans la *Fuite en Egypte* de Broederlam, antérieure de quelques années (scène de droite du rétable de Dijon, Musée de la Ville, comprenant aussi une *Annonciation*, une *Visitation* et une *Présentation*; cf. Panofsky, *Early Netherlandish Painting*, Harvard Univ., 1953, Pl. 51). Au premier plan, au-dessous de la Vierge, on voit une auge rectangulaire d'où s'écoule un filet d'eau. Bien qu'il ne s'agisse pas à proprement parler d'une fontaine de la Vierge mais de la fontaine miraculeusement apparue à la Sainte Famille dans le désert, l'artiste l'a placée tout près du personnage de Marie. Le ruisseau court parallèlement au chemin qu'elle suit, et, pour le spectateur, les motifs de la Vierge et de la fontaine se complètent si parfaitement dans la structure du tableau que ni l'oeil ni la mémoire ne peuvent les séparer l'un de l'autre.

C'est ce que sentirent encore des peintres qui traitèrent le même sujet plus d'un siècle après la mort de Broederlam. Patenier et Joos van Cleve représentèrent tous deux Marie assise sur un tertre et allaitant l'Enfant, tandis qu'à ses pieds coule parmi les fleurs et les herbes aquatiques l'eau d'une fontaine. Joseph est à peine visible à l'arrière-plan (Patenier, *Repos pendant la Fuite en Egypte*, Musée du Prado, Madrid; V. Cleve, même sujet, Musée de Bruxelles. Reproductions dans M. J. Friedländer, *From van Eyck to Bruegel*, Londres, 1956, Pl. 181 et 201). Il n'y a pas lieu, pour ces deux oeuvres, d'examiner la structure des fontaines; elles sont taillées dans le roc de façon rudimentaire et recouvertes d'une dalle qui les protège contre les impuretés. Ce type, commun dans les campagnes, peut aussi être considéré comme une représentation du *fons signatus*. Le rapprochement conscient — la fusion presque — de ce motif avec la figure de la Vierge dans des compositions très voisines, du point de vue iconographique, de celle de Broederlam, confirme l'impression que ce dernier avait déjà voulu relier la fontaine à la personne de Marie.

dans sa gloire; ils pensaient que tout ce qui l'entourait devait porter la marque de la plus extrême élégance, en signe de respect et d'adoration. Tel Stefano da Verona dans sa *Madone au Buisson de Roses* [8] (Fig. 2). Ce peintre, qui ne mourut qu'en 1451, était resté fidèle au "Gothique International"; à cette tendance s'ajoute peut-être ici l'influence de miniatures persanes, comme l'a suggéré K. Clark.[9] Au fond du jardin on aperçoit une fontaine entourée d'anges.[10] Elle se compose d'un petit bassin quadrilobé au centre duquel se dresse une fine colonne supportant une délicate structure gothique, véritable travail d'orfèvrerie. La forme du bassin a pu être inspirée par les bassins polylobés fréquents dans les miniatures persanes, mais cette forme était probablement connue en Europe également pendant tout le Moyen-Age. L'ornement du pilier central reproduit à une échelle très réduite une tour de cathédrale gothique. Cette forme fut empruntée par l'architecture non religieuse et on la retrouve dans les beffrois des Hôtels de Ville de Flandre et dans des demeures privées comme celle de Jacques Coeur à Bourges. Mais c'est surtout la sculpture et l'orfèvrerie qui reproduisirent ce motif indéfiniment au 14ème, 15ème, et même au 16ème siècle. Tantôt il accompagne des statues, de caractère religieux ou non, tantôt il apparaît sous forme de reliquaire (Fig. 3) et d'ostensoir. On prit l'habitude de placer une superstructure de ce genre, ornée ou non de statuettes, au sommet du pilier central des fontaines; il existe aussi des objets d'usage

8   Musée de Castelvecchio, Vérone
9   *Landscape into Art* (Harmondsworth, 1956), p. 25. Des miniatures illustrant les poèmes de Firdousi, Nizami, Omar Kheyyam, Hafiz et Saadi représentaient souvent des jardins royaux, parfois même entourés d'un mur, où les plantes qui parsemaient le gazon formaient des dessins comparables à ceux des tapis. En outre, des tapis somptueux, sur lesquels étaient assis les personnages de marque, mêlaient leurs vives couleurs à celles des pelouses fleuries. On y voyait aussi des fontaines. Certaines de ces miniatures circulaient sans aucum doute en Italie du nord.
10   Et certainement pas "a little triptych-shrine" comme l'a écrit Thomas Bodkin dans la note qui accompagne une reproduction de ce tableau (*The Virgin and Child*, Faber and Feber, Londres, 1945), p. 6. C'est éventuellement à un reliquaire que cet objet pourrait être comparé, mais il apparaît nettement que sa base est un bassin et que les anges tendent les mains vers des jets d'eau. La présence d'un autel ou d'un reliquaire serait tout à fait exceptionnelle, tandis qu'une fontaine a naturellement sa place dans un *Hortus Conclusus*. Le fait que les jets d'eau ne soient pas visibles doit provenir de ce que, peints légèrement et en surface pour produire un effet de transparence, ils se sont obscurcis avec le temps au point de devenir imperceptibles, à moins qu'un nettoyage trop brutal ne les ait effacés, le restaurateur n'ayant pas compris l'intention du peintre.

domestique qui copient la forme de telles fontaines.[11] Toutefois, bien que ce motif ait été aussi adopté par l'art non religieux, il est possible que la configuration de la petite fontaine de Stefano soit destinée à suggérer des sentiments de piété, unissant l'idée de la virginité de Marie à celle de la Communion.

Une fontaine assez semblable se trouve dans une *Nativité,* oeuvre du "Maître de 1410–1415" (artiste originaire de Gueldre septentrionale ou de Clèves).[12] Des anges transportent de l'eau pour la toilette de l'Enfant, soit dans une cruche posée sur l'épaule, soit en balançant deux seaux sur une perche de bois. La fontaine, située au premier plan à gauche, possède une vasque polylobée à pilier gothique — plus lourd et moins fouillé que chez Stefano — montée sur un pied orné de plusieurs renflements circulaires et d'un anneau polygonal. La base est ronde. Dans son ensemble, cette fontaine fait penser à un calice dans lequel on aurait planté une sorte d'ostensoir. On sent que l'artiste a fait de son mieux pour lui donner une allure élégante et recherchée. D'autres détails attestent ce souci, par exemple le beau tapis oriental qui recouvre le lit sur lequel la Vierge est assise.[13]

On peut voir une fontaine identique (à ceci près que sa vasque est ronde) dans une gravure tirée de l'édition de 1510 des *Heures* à l'usage du diocèse d'Angers publiée par Simon Vostre.[14] Cette gravure représente Ste Anne entourée des attributs de la Vierge. Le pilier central de la fontaine est plus élancé que dans la petite *Nativité* du Musée de Berlin, et une palissade de joncs entoure cette fontaine, désignée par une banderole comme "Fons Hortorum".

Ces fontaines en forme de calice possèdent une variété plus simple. La *Madone à la Fontaine* de Jan van Eyck [15] en offre un exemple. Son pied cylindrique est sobrement orné d'anneaux régulièrement espacés; la partie inférieure, assez épaisse, est polygonale. Le pilier central est terminé par une boule d'où l'eau est expulsée par quatre petites têtes de lions; une statuette de lion assis est au sommet. La fontaine, cette fois, n'est pas en pierre, mais probablement en bronze. Une fontaine presque

---

11 Cf. la reproduction d'une pièce centrale de service de table en argent doré orné d'émail transparent, *Apollo* (décembre 1963), p. 115, exécuté en France à la fin du 14ème siècle. L'objet fait partie de la collection du Musée d'Art de Cleveland.

12 Deutsches Museum, Berlin. Reprod. dans Panofsky, *op. cit.,* Pl. 56 No. 110.

13 Le clayonnage qui entoure la hutte, de même que la fontaine, rappellent que Marie est demeurée vierge après la naissance de Jésus.

14 E. Mâle, *L'Art Religieux de la Fin du Moyen-Age en France* (Paris, 1925), fig. 117, p. 220.

15 Musée Royal, Anvers.

identique se trouve dans une *Vierge à l'Enfant* peinte par Jan Provost quelque soixante ans plus tard.[16]

On ne saurait terminer cet aperçu sans mentionner un objet que l'on rencontre souvent dans des scènes d'intérieur telles que l'*Annonciation,* la *Vierge à l'Enfant,* etc. Il s'agit d'une cuvette simple ou ornée de godrons, parfois accompagnée d'une cruche. Sans doute, à première vue, ces ustensiles peints avec un grand soin ne sont-ils pas frappants en tant que symboles de la pureté mariale : la limite est difficile à tracer entre les éléments symboliques d'une scène religieuse peinte au 15ème siècle en Europe du nord, et ceux qui relèvent seulement d'une imitation fidèle de la réalité.[17] Toutefois, la répétition du motif de la cuvette dans des scènes d'un sens très précis indique qu'il s'agit d'un symbole. Panofsky[18] y voit l'équivalent, dans une maison, de la *Fontaine des Jardins.* Il apparaît notamment dans l'*Annonciation* du *Retable de Mérode,* de Robert Campin,[19] qui présente un récipient de cuivre poli suspendu à une chaîne dans une niche, et dans l'*Annonciation* du *Retable de Gand,* des van Eyck,[20] qui comporte une cruche de cuivre accrochée elle aussi dans une niche, et au-dessous de laquelle est placée une cuvette. Ailleurs, la cruche est posée dans la cuvette, comme dans la *Madone au Coin du Feu,* de Campin,[21] ou dans l'*Annonciation* de Roger van der Weyden.[22] Enfin, la cruche peut être assez éloignée de la cuvette, ou la cuvette peut être seule, ainsi que le montrent certaines *Vierges à l'Enfant* de Jan van Eyck.[23]

Exception faite des structures très rustiques rencontrées dès la fin du 14ème siècle et des cuvettes qui sont des substituts de fontaines,[24] les fontaines de la Vierge possèdent donc un pilier central tantôt d'une richesse et d'une complexité gothique, tantôt d'une sobriété toute clas-

16 Museo Civico, Piacenza. Reprod. dans Friedländer, *op. cit.,* Pl. 205.

17 Par exemple le banc orné de petits lions sur lequel s'appuie la Vierge dans l'*Annonciation* du *Rétable de Mérode* (Metropolitan Museum, New-York). S'agit-il d'une allusion au "trône de Salomon" — ou est-ce simplement la reproduction exacte d'un meuble alors commun dans les intérieurs flamands?

18 *Op. cit.,* p. 137.

19 Metropolitan Museum, New-York.

20 St-Bavon, Gand.

21 Musée de l'Ermitage, Léningrad.

22 Panneau central d'un triptyque, Musée du Louvre, Paris, Panofsky, *op. cit.,* Pl. 98.

23 Par ex. "*Ince Hall Madonna*", Nat. Gallery of Victoria, Melbourne, et la *Vierge à l'Enfant* du Städelisches Kunstinstitut, Francfort.

24 Exception faite, aussi, d'un autre symbole de la virginité de Marie, le *Puteus aquarum viventium.* Ce motif, peu susceptible de développements plastiques, a peu tenté les artistes.

sique; leur bassin, dans beaucoup de cas, ne touche pas la terre mais s'appuie sur un pied, ce qui ajoute à la sveltesse de l'ensemble. Ainsi les fontaines de Marie s'associent-elles à sa beauté juvénile.

Il arrive pourtant que l'on trouve un type de fontaines plus monumental, au bassin rond ou polygonal reposant sur le sol. Une gravure tirée des *Heures* à l'usage de Rome, de Thielman Kerver, datant de 1505, représente la Vierge comme une toute jeune fille, debout, les mains jointes, et entourée des emblèmes des litanies.[25] La fontaine, ici encore désignée par une banderole ("Fons Hortorum") a un pilier central assez épais renflé à mi-hauteur. Un petit jet d'eau sort du sommet tandis que quatre autres jaillissent des ornements disposés autour du renflement et retombent dans un bassin hexagonal. Cette structure, rarement rencontrée parmi les fontaines qui illustrent le thème de la pureté mariale, est fréquente, en revanche, parmi celles des *Jardins du Paradis* Céleste ou Terrestre et des *Jardins d'Amour*.[26]

En marge du Fons Hortorum : la Fontaine de Bethsabée

Avant d'aborder ces sujets, il faut noter un thème dont l'iconographie fut influencée par celle du *Fons Hortorum*, et, par suite, de l'*Hortus Conclusus* — c'est Bethsabée se baignant à la fontaine. Sans doute ne s'agit-il pas ici d'emblèmes de virginité. Mais Bethsabée peut y avoir droit en tant que préfigure de Marie.[27] Il arrive même que, par contamination iconographique, la même fontaine soit allouée à la chaste Suzanne (Fig. 4).

25 E. Mâle, *op. cit.,* fig. 111.
26 Dès l'origine, les fontaines mystiques assumèrent des formes telles que vases (emplis de l'eau d'éternité), structures de baptistères, etc. Leur sens était clair. Le rapport est moins évident en ce qui concerne la configuration polygonale, si fréquente, des bassins. Elle dérive des cuves baptismales octogonales ou hexagonales, auxquelles les commentateurs attachaient une signification mystique fondée sur la symbolique des nombres, le *huit* étant associé à la Résurrection ,et le *six*, en général, à la Crucifixion (Cf. Underwood, *op. cit.,* p. 88 sq.). Cependant, ces formes devinrent si courantes que le symbole s'effaça. Au 15ème siècle, il est oublié; nous verrons plus loin que les *Fontaines de Jouvence* sont souvent polygonales, ainsi que les *Fontaines d'Amour*, tandis que les *Fontains de Sang* (où cette forme aurait dû logiquement s'imposer) ne le sont pas toujours. L'analogie partielle des thèmes et la "paresse" qui pousse les artistes à se servir de moules tout prêts pour exprimer des idées nouvelles, contribuèrent à effacer cette géométrie sacrée.
27 Dans la typologie mariale, le couronnement de la Vierge est préfiguré par Bethsabée s'asseyant à la droite de son fils Salomon (III Rois, 2, 19), et Marie est scouvent appelée la "nouvelle Bethsabée". En outre, Bethsabée, dans l'exégèse, représente l'Eglise; elle est pour St Bruno la figure d'Ecclesia purifiée par le baptême (L. Réau, *Iconographie de l'Art Chrétien,* Paris, 1955, I, p. 273).

Pourtant, malgré l'impression de pureté produite par les représentations de Bethsabée au 15ème siècle, la présence de David observant d'une fenêtre la baigneuse nue introduit dans le thème une note amoureuse. La fontaine de Bethsabée se situe, en quelque sorte, à mi-chemin entre les fontaines de la Vierge et les Fontaines d'Amour.

Fontaines du Paradis Céleste et du Paradis Terrestre

Les fontaines du Paradis Céleste se rattachent aussi, dans une certaine mesure, à celles de la Vierge. On les trouve surtout, au 15ème siècle, dans la scène finale des *Chasses à la Licorne* : il est significatif que les artistes se soient sentis poussés à placer ces symboles de la béatitude dans un contexte narratif, agrémenté de détails réalistes.

La licorne, dès les premiers siècles de l'ère chrétienne, fut considérée comme l'un des symboles de l'Incarnation. Cet animal fabuleux avait la réputation de ne pouvoir être capturé vivant, à moins qu'une vierge ne l'apprivoise ; désormais inoffensif, il tombait dans un profond sommeil et les chasseurs pouvaient s'en emparer. Ces précisions, tirées du *Physiologus,* furent diffusées par les Bestiaires et l'on en vint très vite à voir dans la licorne le symbole du Christ et dans la vierge, celui de Marie. Dans l'art, le motif d'une licorne s'agenouillant devant la Vierge, dans l'*Hortus Conclusus,* apparaît vers 1400.[28] Au 15ème siècle, la licorne figure souvent sur des tapisseries illustrant le sujet d'une chasse et, allégoriquement, la Passion et la Rédemption.

A l'occasion du mariage d'Anne de Bretagne et de Louis XII, une série de tapisseries fut exécutée sur ce thème.[29] Le septième épisode représente une licorne blessée au côté mais vivante — tel le Christ ressuscité — emprisonnée dans un enclos pareil à un *Hortus Conclusus*; l'intention de l'artiste était sans aucun doute de montrer le Sauveur interné dans la Vierge.[30] Dans la scène de la capture, licorne et fontaine sont réunies à l'intérieur d'une clairière entourée d'un rideau d'arbres : le Paradis Céleste (Fig. 5). Des chasseurs immobiles et comme étonnés se tiennent auprès de la fontaine à bassin circulaire et pilier central orné de têtes de lions ; on remarque des oiseaux sur la margelle, preuve de la persistance de l'antique motif rencontré dans les plus anciennes représentations du *Fons Vitae,* où les oiseaux s'abreuvant à l'eau d'éternité figuraient les âmes des bienheureux. La licorne trempe sa corne dans le

---

28   Dans un tableau de la Galerie de Weimar. Cf. Clark, *op. cit.,* p. 24.
29   Aux "Cloisters" du Metropolitan Museum, New-York.
30   Le monogramme IHS sur le collier de l'un des chiens (5ème tapisserie) confirme qu'il s'agit d'un thème christologique.

ruisseau alimenté par le trop-plein du bassin — car elle pouvait ainsi, croyait-on, purifier tout liquide.

Quant au Jardin d'Eden, il ne possède pas toujours de fontaine. La Genèse dit seulement qu' "un fleuve sortait d'Eden pour arroser le jardin et de là se divisait en quatre bras".[31] Mais, très tôt, le *Fons Vitae* y fut introduit, le texte biblique se prêtant (et, visuellement, exigeant presque) une telle interprétation. Au 15ème siècle, on trouve fréquemment ce symbole au Jardin d'Eden.

Dans une miniature des frères de Limbourg[32] la fontaine a une importance particulière ; c'est un véritable petit sanctuaire, une rotonde de style gothique qui s'appuie sur des colonnes graciles. Pour la première fois depuis les temps carolingiens, une *Fontaine de Vie* est placée à l'intérieur d'un édicule. Son bassin est hexagonal et son pilier central, épais et cannelé, est orné de mascarons. Les côtés du bassin sont décorés de statuettes dans des niches jumelées.

La fontaine d'Eden des Limbourg est une exception. En général les artistes se contentèrent de répéter le type habituel : bassin rond ou polygonal, pilier central accompagné ou non de l'ornement en forme de petite tour gothique, têtes de lions (Fig. 6). Bosch[33] préféra un bassin carré et combina cette forme à celle d'une vasque ronde.

Echanges iconographiques

Etant donné la parenté théologique des thèmes du Paradis Céleste et du Paradis Terrestre, on comprend qu'ils se soient mutuellement prêté leurs symboles. De plus, dans l'art visuel, les artistes placés devant ces thèmes voisins subissaient l'effet des traditions iconographiques ; il leur parut naturel d'introduire, par exemple, au Paradis Céleste, les quatre rivières de l'Eden (où elles symbolisèrent les Evangiles) ; de transporter les oiseaux du Paradis Céleste (âmes des bienheureux) à la fontaine de l'Eden et à celle de l'*Hortus Conclusus* — même à celle du *Jardin d'Amour,* ou encore d'introduire au Jardin d'Eden le Mur et le Buisson de Roses du Jardin de Marie, la "nouvelle Eve".

Les Fontaines d'Amour

Ainsi qu'on pouvait s'y attendre, des jardins profanes correspondaient dans l'art du 15ème siècle à ces jardins sacrés. "Vergers de plaisir" et

---

31 2, 10. Même au 15ème siècle, il est parfois représenté comme un paysage traversé par un fleuve (relief de Ghiberti au Baptistère de Florence ; miniature de Simon Marmion, MS 9047, Bibliothèque Nationale, Bruxelles, etc.).

32 *Tentation. Chute et Expulsion. Très Riches Heures du Duc de Berry,* Musée Condé, Chantilly.

33 Panneau du *Paradis Terrestre,* Palais Ducal, Venise.

fontaines étaient des thèmes conventionnels de la littérature courtoise. Pour leur donner une expression visuelle, les artistes ne s'inspirèrent pas des jardins et fontaines réels qu'ils pouvaient avoir sous les yeux (une telle supposition serait un anachronisme) mais se tournèrent vers les représentations du Paradis Céleste, Terrestre ou Virginal. Le transfert de motifs sacrés au domaine profane était fréquent à la fin du Moyen-Age : il n'était pas surprenant d'entendre chanter une chanson d'amour sur un air d'église. Si une fontaine dans un jardin symbolisait l'amour divin et les délices de l'âme, cette même image pouvait aussi s'appliquer au "paradis" de l'amour profane. La Vulgate ne traduit-elle pas "Jardin d'Eden" par "paradisum voluptatis"?[34] Les artistes placèrent donc des équivalents du *Fons Vitae* et du *Fons Hortorum* dans des jardins qui devaient évoquer les plaisirs de ce monde, non ceux de l'au-delà.

Il n'entre aucune intention sacrilège dans les représentations de *Fontaines d'Amour* qui apparurent au début du 15ème siècle. L'idéologie courtoise avait fait de la femme une sorte de divinité et de l'amour une sorte de religion, compatible bien entendu avec la Religion. Loin d'être considéré comme avilissant (excepté par les ascètes et les cyniques), l'amour passait pour être la voie indispensable du perfectionnement du coeur, de l'esprit et de l'âme. Le culte passionné de la Vierge, surtout à partir du 13ème siècle, fut en grande partie une sublimation de l'amour courtois. Il est donc normal qu'en retour le vocabulaire religieux ait fourni des métaphores aux poètes pour parler de l'amour humain, et que l'art religieux ait fourni des motifs à l'art profane.

C'est dans un vaste *Jardin d'Amour* que le poète-musicien Guillaume de Machaut reçoit la visite de Dame Nature et de sa suite.[35] Au centre du jardin se trouve une fontaine d'un type familier : vasque ronde posée sur une colonne, l'eau coulant par quatre orifices dans un bassin hexagonal. Ces quatre bouches ont perdu ici tout sens symbolique. Le caractère vertueux du sujet est explicitement indiqué : il s'agissait pour l'artiste d'illustrer "comment Nature, voulant révéler les biens et honneurs qui sont en Amour, vient à Guillaume, lui ordonne de faire sur ce thème de nouveaux dits amoureux et lui donne pour conseillers trois de ses enfants, Sens, Rhétorique et Musique".

Une impression de noblesse et de plaisir serein se dégage également

---

34 Genèse, 2, 8.

35 Miniature anonyme d'un MS des oeuvres de Guillaume de Machaut, Bibliothèque Nat., Paris, Fr. 1584, f. E (reproduite dans *MSS à peintures du 13ème au 16ème siècle*, B.N., Paris, 1955, Pl. XVII). Le jardin est cerné par une route mais *non enclos* : cette miniature, qui date d'environ 1370, n'a pas subi l'influence de l'iconographie de l'*Hortus Conclusus*.

d'un *Jardin d'Amour* attribué à Antonio Vivarini.[36] Des personnages richement vêtus se promènent dans un jardin entouré d'une balustrade de marbre bicolore, derrière laquelle pousse une haie d'orangers. Au centre s'élève une fontaine à vasque ronde dont le pilier central est orné de deux dragons crachant l'eau; au sommet, une divinité féminine ailée et drapée (probablement une allégorie de la Chasteté) est debout sur une sphère flanquée de deux oiseaux. L'idée de chasteté est soulignée par l'hermine que l'une dames tient dans ses bras.

Mais peu à peu, inévitablement, des allusions galantes se glissèrent dans le thème du *Jardin* et de la *Fontaine d'Amour*. Elles sont apparentes dans une miniature du Codex *De Sphaera*[37] où le *Jardin d'Amour*, pelouse fleurie entourée d'un mur de briques roses, a en son centre une fontaine dont le bassin est assez spacieux pour contenir quatre hommes et quatre femmes qui se baignent en folâtrant; sur l'herbe, des jeunes gens chantent en suivant une partition musicale (comme le font souvent les anges dans l'*Hortus Conclusus*), et d'autres jouent de la flûte et du tambourin. Des amoureux s'embrassent. Les *Jardins d'Amour* de caractère érotique se multiplièrent durant tout le 15ème et le 16ème siècle, et la *Fontaine d'Amour* put devenir dans certains cas, l'emblème du péché de luxure.

Jérôme Bosch en donnera, dans son triptyque du *Jardin des Délices*, une image hallucinée.[38] Le panneau central symbolise les plaisirs des sens dans un monde voué à l'Enfer dès sa création. Dans la partie supérieure s'élève une fontaine au milieu d'un grand bassin — d'un lac plutôt — qui donne naissance à *quatre rivières*. Cette fontaine est une construction bizarre qui unit les éléments architecturaux aux formes végétales; son pilier repose sur une sphère où des personnages font des a-

36 National Gallery of Victoria, Melbourne.
37 Biblioteca Estense, Modène.
38 Musée du Prado, Madrid. Fin du 15ème ou début du 16ème siècle.
  La fontaine du *Paradis Terrestre,* que l'on voit sur le volet de gauche, est très différente de toutes les fontaines du Jardin d'Eden déjà mentionnées; nous l'avons à dessein laissée de côté car sa structure et sa signification la relèguent tout à fait à part. Sa base est formée d'une sorte de roue dentée dont le centre évidé abrite un hibou; la superstructure, légère et élancée, est composée d'éléments étranges qui semblent être en croissance et transformation perpétuelle: le symbolisme très personnel de Bosch reste largement mystérieux pour le spectateur, et ses fontaines, toutes géniales qu'elles soient, sont, du point de vue iconographique, des fantaisies. Il y a une autre fontaine au premier plan de ce Jardin, un petit bassin rond où nagent des créatures plus ou moins imaginaires; sur ses bords se trouvent d'autres animaux, dont certains sont bourreaux, et d'autres victimes: notes discordantes dans un Jardin d'Eden, et qui indiquent que le Mal est créé en même temps que la première femme.

crobaties. Deux autres "lacs d'amour", dans ce même panneau, sont remplis de jeunes gens nus des deux sexes, occupés aux jeux les plus divers.

La *Fontaine d'Amour*, qui était au départ un emblème des sentiments délicats, du triomphe des belles manières sur les instincts brutaux, est donc devenue pour Bosch un symbole du péché de la chair. Issue de l'art religieux, elle s'en rapproche ici à nouveau, paradoxalement, en tant que piège du Tentateur.[39]

Les Fontaines de Sang

Ce type de fontaine, profondément mystique, est lié à la personne de Jésus. Un intérêt particulier entoura à partir de la fin du 14ème siècle jusqu'au 16ème tous les détails de la Passion, et une sensibilité nouvelle se développa, que l'on pourrait qualifier de morbide. C'est sous l'aspect d'un martyr ensanglanté que les Chrétiens voulurent désormais imaginer Jésus. Le motif serait né du culte du Saint-Sang, dont le centre se trouvait à Bruges (où quelques gouttes du sang du Christ étaient conservées). De là, ce culte se répandit dans toute l'Europe.[40]

La *Fontaine de Sang* comporte une vasque de forme variable au centre de laquelle se dresse un crucifix; des plaies de Jésus, le sang coule et emplit le bassin (Fig. 7).

Ce nouveau type n'apparut pas d'un seul coup. Bien que des hymnes du 14ème et du 15ème siècle mentionnent déjà les ruisseaux de sang divin et qualifient la Fontaine du Sauveur de "Bain de Vie", l'art ne traduisit que progressivement cette métaphore pathétique. Certaines ouevres appartiennent à une sorte de phase intermédiaire: par exemple l'*Adoration de l'Agneau* du *Retable de Gand*, et un tableau produit dans l'entourage des van Eyck, la *Fontaine de la Grâce et le Triomphe de l'Eglise sur la Synagogue*.[41] Dans la première de ces oeuvres, l'Agneau est debout sur un autel et le sang qui coule de sa poitrine est recueilli dans un calice. Au premier plan se trouve une fontaine à bassin octogonal où l'eau jaillit d'une colonne centrale. L'eau de cette fontaine et le sang de l'Agneau correspondent aux deux principaux sacrements, le baptême et l'eucharistie. En ces deux "moyens de Grâce", les Pères de l'Eglise reconnaissaient l'eau et le sang qui avaient coulé de la plaie

---

39 Le motif garde cependant encore sa forme et son sens traditionnels dans des oeuvres du début du 16ème siècle, telle la tapisserie du Musée des Gobelins intitulée *Le Concert*. Il y règne une atmosphère de sérénité, et la *Fontaine d'Amour* qui constitue le centre de la composition évoque des plaisirs ennoblis par la courtoisie.

40 Mâle, *op. cit.*, pp. 108–115.

41 Musée du Prado, Madrid.

au côté de Jésus et pensaient que le *Fons Vitae* prenait naissance dans
la blessure du Christ; ainsi l'eucharistie, le côté "nourrissant" pour l'âme
du sacrifice de Jésus, était dès l'origine unie à l'idée de purification et de
rédemption évoquée par le baptême. Quant à la *Fontaine de la Grâce*
citée plus haut, elle offre une composition étagée sur trois plans. En
haut, une "Déësis" semblable à celle du *Retable de Gand,* mais l'Agneau
est couché aux pieds de Dieu et n'a pas de blessure; au-dessous de lui
prend sa source le Fleuve d'Eau de la Vie [42] qui traverse la seconde
section du tableau — la prairie du Paradis; *sur son eau flottent des hos-*
ties. Le fleuve se déverse dans une fontaine appuyée au côté extérieur
du mur du Paradis. Le bassin, ici encore, est octogonal; un ornement
doré d'orfèvrerie gothique le surmonte. Les hosties à la surface de l'eau
indiquent clairement que l'idée de l'eucharistie est liée, comme dans
l'Adoration de l'Agneau, à celle du baptême. A gauche (côté des Evangiles) on voit un groupe de fidèles conduits vers la Fontaine par un
pape portant la bannière verte de la Rédemption, tandis qu'à droite
(côté des Epîtres) la confusion règne dans un groupe de Juifs.

Passons maintenant aux *Fontaines de Sang* proprement dites.

Sur un vitrail de l'église de la Trinité, à Vendôme,[43] la Croix est placée dans un bassin hexagonal où se tiennent Adam et Eve. Les quatre
Evangélistes sont assis sur le rebord, tandis que Pierre et Paul sont debout. Au bas de la vasque, au premier plan, on voit une foule en prière.
Un autre vitrail, celui du château de Boumois, depuis longtemps détruit,
représentait une *Fontaine de Sang* assez particulière, dont l'aspect nous a
été préservé par un dessin ancien.[44] Adam et Eve, les mains jointes, sont
plongés presque à mi-corps dans la vasque, de part et d'autre du Cru-
cifié dont le sang jaillit en abondance. De la vasque, son sang coule à
travers quatre orifices dans une piscine rectangulaire. Ces orifices, garnis
de mascarons, symbolisent les Evangélistes. La Vierge et St Jean se
tiennent de chaque côté de la Fontaine. On voit dans la piscine des personnages nus qui viennent d'y entrer, tandis que d'autres sont encore
occupés à se dévêtir.

De nombreuses *Fontaines de Sang* sont accompagnées non de Marie
et de St Jean, mais des saintes Marie-Madeleine et Marie l'Egyptienne —
les deux grandes pécheresses. La Madeleine tient une fiole de parfum,
l'Egyptienne est couverte seulement de ses longs cheveux.

Des artistes imaginatifs apportaient des modifications à ces formules.

42 Apocalypse, 22, 1 : "Et il me montra un fleuve d'eau de la vie, limpide comme
    du cristal, qui sortait du trône de Dieu et de l'Agneau".
43 Mâle, *op. cit.,* fig. 59.
44 *Ibid.,* fig. 60.

Jean Bellegambe, par exemple, remplace les deux saintes par des Vertus aux formes agréables et à l'air engageant, qui attirent les fidèles et les font grimper dans le bassin (Fig. 8). Malgré l'intention certainement sérieuse du peintre, l'effet est quelque peu comique ; des associations profanes et irrespectueuses se présentent à l'esprit : un rapport s'établit, qu'on le veuille ou non, entre les saintes ou les Vertus qui appellent les croyants au "Bain de Vie" et ce que l'on sait de la vie de ces mêmes Madeleine et Marie l'Egyptienne avant leur repentir. La promiscuité des corps dans le bassin de sang n'est pas exempte non plus d'associations érotiques. On pense aux joyeux couples s'ébattant dans le bassin de certaines *Fontaines d'Amour*. Cette confusion était inévitable car il n'est guère possible pour un artiste de représenter de façon radicalement différente la joie qui vient des sens et celle qui vient de l'âme. Il est probable, en outre, que des sujets profanes — en particulier la *Fontaine de Jouvence* — influencèrent à l'occasion l'iconographie du *"Bain de Vie"*.

La Fontaine de Jouvence

C'est un sujet qui relève largement du folklore mais qui, visuellement, est apparenté à la *Fontaine de Sang*. Les thèmes présentent une certaine similitude, puisqu'il y a dans les deux cas régénération par immersion, et l'influence iconographique dut être réciproque.

La vieille légende de la Fontaine de Jouvence était répandue en Europe au Moyen-Age. Au moment de la découverte de l'Amérique, elle connut un renouveau de popularité, car on pensait pouvoir enfin trouver cette fontaine en Floride, région de sources médicinales.[45]

---

45 La tradition de la Fontaine de Jouvence était liée à celle du Fleuve de l'Immortalité ; mais ces deux légendes avaient une origine différente (Cf. Hastings, *Encyclopaedia of Religion and Ethics*, 1913). La première était hindoue, la seconde sémitique. La Fontaine de Jouvence hindoue n'avait pas le pouvoir de rendre immortel mais seulement de restituer aux hommes leur vigueur. La Grèce et Rome croyaient en une sorte de Fontaine de Jouvence, mais située hors du monde, dans un Paradis où les âmes des hommes vertueux ignoraient les maladies et la vieillesse. Pour le Christianisme, la Font. de J. se rattache au symbole christologique de l'aigle. Cet oiseau, d'après le *Physiologus* (Cf. Réau, *op. cit.*, I, p. 85) avait coutume, lorsqu'il se sentait vieillir, de monter jusqu'au soleil, puis de se laisser tomber dans une fontaine où il se plongeait trois fois et dont il ressortait miraculeusement rajeuni. Cette légende, née de l'observation de la mue de l'aigle, fut interprétée comme une allégorie de la régénération par le baptême. Les commentateurs s'appuyèrent sur l'autorité du Psaume CII ("Ta jeunesse sera renouvelée comme celle de l'aigle") et virent dans la fontaine où l'oiseau se plonge le symbole des fonts baptismaux.

Les artistes traitèrent le sujet dans un esprit de légèreté et de gaieté; pourtant ils empruntèrent bien des traits à la *Fontaine de Sang*. Sans doute l'essentiel (Jésus en Croix) n'y était pas; mais les autres caractéristiques du thème mystique pouvaient être adaptées à leur nouveau rôle: les personnages nus dans le bassin ou se préparant hâtivement à y entrer, la joie due à la régénérescence. La vieillesse était à la *Fontaine de Jouvence* ce que le péché était à la *Fontaine de Sang*.

D'autres influences agirent aussi sur les représentations de la *Fontaine de Jouvence;* il faut noter celle des illustrations de traités médicaux concernant l'efficacité des bains sulfureux ou autres (Fig. 9) et celle des miniatures et gravures ayant pour thème les bains publics — ces établissements où l'on pouvait se laver, faire bonne chère et se divertir. C'est de là que proviennent les détails scabreux qui accompagnent souvent les *Fontaines de Jouvence*.

Une gravure au burin de la fin du 15ème siècle attribuée au "Maître aux Banderoles" (Fig. 10)[46] représente la *Fontaine de Jouvence comme* une piscine hexagonale dont un des côtés est remplacé par des marches descendant jusqu'à l'eau. Le bassin porte l'inscription "Hic est Fons Juventutis" et contient sept personnages nus, jeunes et joyeux. A gauche, des vieillards s'approchent de la fontaine en s'appuyant sur des cannes et des béquilles; à droite, on voit de jeunes amants aux gestes fort libres.

La *Fontaine de Jouvence* de Hans-Sebald Beham (Fig. 11),[47] grande composition de la première moitié du 16ème siècle, représentera, en commençant par la gauche, un paysage rural avec une foule de vieillards et d'infirmes qui se dirigent vers la fontaine. Celle-ci apparaît dans la seconde section; elle s'élève au milieu d'un bassin et se compose de trois vasques concentriques superposées (l'artiste s'étant peut-être souvenu de certains projets de fontaines exécutés par Dürer). Le pilier central, dans la vasque supérieure, est en forme de créature grotesque, qui tient à la fois de l'homme, de l'animal et de la plante, et qui jette de l'eau par les oreilles. Cette statue donne à la fontaine un caractère de fantaisie; notons pourtant la présence de deux oiseaux, l'un s'approchant à tire d'aile, l'autre perché sur le bord de la vasque et y buvant — témoignage de la ténacité de la tradition iconographique. La troisième et la quatrième sections de la gravure de Beham montrent des personnages qui s'amusent soit sur la terrasse qui recouvre la piscine, soit dans le grand bassin alimenté par la Fontaine de Jouvence. Ces figures, par

46 A. Bartsch, *Le Peintre Graveur* (1866), X, 2, 4 et 6. Passavant, *Le Peintre-Graveur* (1862) II, 26, 46.

47 Bartsch, *op. cit.*, gravures en bois de H.-S. Beham, no. 165. Passavant, *op. cit.* IV, n. 165.

leur type physique et leurs attitudes, rappellent des oeuvres de Dürer.[48] A l'arrière-plan on aperçoit des chambres avec lits de repos, des salles de jeu, etc.

Ces deux *Fontaines de Jouvence* donnent une idée assez précise de toutes les autres oeuvres de la fin du 15ème et du 16ème siècle qui traitent ce sujet. Nous pouvons dire que, d'une manière générale, elles se rattachent surtout, pour l'iconographie, aux *Fontaines de Sang* dont elles peuvent être considérées comme une variété profane et un peu burlesque.

L'introduction dans l'art d'un motif de nature aussi populaire n'eut toutefois pas pour résultat de "démythiser" le thème de la *Fontaine de Sang*. Bien au contraire, ces fontaines mystiques se multiplièrent dans le courant du 16ème siècle — de plus en plus compliquées et chargées, dans un but didactique, de symboles parfois difficiles à élucider et d'allusions dogmatiques. Ceci ne contredit pas le fait que l'art était las du symbolisme médiéval : dans ces oeuvres tardives, il ne s'agit plus à proprement parler d'art symbolique mais de spéculations intellectuelles. Elles finirent par succomber sous le poids d'allégories ingénieuses, artificiellement plaquées sur une faible charpente artistique.

Conclusion

Des développements caractéristiques se sont donc produits à la fin du Moyen-Age dans le motif de la fontaine, que l'art avait traité jusque là dans un esprit strictement symbolique et dont les implications, bien que nuancées, étaient toujours rattachées à l'idée du baptême et du salut. En considérant l'évolution de ce motif au 15ème siècle en Europe du nord, nous avons pu dégager trois tendances principales : a) une approche plus réaliste et l'introduction d'éléments narratifs; b) l'apparition de contextes nouveaux, aussi bien religieux que profanes; c) un écartèlement de la signification, reflet du trouble d'une époque encore profondément attachée au passé et violemment attirée par les innovations de la Renaissance.

---

48 Tel le *Bain des Femmes,* dessin à la plume exécuté en 1496, Kunsthalle, Brême. Reproduit par W. Waetzoldt, *Dürer and his Times* (Phaidon, Londres), Pl. 117.

ILLUMINATED HEBREW CHILDREN'S BOOKS
FROM MEDIAEVAL EGYPT

By Bezalel Narkiss

To my son Doron on his graduation, with love

A. Children's primary text books

The Midrash tells of Rabbi Akiva, the second century sage, who was forty years of age when he began studying. Together with his son, he went to a teacher and asked to be taught the Torah. He and his son held the board and read the straight A B C, then the reverse Z to A, continuing with the Book of Leviticus, and only then the entire pentateuch.[1] From this and other passages in the Talmud,[2] it would seem that, traditionally children began their reading, either with the first *Parashah* (portion) of Genesis (I–IV, 8), or, with the first three *parashot* of Leviticus (I–XI). While it may be understood why children should commence their study with Genesis, it seems strange to begin with the difficult text of Leviticus, dealing with the specific subject of sacrifices.

Several reasons have been given for this. Rabbi Assi's Midrashic explanation, that since children and sacrifces are pure, purity should deal with the pure, states, no doubt, a *causa post factum*.[2] It seems more plausible that this was the traditional beginning in the schools for priests, or one of the ways to commemorate the Temple of Jerusalem, after its destruction.[3] Whatever the reason, Leviticus was used as a primary text-book for children since the Mishnaic period, and throughout the Middle Ages.

Opinions differ in the Talmudic period as to whether special scrolls containing single *parashot* were allowed to be used for teaching children.[2] Apparently such scrolls did exist in the Mishnaic period though none survived.

The earliest surviving primary text-books which contain the first portion of Leviticus are from the mediaeval Orient. Several such fragments survived in the Cairo *Genizah*, most of which are now in the

---

1   *Avot d'Rabbi Nattan,* VI.
2   Mainly Babylonian Talmud, *Gittin,* p. 60 a.
3   See Nathan Morris, *A History of Jewish Education,* vol. I, Tel-Aviv 1960 (in Hebrew), pp. 171–172.

Taylor-Schechter Collection, at Cambridge University Library, gathered mainly in box K.5.[4]

Text wise, the children's text-books comprise a variation of alphabets, the first *parshiyah* (section) of the Book of Leviticus, and a benediction before the reading of the Torah in the synagogue.

Not all the fragments which will be dealt with here contain these three elements. However, these can be reconstructed. An interesting feature in these small text-books is that most of them are decorated in a system resembling the decoration of oriental Bibles.

B. *The Alphabet, Benediction and Leviticus fragment (K.5.10)*

The first fragment from the *Genizah* to be dealt with contains the alphabet, the benediction, and the beginning of Leviticus. The manuscript, now in Cambridge T-S. K.5.10, is a conjoint double leaf, of which one folio is almost complete (measuring 175 × 175 mm., text space: 135 × 125 mm.) and the rest is a small butt. The text of the complete folio contains on one side verses 1–2 of Leviticus I, written in 6 lines (fig. 1), while at the foot of the other side is written in smaller script the benediction recited before the reading of each Pentateuch *parashah* in the synagogue (fig. 2).[5] Above this the word *hazek*[6] (i.e. strength) is inscribed in bold coloured letters. At the top of the page are two lines consisting of the last two letters of the Hebrew alphabet (*shin* and *tav*), each repeated eight times with different vowel vocalization,[7] every letter decorated with red outlines. The fragmentary conjoint butt preserves only parts of the two top lines of each side. On the folio opposite the benediction page are the ends of what were originally lines containing the first two letters of the alphabet א ב (*aleph* and *bet*) repeated eight times, vocalized, and decorated in the same manner as those already described (fig. 2). On the other side of the butt, opposite the Leviticus text, there are parts of the end of a plain unvocalized alphabet (ק.ר.ש.) *qof, reish, shin*), and the beginning of a line repeating the last letter (ת *tav*), all decorated with red outline (fig. 1).

Missing in this manuscript, therefore, are the beginning of the plain

---

4 See S. D. Goitein, *Jewish Education in Muslim Countries,* Jerusalem 1962 (in Hebrew), pp. 42–43.

5 ברוך אתה יי אלהנו מלך העולם]
       אשר בחר בנו מכל העמים ונ]תן[
       לנו את תורתו ברוך א]תה יי[
       נותן התורה:

6 קְ֗ן—ְ punctuated thus.

7 שָׁ שַׁ שֵׁ שֶׁ שׁוּ תַ תָ תֵ תֶ תָ ת תָ תָ תּוּ

alphabet, the middle part of the "vocalized alphabet" and the continuation of the *parashah*. If we attempt to reconstruct the manuscript, it would seem that is comprised a quire of 6 leaves, of which the middle conjoined leaves (folios 2 and 5) survive. This reconstruction is based on the conjecture that the rest of the letters, between the first two and the last two, would have occupied another double leaf. Judging by the size of the existing vocalized letters on the surviving conjoined leaf, there were presumably four to five lines per page, which could cover the missing letters.[8]

Since the end of the plain alphabet is on the top of the *recto* side of the surviving butt, there must have been another *verso* leaf (fol. 1) with the beginning of this alphabet, possibly also in 4–5 lines. On the *recto* of this first folio there may have been a carpet-page.[9] On the conjoint leaf, the last of this quire (fol. 6), the continuation of the Leviticus text must have been written. A diagram may illustrate this reconstruction:

fol. 1r : Carpet-page

fol. 1v : Beginning of "plain alphabet"

fol. 2r : End of "plain alphabet" קרשת

fol. 2v : Beginning of "vocalized alphabet" א ב

fol. 3r : "vocalized alphabet"

fol. 3v : "vocalized alphabet"

fol. 4r : "vocalized alphabet"

fol. 4v : "vocalized alphabet"

fol. 5r : End of "vocalized alphabet". Benediction.

fol. 5v : Leviticus I, 1–2

fol. 6r : Leviticus I, 2–3

fol. 6v : Leviticus I, 3–4

Diagram A. Reconstruction of first quire of T-S. K.5.10.
———— Extant leaf; — — — — Conjectured leaf.

C. The Carpet-page and Leviticus fragment (K.5.1)

A similar manuscript which does contain carpet-pages is the fragment T-S. K.5.1. An original conjoint double leaf measuring about 175 ×140 mm; text space 135 × 115 mm; Carpet-page space 125 × 100 mm. On both sides of one folio there are portions from the text of Leviticus, while on both sides of the other are carpet-pages. The fragment has no colophon and its date can only be roughly assigned on paleographic and stylistic grounds to a period ranging from the 9th to the 12th centuries. The text, written in 9 lines to the page, begins on the *recto* side with the middle of verse 3 of Chapter I of Leviticus (fig. 3) and ends at the bottom of the *verso* with verse 9 (fig. 4) which is the end of the first *parshiyah* of this *parashah* of Leviticus. Both mutilated carpet-pages have a wide, decorated frame, with a geometrical interlace in the centre of the one, and four inter-twined, double-headed dragons in the other. The very crude geometrical motifs, as well as the floral scrolls in the frames, the palmettes and the open flowers in the backgrounds, do not give any clue as to origin. The colours are reddish-brown, purple-grey and orange. Some silver and gold were used in the illegible inscription in the frame surrounding the geometric carpet-page.

Originally, this manuscript must have started with the geometric carpet-page which contained the inscription (fol. 1 *recto*), followed by the dragon carpet-page (fol. 1 *verso*), then continued with a missing conjoined leaf containing the alphabet, the benediction and the beginning of Leviticus (I, 1–3). The quire was concluded by the surviving text leaf (fol. 4). A diagram reconstructing this quire of four leaves will illustrate it more clearly:

---

8 If there were only four lines to a page, then the 22 letters of the Hebrew alphabet could fit in perfectly: four each to the first five folios and the last two on the remaining leaf which survives. If there were five lines per page it is possible that the five "final letters" (ץ ,ף ,ן ,ם ,ך — *kaf, mem, nun, pei, tzadei*) were also written on a line.

9 The question of decorated carpet-pages, its relation to biblical and educational books will be dealt with later.

fol. 1r : Geometric carpet page

> fol. 1v : Dragon carpet-page
>
> fol. 2r : Alphabet
>
> — — — — — — — — — — — —
>
> fol. 2v : Alphabet
>
> fol. 3r : Alphabet
>
> — — — — — — — — — — — —
>
> fol. 3v : Benediction and Leviticus I, 1–3
>
> fol. 4r : Leviticus L, 3–8

fol. 4v : Leviticus I, 8–9

Diagram B : Reconstruction of T-S K.5.1

D. *The Leviticus fragment with the Colophon (Box 16.378)*

A third example from Cambridge (T-S. 16.378) ends with verse 13 of Chapter I of Leviticus, and it seems that this was its conclusion, since under it the undated colophon appears in smaller script, stating that it was "written by Shlomo bar Sa'adia Halevi the Cantor." [10] This manuscript has conjoined double leaf measuring 180 × 150 mm (fig. 5). The surviving part of the text is written in small square letters in 9 lines, with additional 4 lines for the colophon, although there are only 12 rulled lines to the page. On the opposite page within a primitive double frame of black fish-bone motif is a verse (Proverbs I, 8) and some blessings pointing conclusively to the fact that the book was meant for a studying child, given to him under the direction of his father. It states in black and coloured letters : "Blessed is the scribe, happy is the reader, the youth will rejoice with the help of the Creator. Joyous will be the father of the Righteous, and the parent of a wise will rejoice in him." [11]

[10] לא ימוש ספר התורה הזה מפיך והגית בו יומם ולילה למען תשמור לעשות ככל הכתוב בו כי
אז תצליח את דרכיך ואז תשכל.
וכתב שלמה בר סעדיה הלוי החזן נ״ע.
I am indebted to Professor Norman Golb for bringing this fragment to my attention. We have the intention of publishing together a study of illuminated fragments from the Cairo Genizah.

[11] ברוך הכותב וישמח הקורא ויגל הנער בעזרת הבורא.
גיל יגיל אבי צדיק ויולד חכם ישמח בו.

Similar to the other text-books this manuscript must have contained the vocalized alphabet, the benediction and the first part of Leviticus (I, 1–10). Since only the title and final pages survived, and since the text continues up to the end of the second *parshiyah* in verse 13, it should be assumed that four leaves are missing. The complete manuscript comprised, therefore, a six leaved quire.

E. *The Alphabet with the Candelabrum (K.5.13)*

One more important fragment of a child's decorated school book should be discussed here, in order to complete the picture. Cambridge University Library T-S. K.5.13 (fig. 6) is a conjoined double leaf measuring 140 × 115 mm., with five lines per page. It contains an illustrated carpet-page (empty on its other side) and two pages with the vocalized first five letters of the alphabet, each repeated 8 times, written in alternating red and black lines with reversed colour as outlines. Line ends are decorated with geometric motifs. The carpet-page is not of the usual kind and is most interesting, since it has an illustration of a seven branched candelabrum, standing on a table-like stand, within an arch. An oriental lamp hangs from the middle of the arch, and geometric motifs of the shape of David's star decorate the empty spaces. The main colours are reddish-brown, blue and dusky-gold-ochre. If this manuscript, like the others, contained the alphabet, the benediction and the first *parshiyah* of Leviticus; and if these were written in bold letters five lines per page, the manuscript must have consisted of at least eight leaves. It should be noted that the Candelabrum carpet-page must have been on the verso of the last leaf of a quire.

The date of the "Candelabrum Alphabet" is doubtful. The crude style of the decorated page may allow the assumption of the 11th–12th century, and the script is bewildering. My colleague, Dr. Nehemiah Allony, has pointed out the similarity of the very strangely shaped *aleph,* in our manuscript to the work of a certain Sa'id ben Fargoi of the late 9th century.[12] A comparison of the style and colours of the carpet-page with those of the script and decorative motifs does not allow for any difference in date. The uncertain date of this fragment does not effect its importance, in spite of the fact that so much is missing in this child's first book.

Studying these four examples,[13] it seems that children's primary text-books in the Orient were constructed according to a pattern. They con-

12 See N. Allony, "An Autograph of Sa'id ben Fargoi of the 9th century." *Textus,* VI, pp. 106–117. I am indebted to Dr. Allony for his help and interest in this study.

sisted of vocalized alphabets decorated with colours and motifs, a benediction before the reading of the Torah — the first portions of Leviticus. Last, but not least, decorated carpet-pages were added at the beginning and the end of these small-sized manuscripts.

F. On Carpet-pages

Decorated carpet-pages were a typical feature in oriental illuminated
Bibles.[14] The earliest surviving are from the 9th and 10th centuries. Most
of the carpet-pages of the oriental Bibles contain geometrical and floral
interlacings, while a few have illustrations related to the implements of
the Temple.

These carpet-pages have an additional stylized side motif attached to
their outer border. Similar ones appear in Koran decorations of the
Umayyad and Abbasid periods, where they may have served as a sub-
stitute for tooled bindings. Professor Ettinghausen's suggestion that
carpet-like late classical floor mosaics were the source of the "carpet-
pages" in Hebrew Biblical manuscripts as well as in early Korans, seems
quite plausible.[15] However, the stylized side-motif on the outer side of the

---

13   Other examples of decorated alphabets in the Cambridge University Library are
     T.-S. K.5.8 and K.5.3. The first is a fragment of a single leaf, which has out-
     lined and coloured script on one side only, five lines to the page. It con-
     tains parts of the plain Hebrew alphabet and a reversed alphabet (תשרק etc.)
     both including the final letters. At the bottom is a blessing: ״יי ישמרך מכל רע
     ישמר את נפשך״ "God will protect you from all evil, will guard your soul." The
     second fragment, of two complete conjoined leaves in five lines to the page,
     contains parts of four different combinations of the alphabet, written in co-
     loured, black and outlined letters and with decorative motifs. A fragment of
     a child's own copybook can also be found in the Cambridge Genizah Col-
     lection, T-S. K.5.82. Its single leaf contains two rows of vocalized letters
     (aleph and bet), the end of one combination alphabet (טן, ים, כל), the letters
     which have finals (מ נ צ פ כ) and a drawing of houses and a star. T-S. K.10.26
     contains part of a monumental alphabet, on one side of a leaf, and a com-
     bination alphabet (את בש גר דק) on the other. It is quite different from the
     fragment of an accomplished scribe's doodling, T-S. K.5.9, practising the
     letter mem מ many times, and following it by this cryptic alphabet:

רץ וף זע	הלך ומר
חס טן ים	זנשח חזק
כל חזק	אטבח
אין בכר	גז דו יצכף
גלש דנת	לע מ

14   See B. Narkiss, *Hebrew Illuminated Manuscripts*, Jerusalem, New York, 1969,
     pp. 18–20.
15   See R. H. Pinder-Wilson and R. Ettinghausen, "The illumination in the Cairo
     Moshe Ben-Asher Codex of the Prophets completed in Tiberias 895 A.D.", in

border may be a direct imitation of a leather clasp or a strap, some of which still survive in earlier Coptic bindings.[16]

The "Candelabrum Alphabet" (T-S. K.5.13) follows probably the tradition of Temple-implement pages, such as in the First Leningrad Bible, of 929 A.D. (Leningrad Public Library, Firkovitch Collection, MS II. 17).[17] Two of the carpet-pages of this sumptuous Pentateuch fragment depict in addition to the Candelabrum, the Golden Altar, the Jar of Manna, and the Ark of the Covenant. The Candelabrum and Holy Ark were amongst other implements symbolizing the destroyed Temple. These motifs appear from late Hellenistic times in minor Jewish art object as well as monumental wall paintings in Synagogues and Catacombs, and in later synagogal floor mosaics.[18] We may conclude then, that the decorations of floor mosaics and of Bibles are mile-stones in the symbolic representation of the lost Temple.

The same can be said of geometric and floral carpet-pages, as Professor Ettinghausen has observed. The children's textbooks discussed before, T-S. K.5.1 and T-S. 16.378, which have decorative carpet-pages, are within the tradition of floor mosaics and decorated Bibles.[19]

The earliest surviving Bible with such decorative carpet-pages is a Later Prophets codex copied by the famous masorite Moshe Ben Asher in Tiberias, in 895 A.D., now at the Karaite Synagogue in Cairo.[20] Besides having two carpet-pages with geometrical interlacings and palmette-like side motifs, the manuscript contains many other carpet-pages with floral and geometrical motifs outlined by the *masorah magna* written in micrography (minute script). This is a special feature of Hebrew Bible decorations which was continued in European Bibles.

P. Kahle, *Der Hebräische Bibeltext seit Franz Delitzsch,* Stuttgart 1961, p. 96; and also R. Ettinghausen, *Arab Painting,* Geneva, 1962, pp. 169–170. I am indebted to Prof. R. Ettinghausen for stimulating discussions on this paper.

16 e.g. 8th–9th century binding from Fayyum in Vienna National Bibl. Ms. Rainer Inv. N. 43, and of the same date from el-Usmanein in Berlin Staatliche Museen, Papyrussammlung P. 14018. cf. A. Grohmann and T. W. Arnold, *Denkmäler Islamischer Buchkunst,* Firenze 1929, pp. 40, 42; pls. 16, 18.

17 V. Stassof and C. D. Gunzburg, *L'ornement hébreu,* Berlin and Paris,1905, pls. 2, 3 ;and B. Narkiss, *op. cit.,* pp. 19, 20, 42, 43, pl. 1 A.

18 Such as the wall painting in the Synagogue of Dura Europos, the Roman Catacomb of Villa Torlonia and the floor mosaics of Bet-Alpha, Bet-Shean, and Hulda synagogues. See C. Roth (editor), *Jewish Art,* 2nd edition, Tel-Aviv and New York, 1971, figs. 54, 56, 59, 60, 62.

19 See B. Narkiss, *op. cit.,* pp. 19–20.

20 See P. Kahle, *Der Hebräische Bibeltext seit Franz Delitzsch,* Stuttgart, 1961.

G. Parashat Sh'laḥ-Lekha

Two decorated carpet-pages can be found in a rare illuminated Hebrew manuscript from the East, comprising a complete single *parashah,* dated to 1106–7 A.D.

The manuscript, belonging to the Jewish National and University Library in Jerusalem (MS. Heb. 8° 2230), is a small codex (105 ×120 mm.), of 34 leaves, which deals with the episode of the men sent by Moses to spy out the land of Canaan (Numbers XIII–XV).[21]

The colophon on the last page of the codex (fol. 34, fig. 7), states: "I Yitzḥak ben Avraham Halevi wrote punctuated and masorated[22] with the help of God 1418 Anno Seleucid" (i.e. 1106–7 A.D.).

The text of the codex is written in bold, square, oriental script, generally seven lines to the page. The entire text is vocalized. The scribe planned the page in such a way that it is framed by the *masorah parva* on the side margins, and the *masorah magna* in one line at the top and two at the bottom of each page (fig. 8).

The decoration consists of two carpet pages, one at the beginning (fol. 3, fig. 9) and one at the end of the manuscript (fol. 33v, fig. 7), and of stylized motifs at the different sections and paragraphs of the *parashah.* The binding is 16th century, oriental, brown leather, on wooden

---

21   The text of the manuscript, its punctuations and its masorah have been studied
     by H. Yalon in *Kirjath Sepher,* vol. XXX, no. 2, Feb. 1955, pp. 257–263, with
     two facsimile pages. Yalon found the *masorah* to be of the Ben Naftali rather
     than the prevailing Ben Asher tradition. See also B. Narkiss, *op. cit.,* pp. 20,
     46, 97, pl. 3. A 16th century owner's signature is to be found on fol. 2: "Ehud
     ben Nataniel ben Avraham." The manuscript was donated to the National Library by Mr. A. Tulin of New York, 1951.
     Collation: The first quire is of 8 irregularly bound leaves.

quires II and III are of regular 10 leaves
quire IV of 6 irregular leaves

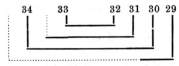

Each quire is numbered from the beginning by Hebrew letters.

22   Wrote the *Masorah Magna* and *Parva.*

boards, blind-tooled with geometric interlacings, showing signs of heavy damage.

The panels of both carpet-pages in the Sh'laḥ-Lekha codex display two differing geometric interlaces in their centres, with wide, decorated frames surrounding them. The side motifs have a somewhat wide base at the point of attachment to their respective panels, and contain three palmettes within a scroll on the opening page (fol. 3), and a single palmette at the end (fol. 33v). Pen scroll decoration outlines the entire page. The main colour of the decorated carpet-page is gold leaf, flaking off, with dark blue as an outline and space-filling colour. The colophon too (fol. 34) has a narrow gold frame decorated in blue surrounded by pen outline.

Stylistically the use of gold and blue in these carpet-pages derives from early 11th century decoration. It resembles, for instance, the geometric micrographical patterns with the spaces coloured in gold and blue in another famous Bible from the Leningrad Public Library (MS. B. 19a), which was copied in 1008–9 A.D. from a Ben Asher Codex.[24] The single palmette motif and the three palmettes in a scroll appear in this Leningrad Bible in a rather similar way to that of our Sh'laḥ-Lekha codex, although in the latter case they are more stylized and linear. The style of these carpet-pages originated probably from illuminated Korans of Egyptian, Persian, Spanish or Syro-Palestinian provenance. From general studies on illuminated Korans, it is difficult to define their exact origin. The style of the decoration in the Sh'laḥ-Lekha codex does appear to have similarities to 12th century Persian illuminated Korans.[25] It is, however, obvious that since the 11th century, Egyptian as well as Spanish illumination is derived from Persian manuscripts.[26]

H. Other decorative motifs in Sh'laḥ-Lekha

The first two text-pages of our codex are decorated with gold bars ending in palmette motifs at the top and foot of the text (fig. 8). The outer

23   אני יצחק בן אברהם הלוי כתבתי ונקדתי ומסרתי בעזרת שדי שנת אלף תי״ח לשטרות
     On the outer margin and side of the frame of the colophon, a later hand added the corresponding year of creation – 4866.

24   See Stassof and Gunzburg, op. cit., Pls. 7 and 17* and B. Narkiss, op. cit., pp. 19, 44, 45, pl. 2.

25   The closest manuscript in style to the Sh'laḥ-Lekha is a 12th century Kufic Koran in Persian now in the Egyptian State Library in Cairo. The decorations of this ms. also contain small rosettes and bars similar to the Sh'laḥ-Lekha codex. Cf. B. Moritz, Arabic Palaeography, Cairo, 1905, pl. 85.

26   Cf. R. Ettinghausen, op. cit., p. 170. This may also be due to the fact that most studies on illuminated Korans deal with manuscripts of Persian provenance.

and inner margins have similar stylized palmettes and open rosettes in gold
and blue with pen outlines. The decorated gold bar as a "*sura*-separat-
ing" heading in early illuminated Korans [27] probably determined the
decoration of bars and panels on the initial text-page of each book of the
Bible. It seems that as early as the 10th century these bars developed
into "endpieces" in Hebrew biblical books, which contained the maso-
retic number of verses.[28] The bar decoration of the two first text-pages
in our manuscript is perhaps a variation on a decorated "head-piece"
in order to achieve symmetry.

The shapes of the stylized floral motifs in the margins of these first
two pages resemble the "*khāmisa maale*" (every fifth verse) and "*ashira
maale*" (ten verses) signs in illuminated Korans.[29] In the first two pages
of our manuscript these motifs are mere decoration, but in the rest of
the text pages they serve as a line-filling device to indicate the seven
parashiyot (sections) into which a Pentateuch *parashah* is divided. At
the end of the *parashah* (fol. 33v) and in other instances (e.g. fol. 18, fig.
10, and fols. 23, 25v) where the *parashiyah* is a "closed" (*s'tuma*) one,[30]
there is an additional decorative device added in the outer margin. This
elongated device is shaped like a cartouche, framed by a gold band with
stylized palmettes at both ends, the whole surrounded by pen outline.
Inside the cartouche is a simple pen decoration with part of the *masorah
parva* and the letter ס (samech) for the word *s'tuma*. In many other folios
small rosettes occur as "line-ending" motifs, probably denoting the
"open" (*p'touha*) *parashiyah* (e.g. fols. 27, 32).

---

27 e.g. A Koran, presented to the Mosque of 'Amr in Cairo in 727, now in the
    Egyptian State Library, cf. Moritz, *op. cit.*, Pls. 8–12, Pinder-Wilson and Et-
    tinghausen, *op. cit.*, p. 96. Ettinghausen, *op. cit.*, p. 169.

28 e.g. The Karaite Later Prophets, cf. Kahle, *op. cit.*, abb. 11; the Karaite
    10 century Pentateuch fragments from Egypt, B.M. Or. 2540, fols. 4,
    7, 7v, 12, 15v, 16v, 18v, 19, 21, cf. R. Hoerning, *British Museum Karaite
    manuscripts, etc.* London and Edinburgh, 1889. Similarly decorated are the
    undated "Gaster Bible fragments" B.M. Or. 9579 and Or. 9580, cf. M. Gaster,
    Hebrew illuminated Bibles of the 9th and 10th centuries, London, 1901. These
    motifs continued into a later period, e.g. a fragmentary Persian 13th century
    Karaite Pentateuch, B.M., Or. 2493, has a decorated panel or bar executed
    in gold and colours, with an attached "side-motif" at the end of each *pa-
    rashah*.

29 D. S. Rice, *The Unique Ibn al-Bawwab Manuscript in the Chester Beatty
    Library*, Dublin, 1955, pp. 12 f. Ettinghausen, *op. cit.*, p. 167, 169.

30 Meaning that the last verse should fill up the line in the traditionally written
    Tora scholl. cf. G. Margoliouth, *Catalogue of the Hebrew and Samaritan manu-
    scripts in the British Museum*, vol. I, pp. 264 ff.

The decorative motifs within the text pages of our manuscript are, like the carpet-pages, traditionally placed in the text, and of Islamic origin as far as their style is concerned. In most illuminated codices of the Bible from Egypt and consequently from Spain and the East, there is a traditional panel and marginal decoration to indicate the beginnings and ends of books, *parashot, parshiyot, haftarot,* Psalms, chapters and other sections. These decorative motifs mainly consist of stylized palmettes, lotus flowers, and later of other non-figurative as well as figurative and illustrative elements.[31]

This little codex of a single *parashah* is therefore decorated in accordance with the Jewish traditional manner of illuminated Bible codices in the East, its small variations still remaining within the scope of this tradition. It is left for us to find out the purpose of such a manuscript containing only one *parashah* of the *Pentateuch.*[32]

I. The Use of a Single Parashah

Logically, this little codex of *"parashat Sh'lah Lekha"* must have been made for someone who was to read this *parashah* in the synagogue, on the appropriate sabbath, celebrating a specific occasion. The *parashah* together with its *haftara* (a portion selected from the Prophets) is read in the synagogue every sabbath, traditionally by a boy of *Bar-Mitzva* (his thirteenth year), at his confirmation or initiation ceremony. Other occasions, such as weddings and engagements, may also call for the reading of the *parashah* in the synagogue. It is thus conjecturable that the little codex was given to a child as a text book from which to study his recitation, or as a commemorative present to a youth. The manuscript does not appear to have been used much, for it is in almost perfect condition.

31 e.g. The Gaster Biblical Fragments mentioned above in note 28. The Damascus Keter, a Bible from Burgos 1260 in the National and University Library, Jerusalem, Heb. 4° 790; cf. B. Narkiss, "Hebrew Illuminated Manuscripts from Jerusalem Collections," *Israel Museum Catalogue of Exhibition,* No. 2, Pl. 4, and B. Narkiss, *op. cit.,* pp. 50–51, pl. 5. An example of a Spanish 15th century manuscript is the Kennicott Bible of 1476 in the Bodleian Library, MS. Ken 1; cf. C. Roth, *The Kennicott Bible,* Oxford, 1957, pl. 7a, 14c and B. Narkiss, *op. cit.,* pp. 74–5, pl. 17. A fragmentary Eastern example is the British Museum Or. Ms. 2493, see Margoliouth, *op. cit.,* I, No. 332 and a Yemenite Bible, British Museum, Or. MS. 2350, see Margoliouth, *op. cit.,* I, 88.

32 H. Yalon in *Kirjath Sepher, op. cit.,* p. 257 states the problem but does not solve it.

Professor S. D. Goitein who mentions other similar decorated single *parashah* manuscripts from the Cairo Genizah,[33] suggests that these were intended for the convenience of adults so that they should not carry heavy books to the synagogue, rather than to commemorate special occasions.

J. Conclusion

If we compare the several manuscripts of "Alphabet and Leviticus *parshiyot*" which have been cited here with the one manuscript of a complete *parashah*, we can conclude that they were intended for different purposes. The "Alphabet-Leviticus" codices were obviously primary books for children who had no training in reading; whereas the "*Parashat Sh'laḥ-Lekha*" was designed for a youth who could read and recite the *parashah* fluently in the synagogue at his *Bar-Mitzva* or betrothal ceremony. Since the reciting of the *parashah* in the synagogue has to be done from the unvocalized Torah Scroll, the "*Sh'laḥ-Lekha* codex" could have been used for the preparation of the recitation in the synagogue and later preserved in commemoration of the event. There may have been a common origin to the "Alphabet" and the "*Parashah*" codices, for they show some similar decorative motifs such as the "carpet-pages", which were determined by illuminated Bibles.

The two types of children's books described here are closely related to the decoration of Bibles in the East. Whereas the single *parashah* manuscript was treated in the same way as a complete Bible, the primary text books borrowed only the carpet pages from the Biblical system of illumination. It is also possible that because these were books intended for children, they were more readily given decorative treatment than were texts of a strictly religious nature.

It seems very reasonable that such school books should be decorated and adorned to catch the child's eye, to divide the material systematically, to endear and soften the bitter yoke of study.[34] Children's decorated school books existed probably from the time men could write, though such text-books were normally discarded when worn out. A papyrus

---

33 S. D. Goitein, *op. cit.*, pp. 50–51.

34 An interesting illustration of sweetening by honey the bitterness of the first lesson is to be found in the *Leipzig Maḥzor* of ca. 1320, from the south of Germany. Leipzig, University Library, MS. V. 1102, vol. I, fol. 131. It illustrates a custom of letting the child lick the honey off a palette of the alphabet, this is related in the "Customs of Rabbi Simḥa of Vitry." See B. Narkiss, Introduction to *Maḥzor Lipsiae,* Leipzig, 1964, pp. 96–97 and Facsimile, Pl. 29.

of the 3rd century B.C., published by Professor C. Nordenfalk[35] is perhaps the earliest fragment of a child's school book. It contains various arrangements of the Greek alphabet, lists of gods and names of rivers, excerpts from Euripides, and Homer as well as some arithmetic. Each list is framed or arcaded by a differently coloured ornamental bar, and therefore easy to distinguish. F. Wickhoff[36] has put forward the idea that early Christian, as well as Byzantine and late Roman book illustrations of the Bible, or Greek and Latin epics, were done for children or rather princes at the Emperor's court. He stresses mainly the sumptuousness of the purple vellum, the gold and silver bold script, the spaciousness of the outline, and illustrations necessary for children, as well as some dedicatory pictures and inscriptions mentioning names of children. He proposes these aspects in explanation of the paraphrased shorthand text of the Vienna Genesis, and the clumsy debased text of the Milan Iliad and the illustrated Vergils in the Vatican, the Paris Psalter, the Joshua Roll, and the Vienna Dioscorides executed for the Princess Julia Anicia. A person of higher learning, a scholar or a priest, would not need illustrations to explain the text, to make it more vivid or to break up the monotonous text pages, as he would not need big bold spacious lettering, unless he wanted a child to follow the text with his little finger.

The need to decorate and illustrate a child's text-book probably inspired the artists' initiative in adorning Oriental-Jewish alphabet and *parashah* books. They used some traditional elements derived from Bible codices, but permitted themselves to interpret these freely and to make some variations in their main scheme.

---

35 Cairo Museum No. 65.445, cf. C. Nordenfalk, "The beginning of Book Decoration", *Essays in honor of George Swarzenski,* Chicago and Berlin, 1951, pp. 9–12.

36 F. Wickhoff, "Die Ornamente eines altchristlichen Codex der Hofbibliothek", *Jahrbuch der Kunsthistorischen Sammlungen,* XIV, Vienna 1893, pp. 196 ff. I am indebted to Prof. Otto Kurz of the Warburg Institute for this reference and to many stimulating discussions on the subject of this paper.

AN UNKNOWN WORK OF MEDIEVAL SCULPTURE IN ACRE

by

MOSHE BARASCH

I

The Municipal Museum in Acre possesses an interesting, and rather unusual work of medieval sculpture, representing an eagle clutching in his claws the head of a large beast, probably a lion (Fig. 1–4). The group, carved in yellowish sandstone, is unfinished. While the front view shows rather detailed carving in some parts (cf. the feathers on the eagle's body, Fig. 1) the other sides are barely touched (Figs. 2–4). The eagle's head has been destroyed. As we know, iconoclastic Moslems, overrunning conquered Crusader colonies, often destroyed parts of Christian sculptures and paintings, but it was generally the heads of human figures that were attacked, while, as a rule, representations of animals remained untouched. In our case, however, the eagle's head was destroyed. The lion's head remained unharmed.

Nothing is known of the work's provenance. We don't know where it was found (although one assumes that it was discovered in Acre) or how it came into the Museum. On the sculpture itself no signs of signature or dating can be discerned, nor is there any clear indication of the function it was intended to fulfil. Needless to say, no text can be related to this group. The investigation of this work of art therefore rests completely on an analysis of its style and an interpretation of its iconography. We shall start with a brief description.

The first, and probably strongest, impression one gets from looking at our work is that of frontality. The eagle, straddling the lion's head, so completely spreads his wings that he creates a perfect plane. The bulging body of the eagle, placed precisely in the middle of this field, exactly follows the axis of the plane, and thus produces an almost perfect instance of frontality. Planar frontality was also, as we shall immediately see, an important technical principle, and governed the process of execution. It is, of course, impossible to determine the position of the eagle's head but it seems likely that the head, too, followed the central axis of the eagle, and was thus perfectly frontal.

Planar frontality does not exclude rather deep carving. Such carving can be observed both in the grouping of the main masses (the eagle's belly, his thighs) and in the shaping of the decorative patterns in the feathers of belly and wings. The carefully rounded, but pronounced bulging of the eagle's body, and the plastic protuberance of his legs clearly prove that the artist who produced this group was capable of conceiving his work in terms of volume as well as of frontal planes. Deep carving also creates some specific light-and-shade effects, which at least soften the character of rigid frontality. The scales on the wings (particularly the wing on the right, Fig. 1) and on some parts of the belly create lively optic effects, which clearly go beyond mere linear pattern. It is obvious, I believe, that both the plastic masses and the optical effects resulting from the deep carving of details impart to the eagle a certain degree of naturalism which is not characteristic of the outline in itself.

In spite of such naturalistic tendencies, however, one clearly notices a certain expressive restraint in this shaping of the eagle. It is true that we lack some crucial information for the perception of expression: we don't have the eagle's head, and — more important — we don't know the precise attitude of his claws, whether lightly perched on the lion's head, or deeply sunk into his mane. But the eagle's straddling pose definitely bears the character of domination or conquest, and this concept is articulated in the lion's head, as we shall immediately see. In the carving of the eagle, however, the artist did not reveal these expressive qualities, but rather hid them behind a formal treatment. It might appear that he would have liked us to remember that the bird has a heraldic quality.

That the artist was capable of much more dramatic style than can be guessed from a study of the eagle can be recognized in the lion's head. It is true that the head was not finished (as opposed to some parts of the eagle which show the polishing belonging to the last stage of carving), and perhaps many features that now strike us as dynamic and strongly evocative would have disappeared had the artist completed his work. But even if we restrict ourselves to such features that would not have changed, we must still reach the conclusion that the lion is not of the same expressive quality as the eagle.

Looking carefully at our work we discover some subtle differences between eagle and lion which form a background for the more obvious contrast. First one notices that, while the eagle is symmetric and frontal, the lion is not. Although the eagle rests on the lion's head, the axes of the two creatures do not correspond. Compared to the axis of the eagle's body and wings, the lion's head is slightly oblique and turns slightly to the right. Therefore, the eagle's right claw is placed roughly above the lion's eye, while the other claw is placed behind the ear.

A certain degree of asymmetry mey be observed in the head itself. Thus, one of the eyes is firmly closed (Fig. 1, the eye to the left)
while the other is half open. The nose, and particularly the upper lip,
are clearly asymmetrical, slanting towards the right. This asymmetry,
ascending towards the right in its general tendency is further articulated
in the wrinkles of the lion's forehead.

The lion differs from the eagle also as far as expression is concerned.
The restraint in expression which we have noted in the eagle does not
hold true for the lion, which is represented as suffering. This is not only
the impression of the modern beholder, but also the medieval artist's
intention since the diagonal mouth was an accepted formula for the expression of pain. The physiognomic expression of the lion is, then, an
articulation of his position as the conquered, subjugated animal. The
expressiveness of the lion renders the restraint in the shaping of the
eagle even more purposeful.

An interesting aspect of the Acre group is that it provides an excellent example for the study of medieval sculptural techniques and of
stages in the process of carving. In analyzing our work we can clearly
distinguish three different stages of carving, each of them with its own
function and characterized by a different format of shapes.

(a) Looking at our work in the round we observe first that originally,
i.e. in the first stage of carving, it had a cubic shape. At the back (Fig. 4)
and the two narrow sides (Figs. 2, 3), where the stone has been barely
touched, the cubic shapes are still clearly visible. The back of the group
is a large cube; the upper edge of the wings forms a large plane. At this
stage the artist, working with very coarse tools, apparently had no intention of indicating even in the most general outlines, the shape which
the group would eventually assume. The only specific forms indicated
at this point are the eagle's wings (see the two narrow sides, Figs. 2, 3).
Characteristically, the wings are also conceived as stereometric shapes,
meeting the rest of the block at right angles.

A careful study of our work suggests that the Acre sculptor, at least
in the initial stages of carving, thought in terms of a system of more
or less independent planes meeting at right angles, and perhaps connected by oblique passages, rather than in terms of organic shapes, or
rounded transitions; he conceived of each plane as an independent unit
rather than of the sculpture as a whole. Even in the more advanced stages
of execution the plane still remained the basic unit, as can be seen in
our group: while the frontal view was carved, so-to-speak, up to the
last detail (see for instance the pattern on the belly and wing feathers),
the other planes were left in a raw state.

(b) The second stage of carving can best be discerned in the profile views of the lion's head (Figs. 2, 3). Here the artist applied finer tools than in the first stage, though the carving is still quite rough. The shapes still lack soft transitions, and, of course, any kind of polishing, but the individual surfaces are considerably smaller, and — most important — they do suggest the basic anatomic forms of the figure portrayed. While the first stage of carving is governed by stereometric shapes, in the second stage the artist's hand, in carving the stone, already follows the forms of nature. This can be seen with particular clarity in the lion's mane (Figs. 2, 3) and in the "wrinkles" of his man-like forehead (Fig. 1), but it can also be perceived in other parts of his head. Even where the individual form is still geometric, the combination of such geometric surfaces is meant to suggest the anatomic structure of a lion's head.

Perhaps part of this following of nature which is characteristic of the second stage is the introduction of rounded, swelling forms. Although in themselves these rounded forms are not necessarily true to actual natural shapes, they have a more organic quality than do the stereometric shapes of the first stage. The rounded, swelling forms in our group are notably the eagle's body and thighs.

(c) The last stage is, of course, that of finish and polishing; in our group it can best be observed on the eagle's belly and wings (Fig. 1). Here the artist used fine, sharp tools, but nowhere, apparently, did he intend to carve deeply into the stone. The stage of decoration is dissociated from that of shaping structure.

It is interesting to observe that the decoration itself has a definitely linear character; the artist does not betray an intention of including plastic values, effects of light and shade, etc., in his range of decorative motifs. Moreover, the decoration itself tends to some kind of geometric pattern, and definitely has no organic quality. While in the second stage of carving the artist came closer to nature, in the third stage he clearly did not progress in the same direction.

II

The basic theme, or motif, of our group may be summarily described as the victorious eagle resting on the head of a defeated, vanquished lion (or of another large beast). For a better understanding of our work it may be useful to inquire briefly into the history of this motif.

While the fight of the eagle and the snake has been brilliantly investigated,[1] no attention seems to have been paid to the eagle overcom-

1 Cf. Rudolf Wittkower, "Eagle and Serpent: A Study in the Migration of Symbols," *Journal of the Warburg Institute,* II (1938–39), pp. 293–325.

ing a lion, or similar beast, as an independent theme of artistic representation. The latter theme is certainly not as common as the former, but
there is a considerable amount of pertinent material which would warrant a special study. The following remarks are not intended to provide
the outlines of such a study; only a few works will be mentioned for
their possible direct bearing on the connotation of the work of art which
is the subject of our discussion.

In late Antiquity — and perhaps particularly in the eastern parts
of the Mediterranean — the motif of the eagle conquering another beast
seems to have been quite common. It was represented on a large variety
of objects and in different media during that period, although, as Cumont observes, the meaning of the motif is still largely obscure.[2] In these
representations, the eagle does not generally rest on the isolated head
of the conquered beast, but on its back, and thus the whole animal supporting the eagle is depicted. The variety of these subjugated animals is
rather large. Many late Hellenistic and Roman ex-votos showing an
eagle perched on the back of a stag, a goat, or a bull have come down
to us.[3] This combination seems to have been so common that it appeared on certain coins, especially on Alexandrian pieces.[4] Some Satrapic
coins of Asia Minor are of great interest in our context: here the eagle,
instead of resting on the back of a stag or bull, is actually perched on
a lion.[5] The motif appears in different countries and regions of the ancient world including, in our area, both Cyprus and Palestine.[6] We
should also remark that, while usually the whole figure of the dominated
animal is represented, there are cases in which the beast vanquished by
the eagle is reduced to its head alone.[7]

As has been said before, the precise meaning of the motif is not clear:

2 Franz Cumont, *Etudes Syriennes*, Paris, 1917, p. 117: "... dont [i.e. the eagle
   on the head of a quadruped] la signification est d'ailleurs mal éclaircie".
3 Cf. S. Ronzevalle, "Notes et Etudes d'Archéologie Orientale, X. L'aigle funéraire
   en Syrie," *Mélanges de la Faculté Orientale Beyrouth (Syrie)*, V (1912), p. 226
   ff.; F. Cumont, *Etudes Syriennes*, p. 51, note 1.
4 Cf. Lajard, *Recherches sur le culte de Vénus*, p. iv, no. 7. And see Ronzevalle,
   p. 227, note 2.
5 The coins are reproduced in Babelon, *Traité des monnaies grecques et romaines*,
   pl. 113, no. 4.
6 For Cyprus, cf. Babelon, *Traité des monnaies grecques et romaines*, pls. 128,
   n. 5; 129, n. 5. And see Ronzevalle, p. 228. For Palestine, cf. the coin of Gaza
   reproduced in Babelon, pl. 124, nos. 1 and 2.
7 The reduction of the conquered animal to its head alone is apparently an old
   usage, though it is not very frequent. Cf. eg. the eagle with the head of a
   horse on an ex-voto consecrated to the god Turmasgada, in Stuart Jones,
   Sculptures of the Museo Capitolino, p. 60, no. 27. Cf. also Ronzevalle, p. 227 ff.

yet obviously it indicates a victory of the eagle over the other beast, —
or so at least it must have been understood by medieval spectators.

In medieval art our motif appears in a variety of forms which is
probably even wider than that of the ancient world. Only the main
types, or those immediately related to our work, will be outlined here.

(a) A quite widely disseminated version of our motif is the eagle on a
hare. Originating in the old world, probably even before classical Antiquity,[8] in the Middle Ages, it appears frequently both in Byzantine and
in western art. A good Byzantine example is the eleventh century marble
slab now in the British Museum (Fig. 7). Since in medieval symbolic
imagery the hare sometimes symbolizes the quick course of human life,[9]
the eagle standing above it may perhaps have the meaning of salvation.
But this was certainly not the only meaning of the eagle and the hare.
On some western representations [cf. the strongly expressive depiction
of the motif on the wall of Castel Ursino in Catania (Fig. 8)[10]] the eagle
holds a slain hare in his talons, and is clearly the rapacious and triumphant bird rather than the symbol of salvation.

(b) The association of an eagle with a human being is, of course, well
known in medieval art. Even if we disregard the most common versions
of this motif (primarily St. John with his eagle, but also the eagle of
the Apotheosis, or Ascension) we still find it frequently represented, and
we notice that it appears in a particularly wide variety of contexts and
with diverse expressive qualities. To give but a few random examples
I shall mention the famous capital of Vezelay where an eagle holds a
human being (probably Ganymed) in its beak, probably in order to
carry him up into the air[11]; or the puzzling representation in St. Pierre

8   Cf. Wittkower, "Eagle and Serpent," p. 318, who rightly says that the material
    deserves a special treatment. Examples are known from Susa and Babylon, as
    well as from Greek coins and Roman art. For Christian examples, cf. Strzy-
    gowsky, *Amida*, 1910, pp. 347 ff., 367, 369; A. Calderini (ed.), *La Basilica di
    Aquileia*, 1933, p. 271; Gabelentz, *Mittelalterliche Plastik in Venedig*, 1903,
    p. 111.
9   Cf. Franz Xaver Kraus, *Realencyclopädie der christlichen Altertümer*, I. p. 651.
    And see also Wittkower, "Eagle and Serpent" p. 318.
10 This sculpture has been recently published in the important study by Josef
    Deér, "Adler aus der Zeit Friedrichs II.: *victrix aquila*," in Percy Ernst
    Schramm, *Kaiser Friedrichs II. Herrschaftszeichen* (Abhandlungen der Akademie
    der Wissenschaften in Göttingen, Philologisch-historische Klasse), Göttingen,
    1955, pp. 88–124, and figs. 40–84. The eagle of Catania is reproduced in figs.
    66 a, b.
11 Capital of the first column to the south. Cf. V. H. Debidour, Le Bestiaire
    Sculpté du Moyen Age en France, 1961, fig. 403. For the subject matter of this
    capital, cf. J. Adhémar, *Inиuences antiques dans l'art du moyen age français*:

de Chauvigny, where we see a rapacious bird (obviously meant to be an eagle) strangling a human being in its enormous beak and at the same time forcefully tugging at the feet with its talons.[12]

In curious contrast to these scenes of unrestrained violence is the almost perfectly classical representation of an eagle perched on the head of a beautiful, dignified old man which forms part of the large pulpit in the Cathedral of Salerno (Fig. 9).[13] We cannot here go into a discussion of the forms and meanings of the motif of an eagle with a human being, but we should like to note the close relationship in composition between the group in Acre and the detail of the Salerno pulpit just mentioned.

(c) Another version, quite rare, but perhaps significant in our context, shows the eagle holding a dragon in his talons. This offshoot of the very frequent theme of the eagle fighting the serpent has a certain similarity with our group, both in composition and perhaps also in meaning. In visual rendering we know it from late medieval times but in literary formulation it appears at a much earlier period.[14] In the text it seems to be related to the well-known verse of Psalm 91 : 13, to which we shall later return.

(d) I should like to conclude this brief list of variations of our motif with a "type" which is known in only a very few instances but which is closest to our work because it represents an eagle actually perched on a lion. Although this is rare, examples of it are known both in Europe and in the Holy Land. One of the most articulate is found in a historiated Crusader capital of the El-Aksa Mosque in Jerusalem (Fig. 5).[15] Here we see some fantastic birds, probably representing eagles, standing on the backs or flanks of lions. The whole composition as well as the

Recherches sur les sources et les thèmes d'inspiration (Studies of the Warburg Institute, VII), London, 1939, p. 222, and fig. 73. It is interesting that the eagle here carries an animal of prey in his claws.

12 Cf. Debidour, *Le Bestiaire Sculpté*, fig. 205.
13 Cf. Deér, fig. 62.
14 Wittkower, "Eagle and Serpent," pl. 54 f. reproduces an illumination of a fifteenth century German Book of Dreams (British Museum, MS Add. 15606), but he correctly stresses that the motif, in its countless variations, has a long life. Cf. for instance, the *Sermons* of Pseudo-Ambrose (Migne, *Patrologia Latina*, xvii, col. 695 which, *inter alia*, reads: "Et ut aquila serpentes devorat ... ita et Christus Dominus noster, percusso dracone, id est, diabolo lacerato, quod humanum sibi corpus assumit, peccatum illud quod hominem tenebat obnoxium, tamquam perniciosum virus exstinxit."
15 Cf. Camille Enlart, *Les Monuments des Croisés dans le Royaume de Jérusalem*, Paris, 1927, pl. 115 bis, fig. 359.

individual creatures are highly ornamentalized; the capital radically differs from our group both in style and in the situation portrayed. An actual combat between the beasts is represented, as can be seen from their violent movements, and the turned heads and twisted necks of both eagles and lions. In contradistinction to this violent scene, the Acre group represents the victorious eagle, in a rather heraldic manner, even without reference to the fight by which the victory was achieved.

So far as I know, Enlart is the only scholar who has, briefly, investigated the El-Aksa capital,[16] comparing it to the famous twelfth century capital in St. Benoit-Sur-Loire [17] which does indeed show some striking similarities. In the French capital, which is less ornamental in style than that in Jerusalem, the eagles are even more clearly attacking the lions, actually biting their necks.

Enlart remarks in passing that "the origin of the motif certainly is a pattern on a textile or an ornamental sculpture coming from the Orient" which has been adopted by western artists.[18] Unfortunately he does not indicate his reasons for this assumption, but in itself it does not seem unlikely. In twelfth century western French art one occasionally finds a piece of sculpture which recalls some features of the El-Aksa capital and is clearly of Oriental origin. The best examples are found in the Cathedral of Bayeux.[19] Some of the groups of fantastic animals which obviously betray Oriental influences do indeed have some thematic, and perhaps even compositional, relation to the El-Aksa capital. See especially the relief of a rapacious bird (probably an eagle) flying over a lion while holding a skull in its talons. However, when we compare the Bayeux reliefs with the work of art here under discussion, the distance is even wider than between our work and the El-Aksa capital. The Bayeux artist portrayed scenes of strenuous fighting, and emphasized the atmosphere of actual violence by giving highly dramatic, twisted movements to his beasts. Compared to such representations, our group (although clearly less geometric and ornamental) betrays an almost serene spirit of detachment; it appears as a noble, heraldic monument.

A work of great interest to our inquiry and closer to our group is the Relief with Eagle and Lion, a twelfth century work from Central Italy, now in the Boston Museum of Fine Arts (Fig. 10).[20] The panel

16   Enlart, I, p. 125.
17   Enlart, pl. 115 bis, fig. 358. For the capital in St. Benoit-sur-Loire, cf. also Adhemar, *Influences antiques,* fig. 37.
18   Enlart, I, p. 125.
19   Cf. Debidour, *Le Bestiaire Sculpté,* figs. 95–98.
20   Cf. Walter Cahn, "Romanesque Sculpture in American Collections. VI. The

shows an eagle with outspread wings gripping a recumbent feline quadruped in its claws. In general composition it is closest to the type "Eagle on Hare", but the vanquished animal is quite clearly meant to be a lion.

Another Crusader monument in Jerusalem offers perhaps even closer resemblances to our work. I refer to a capital in the Mount Zion Monastery in Jerusalem (Fig. 6).[21] Here we see three birds in a row; those to the right and left stand on scrolls, while the central bird (smaller than the others, but represented in frontal view) is standing on an object which looks like a human head. Both the birds and the objects on which they are standing, partly damaged by iconoclastic Moslem conquerors, are rather poorly preserved, and do not permit us to draw any really valid comparisons with the work of art here under discussion. We cannot even be sure that the birds are meant to be eagles, although this seems to be very likely. What can be seen of the Mount Zion capital appears stylistically rather different from the Acre sculpture. But the Jerusalem capital proves that the motif of an eagle standing on a head (a motif whose occurrence in European art we shall shortly discuss) was also known in the Holy Land.

The history of the motif does not suggest any definite interpretation of the Acre group, nor does it provide a basis for attributing our work to a specific region or school. What seems to be fairly clear is merely that the motif itself, in its basic elements and normal configuration, was known in European art of the late twelfth and thirteenth centuries. We may, therefore, be sure that when the Acre artist carved our group he did not invent the theme, or even the composition, but followed a more or less established pattern.

It should, however, be noted that this pattern was established only in very broad and general outlines, and left room for much variation. From the examples discussed we have seen that in the late twelfth century the eagle could be perched on the body of a whole animal or only on its head, that the creature supporting the eagle could be a hare, a lion, or even a human being, that it could be alive or dead, etc.

Apparently the meaning of the motif was not less fluid than the specific elements composing it. We shall later return to questions of mean-

Boston Museum of Fine Arts", *Gesta*, IX, 2 (1970), fig. 10. Cf. also *Classical and Medieval Sculptures ... Part III of the Joseph Brunner Collection*, New York, 1949, p. 147, no. 605. See also *Bulletin of the Boston Museum of Fine Arts*, Autumn-Winter, 1957, p. 59. I am grateful to Professor H. W. Janson of New York University for having brought to my attention this example.

21   Enlart, *Les Monuments des Croisés*, II, Paris, 1928, p. 257, fig. 332. So far as I know, this capital has never been investigated.

ing. Here it will suffice to remark that the eagle could be understood as redeeming the creature in its claws, as killing it, or as treading upon it.

It is obvious, finally, that our motif was not related to a specific object, whether liturgical or secular, or to a definite place in the building. We know that it appeared on pulpits, on capitals, or as a kind of decorative sculpture placed in a wall-niche. It cannot even be said that it belonged exclusively either to the realm of religious or of secular objects or imagery.

Summarizing all these considerations, we may say that our group clearly belongs to a tradition, but that this tradition itself was so versatile and "open" that most of the problems set by our specific work of art remain to be solved by direct investigation.

III

Before attempting to attribute our group to a particular school of medieval European art it might be useful to describe briefly the major types of eagle representation in sculpture around A.D. 1200. Our image, especially the eagle himself, obviously has many roots in religious as well as heraldic imagery of the period. But since we shall later attempt to show [22] that, in its iconography at least, our group cannot be derived from the religious sphere, we shall concentrate mainly on eagle representations in the realm of heraldic imagery.

Needless to say, even within that rather limited field we find a rather large variety of types. Stripped to mere essentials, we find in European heraldry around A.D. 1200 three major types of eagle representation, roughly corresponding to the three major cultural areas of the period; we have a Byzantine type of eagle, an Islamic type, and finally a west European type.

The Byzantine type of eagle is perhaps best represented in the eleventh century marble slab now in the British Museum (Fig. 7).[23] Here the eagle is of a rather heavy type, his legs are affixed to the body in a rather unnatural way, the tail is broad and fan-like, and, most important, the tops of the wings are rounded. These characteristics of the Byzantine type prevail in media as different as the marble slab just mentioned and

---

22   See below p. 91 ff.

23   Cf. Ernst Kitzinger, *Early Medieval Art in the British Museum,* London, 1940, pl. 34. Kitzinger (p. 109) believes that the eagles to the right and left of this slab are "grasping" hares, apparently, then, in the process of seizing, catching them. Deér, p. 91, believes that the eagle in the centre of the marble slab betrays the influence of Islamic models.

silk cloth.[24] It is hardly necessary to remark that the Byzantine eagle is also found in western art. Suffice it to mention the Eagle Capital of Gelnhausen.[25] The eagles of this capital are, except for one feature, clearly patterned after Byzantine models, and probably represent the official form of the "Reichsadler".[26]

The heraldic eagle in Islamic art tends more towards a stylization in vegetational forms. The Islamic type found its way into the medieval art of Western Europe, and it is of course only because of these influences that it is mentioned at all in this paper. While the Byzantine eagle is short and heavy, the eagle of the Islamic type is slender and light; its rounded, sometimes capricious outlines often reveal an extreme elegance. As can be seen on an eagle carved on a ceremonial sword [27] the tail is highly formalized, recalling the shape of a blossoming flower. The upper parts of the wings are not rounded, as in Byzantine art, but are shaped in "volutes", another form of a definitely vegetational character. It has been shown [28] that this specific type of eagle had a particular appeal in western heraldic imagery, and even deeply influenced the "Reichsadler". Needless to say, it led far away from the antique origin of eagle representations in European art.

The specifically western type of eagle, which in many respects is directly related to ancient models, emerged mainly in Italy. But it can be located with greater precision even within Italy itself. It is principally

24 Cf. Deér, fig. 44, Cf. also V. J. Deér, *Der Kaiserornat Friedrichs II*, Bern, 1952 (Diss. Bernenses), p. 72, note 92.

25 For the capital of Gelnhausen (ca. 1180/90), see Deér, Fig. 43. For eagles on capitals, cf. K. Nothnagel's entry "Adlerkapitelle" in *Reallexikon zur deutschen Kunstgeschichte*, I, 1937, cols. 180–187. And cf. also Ernst Kitzinger, "The Horse and Lion Tapestry at Dumbarton Oaks; Appendix: List of Early Byzantine Animal and Bird Capitals", *Dumbarton Oaks Papers*, III (1946), p. 60 ff., figs. 90–102. It should be stressed that such eagle-capitals are particularly frequent in Southern Italian sculpture.

26 Cf. Deér, "Adler aus der Zeit Friedrichs II", p. 91 ff. The feature which provides the exception is, of course, the wing, which is shaped in the "Islamic" form. Perhaps also the position of the eagle's legs (parallel instead of straddling) differs from the Byzantine model.

27 For this eagle, cf. Deér, fig. 48. The Islamic type of eagle is also frequently distinguished by its bearing the Persian "diadem", — cf. Kurt Erdmann, "Die Entwicklung der Sasanidischen Krone. Exkurs II: "Das Diadem," *Ars Islamica*, CV/XVI, (1951), p. 117 ff. For the influence of Islamic eagles on Byzantine art, cf. Andre Grabar, "Les succès des artes orientaux à la cour byzantine sous les Macédoniens," *Münchener Jahrbuch der bildenden Kunst,* Dritte Folge, II (1951).

28 Cf. Deér. p. 91 ff., who stresses that even in Byzantine art, the eagle reveals influences of Islamic stylization if its function is primarily heraldic.

in Norman Southern Italy, with its capital in Palermo, and in the cities of Campania that in the twelfth century we already find so-called "realistic" eagles, based on Roman models.

These early South Italian eagles do not fulfil any specifically heraldic functions, but appear mainly on pulpits, candles, and capitals. They are thus of a more sculptural character than both the Byzantine and the Islamic eagles, and for that reason, too, are closer to our group.

One of the earliest eagles of this type may be found on the Easter Candle of the Palatine Chapel, a work datable to the period of Roger II and clearly influenced by Roman candelabra.[29] More important in our context are the eagles carved on the ambos of the Cathedral in Salerno, in the late twelfth century.[30] They display, in the naturalistic modelling of the body as well as in the representation of the feathers, a remarkable similarity to the ancient eagles that could, of course, be seen at that time in Southern Italy.

Very interesting for the purpose of this study is a detail from the large pulpit in Salerno Cathedral, representing an eagle resting on top of a human head (Fig. 9).[31] This rather early eagle (probably created ca. 1170) displays varying influences. The volutions (however slight) of the wings recall the vegetational stylization of Islamic art; the strong, short and pronounced legs remind us of Byzantine models; and the sharply crooked beak confers on it a typically medieval feature. And yet, this eagle is clearly permeated by a spirit other than that discernible in all the types mentioned. It is largely influenced by antique models, and although the rigidly frontal position gives it a heraldic character, the eagle strikes us as "naturalistic".

The Protorenaissance in Southern Italy produced many eagles that show this typical combination of antique model, heraldic position and naturalistic spirit. Deér has called attention to an eagle carved on top of an early thirteenth century capital in the cloisters of Monreale, which is clearly patterned after the eagles of the Roman legions.[32] Another thirteenth century example of great expressive force has been published by

29   Cf. A. Venturi, *Storia dell' Arte Italiana*, III figs. 506–598. P. Toesca, *Storia dell' Arte Italiana*, Turin, 1927, fig. 586. And see Deér, p. 102.

30   For the two pulpits in Salerno Cathedral (erected about 1171–1181), cf. G. H. Crichton, *Romanesque Sculpture in Italy*, London, 1954, p. 137 ff.

31   Cf. Crichton, pl. 85b (for a general view of this specific group in the whole pulpit) and Deér, fig. 62 (for a detail of the eagle and the human head).

32   This eagle is found on top of the famous Mithras Capital of Monreale. Cf. Deér, fig. 65. So far as I know, the eagle has not attracted much attention while the capital itself has been discussed several times.

Deér, a monumental piece of sculpture representing an eagle holding a slain hare in his talons. The sculpture decorates a wall-niche of the Castello Ursino in Catania (Sicily),[33] and was probably produced in the middle of the century. To my mind it betrays some rather "soft" qualities. The carving is much deeper than in our group, and the wings are not spread out so as to form a surface more or less continuous with the body, but are rather placed at an angle to it. The carving of the feathers, especially on the body, is much softer. All this gives the group a highly naturalistic, immediately dramatic character, but makes it appear less of a heraldic sign.

Eagles of a roughly similar type were represented in various media in South Italian art of the twelfth and thirteenth centuries. An early example is the relief on the sarcophagus of the Empress Constance (died 1198), the mother of Frederick II. Here we seen an eagle [34] that clearly displays traces of stylization in the heraldic manner of the time (see especially the volute form of the wings). But its frontal position, protruding thighs, and short, heavy legs distinguish it from the elegant type of the purely heraldic eagle, and grant it some kind of monumentality.

South Italian cameos, usually somewhat later than Constance's sarcophagus but still belonging to the same period, show basically the same type of eagle. Several of these cameos are influenced by imagery on coins, and show the transformation of the profile or three-quarter view into a fully frontal eagle with outspread wings, a really majestic symbol.[35]

Coins are, of course, an important medium for the study of eagles. Particularly significant also are the gold coins, the so-called *Augustales*, of Frederick II, many of them bearing the image of an eagle on the obverse. On these coins the eagle is usually represented either in profile or in a kind of serpentine movement with a sharp turn towards the left. Although the style of these representations differs greatly from the Roman models, the postures of the eagles often go back to antique sources. In spite of the definitely medieval character of the coins, they provide the earliest significant examples of eagle representations which

33 Published for the first time by Deér, fig. 66a, b. See also *ibid.*, p. 105, for the dating of the sculpture (apparently in the "forties" of the thirteenth century).

34 Cf. Deér, fig. 67, and p. 104.

35 Cf. in general, H. Wentzel, "Mittelalterliche Gemmen," *Zeitschrift des deutschen Vereins für Kunstwissenschaft,* VIII (1941), p. 98 ff.; J. Deér, "Der Basler Löwencameo und der süditalienische Gemmenschnitt des 12. und 13. Jahrhunderts," *Zeitschrift für schweizerische Archäologie und Kunstgeschichte,* CIV (1953), p. 129 ff.

are clearly directed towards Antiquity. A good example is the rather unusual coin, now in Vienna (Fig. 11),[36] where the eagle is patterned after the emblem of the Roman legions. Seen in full frontal view, the eagle spreads his wings, and only his head is turned towards the left, a traditional feature in Staufic eagle imagery. The eagle on the seal of Frederick, the son of King Manfred, has a similar form.[37]

Southern Italy was not the only province where such eagles were carved in the twelfth and thirteenth centuries. We frequently find them in Tuscan sculpture, mainly on pulpits. It suffices to mention the eagle on the pulpit of S. Miniato in Florence,[38] or, to give a more primitive example, on the pulpit in Gropino.[39] In these pulpits the eagle, who usually stands on a human figure (the symbol of St. Matthew) in his turn standing on a lion (Mark), supports the lectern. (Needless to say, the function of the eagle as a support of the lectern is not restricted to Tuscany, — cf. the pulpit in the Cappella Paltaina in Palermo.) [40] But although such eagles appear in other provinces of Italy as well, none of these provinces (nor any other European country) has a tradition comparable to that of Southern Italy as far as both artistic achievement and the articulation of forms are concerned. Moreover, the eagles of South Italian sculpture represent a very definite attempt at reviving the antique model and spirit.

It is not our task to trace the history of the eagle in thirteenth century sculpture, but we must at least mention the wonderful eagles on Nicolo Pisano's pulpits in Pisa and in Siena. As in the other Tuscan examples just mentioned, here too the eagle supports the lectern. But while Pisano follows Tuscan traditions in the placing and function of the symbolic bird, in style, broad conception and expressive character his eagles are much closer to those of Southern Italy than to the nearby Tuscan representations. It has been pointed out (convincingly, I believe) that Nicolo Pisano's eagles cannot be derived from the traditions of religious art; they also cannot be explained as following on from the heraldic

36 Cf. Deér, "Adler aus der Zeit Friedrichs II", fig. 73, and p. 104 f. For the classicizing tendencies and classical models of these coins, cf. Ernst Kantorowicz, *Kaiser Friedrich II,* Ergänzungsband, Berlin, 1931, Exkurs I. Cf. also H. Wentzel, "Italienische Siegesstempel und Siegel all'antica im 13. und 14. Jahrhundert," *Mitteilungen des kunsthistorischen Instituts in Florenz,* VII (1955), p. 73, and, for the general context, see Erwin Panofsky, *Renaissance and Renascences in Western Art,* Stockholm, 1960, p. 101.

37 Deér, fig. 84, and p. 123.

38 Crichton, *Romanesque Sculpture in Italy,* pl. 73a.

39 Crichton, pl. 75, and pp. 118, 120.

40 Cf. Crichton, pl. 89.

imagery of Pisa. But they do seem to derive from the South Italian, Hohenstaufic political emblems.[41] These eagles may well be the application of political imagery to religious art. That this was perhaps consciously done may be inferred from a comparison of the representation of the animals in the panels of the Baptismal Fonts (both in Pisa and Siena) and the eagles. The animals display a surprising realism, not only in texture, but also in behaviour and movement; thus one goat scratches itself, another sniffs at the Virgin's mantle, etc. It has rightly been stressed that Nicolo Pisano here displays an acute observation of real life.[42] In contradistinction to such observation of everyday life, the eagles on these pulpits are endowed with a purely majestic spirit which is closely linked with heraldic imagery. In spite of their naturalistic texture these eagles remain elevated symbols.

It is to this South Italian tradition of representing the eagle as a theologico-political symbol that we wish to attribute our group. Such an attribution cannot be proved by one single clear-cut argument, but it can be supported, I think, by combining the different aspects of our sculpture.

The eagle in Acre combines elements from different artistic traditions. It is seen in full frontal view ,the wings are spread out, the body is bulky, heavy, and protruding, the thighs are short but very prominent, the talons themselves (as far as can be inferred from the present state of the work) are rather large and heavy. All these features recall the tradition beginning with the relief on the sarcophagus of the Empress Constance. But in contradistinction to that early image, the wings of our eagle are not shaped in the volute form which is typical of the sarcophagus relief; they also do not suggest the perfectly arched shape of the Byzantine eagle's wings, but vividly recall the rather slight curve and the somewhat geometric, angular shape of the eagle's wings on the

41   Cf. Deér, p. 107 ff. As proof for his thesis Deér calls attention to the fact that the eagle on Nicolo's pulpit in Pisa holds an animal in its claws, and the eagle of the Siena pulpit shows the turning of the head towards the left, which is a regular feature of Staufic heraldic symbolism. Needless to say, the establishing of such a connection (if it can indeed be established) does not necessarily mean a renewal of the old discussion as to Nicolo's Apulian origin. In thirteenth century Tuscany there were enough southern models available to explain an influence without necessarily requiring that Nicolo be born in the south.

42   Cf. Hans Graber, *Beiträge zu Nicola Pisano*, (Zur Kunstgeschichte des Auslandes, Heft 90), Strasbourg, 1911, p. 56. See also A. Möller, "Das Naturgefühl bei Nicolo Pisano," Repertorium für Kunstwissenschaft, XXVIII (1905), p. 1 ff.

golden *Augustalia* in Vienna, and especially of Nicolo Pisano's eagle in the Baptistery in Pisa.

The slightly angular wing (clearly distinguishable both from the massive arched wing of Byzantine art and from the volute-shaped wing of Islamic traditions) does indeed seem to have been a characteristic feature of at least one tradition in Italian twelfth century sculpture. In an earlier, and much cruder version we find it in the angels of Monopoli.[43] The same type of wing, its shape now softened and probably closer to that of our eagle, can be seen in the bird supporting the lectern of the pulpit signed by Guglielmo, a pulpit that was created in 1158–1162 in Pisa, and is now in Cagliari, Sardinia.[44]

Judging according to the form of the wing (obviously an important feature) the eagle of Acre seems to belong to that Italian tradition, and seems to stand somewhere midway between Frederick's golden coin and Nicolo Pisano's supreme work of sculpture.

The design of the individual feather, the basic decorative unit of our eagle, also suggests, I believe, an origin in Italian art of the early thirteenth century. The closest comparison in this respect seems to be a Bronze Eagle, now in a private collection (Fig. 12), which was cast in Southern Italy in the period of Frederick II, and probably actually served as a military emblem.[45] Needless to say, these layered, scalelike forms occur in the representations of eagles all over Europe, but in France and Germany the scales are usually flat.[46] As compared to such northern works, Italian representations, influenced by antique models, show a deeper, more plastic carving of the scale, and it is precisely this quality which our work has in common with them.

Eagles *all'antica* occur, of course, not only in Italy, but also, though less frequently, in Southern France. It might therefore be useful to compare our eagle to a twelfth century example which among French representations, comes closest to it, the eagle from the facade of Saint Gilles-du-Gard.[47] The structure of the body, the position of the legs (straight and parallel in St. Gilles, straddling in Acre), the form of the

43 Cf. A. Kingsley Porter, *Romanesque Sculpture of the Pilgrimage Roads*, (Reprint, New York, 1966), ills. 159–162.

44 Kingsley Porter, ill. 186; Crichton, *Romanesque Sculpture in Italy*, pl. 53. This pulpit has aroused much discussion, briefly summarized in Crichton, p. 98 f. The shape of the eagle does not seem to save attracted much attention.

45 Cf. Deér, figs, 76, 77, and pp. 108–111.

46 The flat scales of northern eagles can be seen, for example, in the eagle of the Bronze Lectern in Hildesheim. Cf. Deér, fig. 49 a-b.

47 Debidour, *Le Bestiaire Sculpté*, fig. 296.

wings (broadly undulating in France, slightly angular in Acre), the quality of carving extremely soft, almost "painterly" in France, ornamental and linear in Acre) differentiate between the two eagles. In all these respects, the Acre work seems to be much closer to Italian models.

The Bronze Eagle just mentioned (Fig. 12) does not belong to exactly the same type as ours. Its wings are of the volute shape, and it turns its head sidewards — both features frequently recurring in heraldic imagery influenced by Islamic traditions. This may to some extent be due to the fact that in bronze casting (as in many other kinds of metal work) Islamic influences were more easily absorbed than in stone carving. However, the ornamental design within the individual feather is practically the same in the Bronze Eagle and in our group : a regular, linear design, which stands in marked contrast to the soft texture in St. Gilles.

The general character of the eagle, — its physiognomic type, so-to-speak — is of course less clearly definable than such individual features as wings or feathers. But so far as these qualities can be discussed, they would also seem to suggest the origin of our eagle in South Italian art. The Acre eagle clearly belongs to the Antiquity-imitating type which, as we know, developed quite early (second half of the twelfth century), mainly in Southern Italy. It appeared also, in a somewhat different form, in the south of France, but we have already seen that the eagle of Acre differs from those of Southern France.

In Italian art, however, we find many representations of eagles which reveal significant affinities with our work. The comparatively small head of the Acre eagle,[48] the general shape of his body, broadening towards the base, and the short but rather heavy thighs are features frequently found in Italian representations of eagles. See, for instance, the eagle on the pulpit of S. Ambrogio in Milan,[49] or the eagle supporting the lectern in the pulpit of Barga (Lucca).[50]

The posture of our eagle may also be of some significance in establish-

---

48   While the exact size of the head cannot be established, of course, it seems obvious that it must have been rather small.

49   Cf. Kingsley Porter, *Romanesque Sculpture of the Pilgrimage Roads,* ill. 175; Crichton, *Romanesque Sculpture in Italy,* pl. 25. Remarkable in this eagle are both the small size of the head and the scales, which are similar to those in Acre. The wings of the Milan eagle are larger than those of the eagle in Acre, but they have basically the same shape. The similarity of the wings in Acre and Milan becomes obvious when we compare them with the wings of the eagle in St. Gilles (cf. note 47).

50   Kingsley Porter, ill. 246. Besides the large eagle supporting the lectern there are also smaller eagles on the capital beneath the pulpit. In the larger eagle the wings are somewhat narrower and less angular than in Acre, but the head

ing its origin in Italian art. In Acre the eagle is represented in what may be termed a moderately straddled attitude. It is thus opposed to the extreme straddling of Byzantine eagles, on the one hand, and to a parallel placing of the legs, on the other, the latter position being particularly frequent in eagle representations of northern Europe. The "moderately straddled" position is typical, or particularly frequent, in Italian art, although it may be found in other European countries as well. An example of specific interest in the present context is the mosaic in the so-called Roger-Chamber in the Royal Palace of Palermo (Fig. 13).[51] Here the eagle, catching a hare, is clearly a royal symbol, and its heraldic function is expressed both in the turning of the crowned head and perhaps also in the slightly voluted form of the wing. It is a good example of a slightly straddling bird, combining, I believe, the majestic expression inherent in the straddling posture (particularly if the eagle bestrides a captured animal) with a feeling for organic nature, which prevents an exaggeration of the attitude.

In view of all these considerations (the general motif, the form of the wing, the decorative patterns, and the eagle's posture) it seems feasible to assume that the eagle in our work was carved either by a south-Italian artist, or by an artist using a South Italian model.[51a]

Can the lion, or whatever other beast the isolated head in our group may represent, also be attributed to the artistic tradition of the same broad region? It is difficult to give a definite answer. Needless to say, lions are frequent in the late Romanesque and Gothic art of all parts of Europe (although in Italy they are at that time probably more common than in any other country) and their representation displays a large variety of types. One should keep in mind, moreover, that the lion in

is also very small, the shape of the body is similar, and the regularity of the scales is also reminiscent of the Acre sculpture.

51 Cf. Deér, fig. 85. O. Demus, *The Mosaics of Norman Sicily*, London, 1950, p. 185, note 6, assumes that the eagle is a later addition, and Deér, p. 105 f., proposes the possibility of a connection with the Stauffic eagle.

51a There was, of course, more than one type of eagle in South-Italian art of that period, and we find eagles which differ entirely from ours, and from the others mentioned. See, for example, the eagle from the pulpit in Bitonto (Bari), signed by Niccolo and dated 1229 (Kingsley Porter, ill. 244); the eagle of the pulpit of S. Maria del Lago in Moscufo (Chieti), signed by Nicodemus and dated 1159 (Kingsley Porter, ill. 180); and the rather late (1272) eagle from the Cathedral of Ravello (Deér, fig. 61). In all these eagles the head is much larger than in Salerno (our fig. 9) and probably also in Acre, the wings are "closed" while in Acre, Salerno, etc., they are heraldically spread out, the pattern of the scales is much rounder, and — most important — the legs are not portrayed in the straddling position, but are parallel.

our group has remained in a rather fragmentary state (he is clearly in a more initial stage of carving than the eagle) and it is difficult to compare him with accomplished sculptures. Many of the features which now seem very characteristic (e.g. the broad strigilation of the lion's mane) might well have disappeared, or been transmuted into more decorative forms, had the artist completed his work. The following observations, therefore, are made with more than the usual hesitation.

It should be said first that the capital in the El-Aksa Mosque (Fig. 5) as well as the related capital in St. Benoit-sur-Loire, i.e. works that have some relationship to the Acre group in theme, reveal an altogether different lion physiognomy. This can only partly be accounted for by the fact that in these two capitals the lions are represented fighting the eagles while in the Acre group the lion is vanquished, and supports the eagle in passive suffering. The main reason for the difference in physiognomy is, of course, that the lions of the El-Aksa Mosque and of the Acre group are derived from different artistic traditions. But in European sculpture of the twelfth and thirteenth centuries we find several representations of lions that might bear a relationship to our work, and I shall briefly mention some of them.

Some rather surprising similarities to the lion in our work can be seen in an early Burgundian capital from Anzy Le Duc.[52] In this grotesque mask we see the open mouth with hanging tongue, the flat nose, the round eye-balls, and the strigilation of the hair–features which are characteristic of the beast's head in our work. But in spite of such similarity in individual elements, the spirit seems to be altogether different. The carving in Anzy-le-Duc is flat and linear, in Acre it is deep and plastic.

Several characteristic features of our work, such as the slightly diagonal mouth of the lion, or the hanging tongue, are found in European sculpture of the period. Thus the lions supporting the famous Episcopal Throne of Bari show the diagonal mouth, which probably was a formula for representing pain.[53] See also the asymmetric shape and dramatic expression of the lions in *Daniel in the Lions' Den* in St. Trophime, Arles (particularly the lion to the left).[54]

The monumental lion of Venosa (Potenza)[55] is different in physiognomic type and carving from our head, yet they have some significant

52   Kingsley Porter, ill. 17.
53   Cf. Moshe Barasch, "A Holy-Water Basin in Acre", *Proceedings of the Israel Academy of Sciences and Humanities,* IV (1970), p. 230, for a discussion of this formula.
54   Debidour, Le Bestiaire Sculpté, fig. 150.
55   Kingsley Porter, Ill. 171.

elements in common. The lion of Venosa shows the hanging tongue, and perhaps the strigilated hair should also be noticed. The mane of the Venosa Lion is more ornamental than that of our group, but had our lion been finished, one may suppose that the hair would have presented a similar character.

Perhaps one should also recall the lions supporting the pulpit in Pistoia.[56] They are certainly not of exactly the same type as in Acre, but they reveal, I think, a kind of family likeness, both in physiognomy and in expression. This type persisted, and can probably be discovered in some works of Nicolo Pisano.[57]

Summing up, then, while the lion in our work does not clearly indicate a given school as its source, it reveals some rather broad relationships to South Italian sculpture.

IV

In turning from an analysis of style to an investigation of iconography, the specific character — perhaps even the uniqueness — of our work immediately becomes evident.

The iconographic problem posed by our group is quite interesting. Needless to say, both the eagle and the lion are the animals most frequently portrayed in symbolic contexts. In secular as well as in religious iconography an almost inexhaustible variety of meanings is attached to them. When one investigates the iconographic meaning of an eagle or a lion in a specific work of art one is, therefore, faced with an *embarras de richesses* rather than by a scarcity of possible interpretations. On the other hand, however, our group seems to have a definitely distinct feature, namely, the particular relationship between the two animals. To my knowledge, there are no medieval representations of an eagle and a lion that show the two beasts in precisely the juxtaposition which we find in the Acre sculpture. Obviously, then, in attempting to interpret the meaning of our group it will not be sufficient to discuss the character of the two beasts separately, but we shall have to understand what was meant by their quite specific relationship.

Before attempting to analyse the meaning of our unusual image we should briefly comment on a motif which at a first glance might seem to resemble the theme of our work, but which, I believe, is intended to convey an altogether different message. In medieval art eagle and lion representations belong, of course, to the realm of the symbols of the

---

56 Crichton, pl. 69.
57 For Nicolo Pisano's lions, cf. H. Graber, *Beiträge zu Nicola Pisano,* p. 8 ff.

Evangelists. In twelfth and thirteenth century works of art two Evan-
gelical symbols, and among them, of course, the eagle of St. John and
the lion of St. Mark, are often arranged one on top of the other. This
type of composition appears in all types of works and media, but for
our purpose the pulpits are probably the most important. A good example
of such an arrangement (and one that, in fact, may have something to
do with our work) is the pulpit in the Camposanto in Pisa, representing
a *Majestas Domini* and signed Buonamico.[58] Here, at the right hand
side of the relief, we see the eagle hovering quite closely above the lion.
However, even at a first glance we can see the basic difference between
the two compositions : in the Pisan pulpit the eagle is placed above the
lion, but he does not stand on the lion's head or dig his talons into the
mane; the lion himself is as majestic as the eagle, and does not show the
suffering expression that we observed in Acre. In short, in spite of a
certain superficial similarity in composition, the relationship between
the animals is altogether different. The symbolic representation of the
Evangelists never depicts one animal as victorious over the other. But
it is precisely this motif of the eagle fighting and overcoming the lion
that, as we have tried to show, is the true theme of the Acre group.

As we have said above, the main iconographic problem of our work
is posed, not by the individual animals, but by their specific combination; it is, therefore, this configuration that should be studied. On the
other hand, the image of an eagle clutching a lion's head in his talons
is both unusual and far from self-evident in intention, and any attempt
at interpretation will have to rely, at least to a certain extent, on aspects
of the meaning of the individual animals.

The lion is, of course, one of the principal heraldic beasts, appearing
on innumerable occasions in symbolic functions and contexts. The meanings usually attached to the King of animals, as everybody knows, are
those of royal dignity, of valour, and of domination. In the religious
imagery of the Middle Ages, especially in the west, he often represents
the Saviour. Usually, then, the lion has a "positive", dignified meaning, which stands in marked contrast to his appearance in our sculpture.
How can this beast, one asks, be shown in such an inferior position, and
subjugated by the proud eagle?

Even the lion is no exception to the rule that in iconography the
meaning of all animals (and of almost all other figures) is ambivalent.
Besides the dominant tradition of presenting the lion as a royal symbol
one finds, in fact, both texts and visual representations (though the lat-

58 For a reproduction, cf. Kingsley Porter, ill. 181.

ter are less frequent) in which he appears as a blood-thirsty, dangerous beast, a symbol of death, a veritably demonic figure. It may be useful in the understanding of our work to recall a few of these texts and representations.

In religious imagery especially the lion is sometimes understood as the demonic beast that must be overcome. In Biblical texts, even where the lion appears as a royal symbol, he is not unequivocally "good". Thus Proverbs XX, 2 says:

"The dread wrath of a king is like the growling of a lion;
he who provokes him to anger forfeits his life.

Even when the lion appears in a redeeming context he evokes fear and trembling, as indicated, for instance, in Hosea XI: 10–11:

They shall go after the Lord,
he will roar like a lion;
Yea, he will roar,
and his sons shall come trembling from the west
They shall come trembling like birds from Egypt,
and like doves from the land of Assyria;
and I will return them to their homes, says the Lord.

In Scripture the lion is frequently a personification of mortal danger; he is feared in the same way as death.

Deliver my soul from the sword,
my life from the power of the dog!
Save me from the mouth of the lion,
my afflicted soul from the horns of the wild oxen

prays the Psalmist (Psalm XXII: 20–21), and Isaiah (38: 13) says

I cry for help until morning;
Like a lion he breaks all my bones;
from day to night thou dost bring me to an end.

From the image of death to the symbol of sin is but one step. In Christian literature, one sometimes finds the lion as a designation of sin, the most famous formulation being that of the First Letter of Peter, (V: 8) which reads:

Be sober, be watchful. Your adversary the devil prowls
around like a roaring lion, seeking someone to devour.

The conception of the lion as a Satanic beast, to be overcome by forces

of redemption, is already indicated in the Old Testament. The famous
verse of Psalm 91 : 13 reads :

You will tread on the lion and the adder
The young lion and the serpent you will trample under foot.

The young lion and the serpent you will trample under foot. There is
no need to trace here the story of this motif, in which Christ's triumph
over the forces of darkness is represented as his trampling on the beasts
among which a lion is conspicuous. It is one of the oldest motifs, to be
found on Early Christian lamps (one of which is now in the Museo
delle Terme in Rome), on mosaics, on small reliefs. As one knows, the
tradition of this motif reaches to the famous *Beau Dieu* from Amiens.[59]
In all these representations the lion, as far as he can be identified, stands
for sin and vice.

Another interesting context in which the lion may stand for sin overcome by virtue is provided by the figures of lions bearing columns in
the pulpits and portals of churches, an image frequently encountered in
Romanesque art. It has been suggested (convincingly, I think) that these
lions bowing their heads, and making a supreme effort to sustain the
burden of the columns, represent hostile forces overcome by faith.[60] In
Arles this is perhaps made particularly clear by the addition of serpents
and other crawling beasts which creep up from beneath the lion's belly.[61]

---

59   The early Christian lamp is reproduced in *Realenzyklopädie der christlichen
     Altertümer*, II, p. 734, fig. 434, and in A. Venturi, *Storia dell'Arte Italiana*, I,
     p. 437. fig. 424. Another interesting example, a Diptychon plate, from the
     seventh or eighth century, is reproduced in Reusens, *Eléments d'archéologie
     chrétienne*, Louvain, 1888, I, p. 254. Interesting remarks are to be found in
     Joseph Sauer, *Symbolik des Kirchengebäudes und seiner Ausstattung in der
     Auffassung des Mittelalters*, Freiburg, 1902, p. 316. For the *Beau Dieu* in
     Amiens, cf. Emile Mâle, *L'Art religieux du XIII siècle en France: Etude sur
     l'iconographie du Moyen Age et sur les sources d'inspiration*, Paris, 1898, p. 61.
60   This has been suggested by Sauer, *Symbolik des Kirchengebäudes*, p. 348. So
     far as I know, Sauer's interesting suggestion has not been taken up by any
     modern scholar. In his support one may perhaps cite the fact that, at roughly
     the same time, figures bearing burdens, supporting heavy loads (cf. the so-
     called "Atlantes") are usually figures of sinners. Cf. Horst W. Janson, "The
     Meaning of the *Giganti*" *Atti del Congresso Internazionale sul Duomo de Mi-
     lano*, Milano n.d., p. 61 ff. The Atlantes are explicitly designated as images of
     sin or vice in Piacenza Cathedral, where the small Atlantes supporting the
     lintel of the main portal are inscribed USURA and AVARITIA (cf. Crichton,
     Romanesque Sculpture in Italy, p. 39).
61   Kingsley Porter, ills. 1369, 1371, 1373, Cf. also ill. 1325 a (St. Gilles). And
     cf. Sauer, p. 348.

So wide-spread was the conception of the lion as a symbol of sin that a mid-thirteenth century German mystic, Mechthild of Magdeburg, uses it when describing the four cardinal sins as represented by four different animals: the ape stands for wordliness, the bear for fornication, the wolf for greed, and the lion for pride.[62] It seems that at times the identification of the lion with sin became so self-evident that David conquering the lion is described in a medieval reliquary as "David triumphing over Satan".[63]

The sinful character of the lion is expressed not only metaphorically, but sometimes also more directly. Honorius of Autun stressed the ambivalence in the meaning of the lion. Expounding verse IV : 8 of the Song of Solomon (Come with me from Lebanon, my bride; / come with me from Lebanon. / Depart from the peak of Ama'na, / from the peak of Senir and Hermon, / from the dens of lions, / from the mountains of leopards) Honorius says that the lion sometimes signifies Christ, sometimes the devil.[64] In discussing the image of Christ trampling upon the beasts he gives an interpretation which is, I believe, of great importance in our context. In his *Speculum Ecclesiae* we find a sermon for Palm Sunday which explains in detail the meaning of the creatures mentioned in Psalm 91 : 13. In Honorius' interpretation the dragon represents the devil, the basilisk is a symbol of death, the adder stands for sin, and the lion is a personification of the Antichrist.[65]

Can we indeed consider the head of the conquered beast in our group, whether we choose to interpret it as the head of a lion, of a dragon, or of some other imaginary monster, as representing an important demon, perhaps even the Antichrist? What speaks in favour of such a supposition?

I should like to state immediately that there are no compelling reasons for accepting this hypothesis, that is reasons which would exclude the possibility of a different interpretation. Yet in carefully considering our sculpture, we are reminded of traditions of symbolism, and of literary and visual imagery which, although perhaps not codified in a universal-

---

62 Cf. P. Gall Morel, *Offenbarung der Schwester Mechthild von Magdeburg, oder das fliessende Licht der Gottheit*, Regensburg, 1869, I, xxxviii, p. 17. See also H. W. Janson, *Apes and Ape Lore in the Middle Ages and the Renaissance*, (Studies of the Warburg Institute, xx), London, 1952, p. 66 note 103.

63 In the reliquary of Begon in Conques. Cf. Debidour, *Le Bestiaire Sculpté*, p. 290.

64 See *Expositio in Cantica Canticorum*, secundus tractatus, cap. 4, which reads: "Leo significant aliquando Christum, aliquando diabolum, aliquando superbem principem" (cf. Migne, *Patrologia Latina*, CLXXII, col. 418 C ff.). And see also Sauer, *Symbolik des Kirchengebäudes*, p. 60.

65 *Speculum Ecclesiae* (Migne, *Patrologia Latina*, CLXXII, col. 913).

ly accepted and commonly applied form, maintained a strong vitality, and deeply influenced medieval imagination. Drawing on such, sometimes only half-visible, currents of imagery may help us in our attempt to understand the unusual motif of our group.

Several features in these symbolic traditions suggest a possible connection of the lion, as represented in our group, with images of the Antichrist. The isolated head itself might have had such a connotation. In medieval fantasy, the Antichrist was pictured in a rather large variety of shapes and guises.[66] One of the images symbolizing him was the isolated head. Thus Hildegrad of Bingen relates that the Antichrist's head attempted to leap to the sky (that is, to assume domination) from a dirt-heap, but was struck by a thunderbolt, and tumbled down, spreading fog and the smell of plague.[67] At another point of her treatise she says that the Antichrist dies by striking his head with great force, apparently on some rock.[68] The fact that in our group only the head of the conquered animal is represented may have something to do with the emphasis placed on the Antichrist's head in these traditions.

Medieval imagery, in fact, provides occasional examples of a connection between the Antichrist and the lion. Such links cannot be regarded as the main tradition (the predominant image of the Antichrist is clearly human), yet they are significant enough to deserve consideration.

In Scripture we already find a suggestion of a link between the Antichrist and the lion. Of the apocalyptic beast which symbolizes the Antichrist it is said that its mouth is like a lion's mouth (Revelations 13 : 2). In the writings of the early fathers the Antichrist is sometimes described as a lion, although for reasons different to those suggested in *Revelations*. It is the majestic, rather than the frightening, aspect of the lion that makes him an appropriate metaphor for the false Messiah. Since the Antichrist is an image of Christ, the description of Christ as a lion requires that the Antichrist too be considered as a lion. Hippolytus, in

---

66 Cf. Aurenhammer, "Antichrist", p. 151 ff., esp. p. 153 ff.; Oswald Erich, "Antichrist", *Reallexicon zur deutschen Kunstgeschichte*, I (1937), col. 720 ff. A rich collection of material is in the still useful work by W. Bousset, *The Antichrist Legend*, London, 1896.

67 *Liber Scivias* III, 11, as quoted by Aurenhammer, p. 154.

68 "For when he shall have fulfilled all the pleasure of the devil, the beguiler. ... shall gather all his host and say unto the believers in him that he intendeth to go aloft — and lo! as if stricken by a thunderbolt suddenly coming (down) he strikes his head with such force that he is cast down from that mountain and delivereth his soul unto death", quoted by Bousset, p. 149.

his treatise *On the Antichrist,* says: "A lion is Christ, and a lion is the Antichrist." [69]

In the Middle Ages it is the terrifying qualities of the lion that warrant the comparison between the Antichrist and the King of animals. Hildegard of Bingen describes the Antichrist as a creature composed of different animals. ". . . his nose and mouth are those of a lion; frighteningly he opens his mouth, and terrifyingly he sharpens his iron teeth." [70]

A few isolated representations indicate that the specific motif must also have been known in the visual arts. In the *Hortus deliciarum* the second apocalyptic beast wears the head of a lion, a nearby inscription reading: "bestia quie apparuit est antixqs." [71] In another miniature of the *Hortus deliciarum* the Antichrist is depicted as a child sitting on the lap of a Satan in human shape, with bird's talons and a lion-like head, the inscription reading *Lucifer ut Satanas* and *Antixqs.*[72]

There is further detail in our sculpture which deserves careful consideration. As we have already had occasion to notice, there is a certain irregularity of the beast's eyes; one is smaller and firmly closed, the other larger, more protuberant and opened. Now, this particular irregularity appears in early literary descriptions of the Antichrist. In the *Apocalypse of Ezra* the Antichrist is imagined in the following way: "The form of the face of him as of a field; his right eye as the morning star, and the other one that quaileth not . . ." [73] This apparently goes back to Jewish sources. In the Midrash *va'Yosha* the false Messiah is described in the following words: "He shall be baldheaded, with a small and large eye . . ." [74]

In general the absence of a member is quite typical of late antique and oriental demonic figures,[75] but it is a feature to be found also in

---

69 Cf. Bousset, p. 25.

70 Cf. H. Aurenhaummer, "Antichrist", *Lexikon der christlichen Ikonographie* Bd. I, pp. 151–156.

71 Cf. R. Chadraba, "Antichrist", *Lexikon der christlichen Ikonographie,* col. 119–122.

72 Chadraba, *ibid.*

73 Cf. Tischendorf, *Apocalypses Apocryphae,* xxix. And see Bousset, *Antichrist Legend,* p. 156.

74 Quoted after Bousset, *Antichrist,* p. 156. Cf. also *Questiones ad Antiochum Ducem* 109, Migne *Patrologia Graeca,* XXVIII, col. 663–666, which reads: "And he received a certain sign in one hand and in one eye". Quoted after Bousset, p. 157, who also calls attention to a similar formulation in the *Apocalypse of Zephania.*

75 In a Greek gnostic text, The Testament of Solomon, a demon has only one wing (Migne, *Patrologia Graeca,* CXXII, col. 1356); in magical literature, a demon is called "The one without one breast" (cf. F. Pradel, *Griechische und*

medieval imagery.[76] In our context it is particularly interesting to notice that in medieval traditions, both visual and literary, demons are frequently imagined as one-eyed. In medieval art we indeed find many representations of demons who are missing one member, and there are also depictions of one-eyed demons.[77] Moreover, we know of depictions of the Antichrist that display this very feature. Thus, in some illuminations to *Revelations* X: 2 and X: 7–10 (the conquest of Jerusalem) the Antichrist is portrayed as a warrior wearing a crown, and, according to the Jewish traditions just mentioned, with a large right eye; the other eye is sometimes scratched out.[78]

Let us assume that our interpretation is correct, and that the animal's head — whether it is that of a lion or of some imaginary monster — does indeed represent a major demon, or perhaps even the Antichrist himself, — how are we then to understand the eagle? What, or whom, does it represent?

A systematic discussion of eagle symbolism would clearly go far beyond the limits of this study. As is well known, after the lion the eagle is the most common symbolic beast, and frequently appears in emblematic imagery. The meanings attached to the eagle, although probably less diversified than those for the lion, constitute a rather extended scale. Even if we "limit" ourselves to the Christian middle ages, we are still faced with a variety of meanings too wide to be surveyed in the present paper. In any event some aspects of the eagle's symbolism are too well known to be repeated here. We shall, therefore, briefly discuss only a few of those symbolic meanings of the eagle which may have a direct bearing on our group.

Since our sculpture clearly represents the victory of the eagle over his enemy it will probably be useful to start with some observations on the victor symbolism of the eagle. As everybody knows, in classical Antiquity, and particularly in the Roman Empire, the eagle had a political and mili-

---

süditalienische Gebete, Beschwörungen und Rezepte des Mittelalters (Religionsgeschichtliche Versuche und Vorarbeiten, III Band, 3. Heft). Giessen, 1907, p. 339. The headless demon of late Antiquity is famous — cf. K. Preisendanz, *Akephalos der Kopflose Gott* (*Beihefte zum "Alte Orient"*, 8), 1926. Much interesting material is collected in Meyer Schapiro, "From Mozarabic to Romanesque in Silos", *Art Bulletin*, XXI, 1939, p. 330, note 48.

76 Cf. Pradel, p. 339; Schapiro, p. 330 ff.

77 For a rich collection of examples, cf. Schapiro, note 48. For one-eyed demons, cf. the article "Einäugigkeit" in *Handwörterbuch des deutschen Aberglaubens*, II, p. 694 ff. For a possible application of such one-eyedness to the representations of sinners and demons in profile, cf. Schapiro, *loc. cit.*

78 Cf. Aurenhammer, p. 153.

tary significance. The eagle of the legions was the emblem of Roman power and majesty.[79] Many literary sources throughout Antiquity describe the eagle as the bird of victory. Thus Dio Cassius relates that in Caesar's fight against the younger Pompey the eagles of Pompey's legions dropped golden thunderbolts from their talons into his camp, and then flew off to the camp of Caesar, indicating that the victory would be with the latter.[80] A similar story had already been told by Homer, with the difference that here the eagles dropped serpents instead of golden thunderbolts.[81] The fight of the eagle and the serpent has been admirably studied by the late Rudolph Wittkower who showed that when the motif of the eagle conquering the serpent appeared on the Triumphal Arch in Nola the eagle was clearly an emblem of victory and triumph.[82]

In the Middle Ages the eagle retained these specific symbolic meanings. In the field of political and military symbolic imagery it remained the royal bird (appearing as such on the decoration of crowns and thrones),[83] and the creature chosen for depiction on military standards and insignia.[84] More generally, the eagle lived in the medieval imagination as the strong and rapacious bird capable of overcoming any other beast. Both in Byzantium and in the west we find representations of the eagle holding a dragon or some other prey in his talons, or victoriously perched on a frightened hare.[85] Whatever the precise meaning attached to the

---

79 Cf., inter alia, Otto Keller, *Thiere des classischen Altertums*, 1887, p. 242 ff. The article by Karl Sittl, "Der Adler und die Weltkugel." *Jahrbücher für klassische Philologie*, Supplement XIV, 1884, pp. 1–51, was not available to me while writing this paper.

80 *Roman History*, XLIII, 35 (Loeb Classical Library, IV, p. 275). Cf. Wittkower, p. 308 ff.

81 *Iliad*, CII, 201 ff. And see Wittkower, p. 308.

82 Cf. Wittkower, p. 310, and pl. 51k. See also E. Löwy, "Die Anfänge des Triumphbogens," *Jahrbuch der kunsthistorischen Sammlungen in Wien*, II, 1928, p. 2.

83 For eagles on crowns, cf. Schramm, "Die Fragmente dreier in Polen erhaltener Kronen," *Kaiser Friedrichs II, Herrschaftszeichen* (cf. above, note 10), p. 59, ff., 74 ff., and "Erhaltene Kronen der Staufer," *ibid.*, p. 135. For eagles on thrones, cf. Deér (see above, note 10), p. 118 ff.

84 For eagles on medieval standards and insignia, cf. Percy Ernst Schramm, *Kaiser, Rom und Renovatio* (Studien der Bibliothek Warburg, XVII), II, Leipzig–Berlin, 1929, pp. 96, 98 (text of *Graphia aureae urbis Romae*), and see also *ibid.*, I, p. 264 (referring to Benzo of Alba's description) and p. 298, referring to Hildebert of Lavardin.

85 Deér, p. 94, points out that the *Reichsadler* frequently holds some prey in its claws, and mentions monumental examples from the inner court of the castle of Barletta, from the castle of Bari, etc.

eagle in each particular case — and the specific meanings certainly vary from case to case —, their common quality is that the eagle symbolizes victory.

In this context one should perhaps also recall the antique motif (particularly frequent in the first Christian centuries in the eastern part of the Mediterranean) of the eagle holding a crown in his talons or in his beak.[86] Since this is the crown that is to be placed on the head of the victor, the whole motif constitutes an additional link between the eagle and victory symbolism.

The Middle Ages could have derived the association of the eagle with victory not only from classical traditions, but also from northern beliefs. In northern mythology the eagle is, of course, the bird of struggle and victory: he is also the symbol of heroism. The hero appears to his wife in a dream as an eagle. The giant Hrälsweg ("devourer of corpses") sits in the guise of an eagle at the edge of the sky, and causes storms by agitating his wings. The names of Germanic warriors frequently refer to eagles, specifically stressing the bird's aggressive nature. The belief that the eagle, when attacking his enemies, aims at the face,[86a] perhaps also has some significance for our purpose.

In Christian religious symbolism the eagle acquired a wide range of meanings, partly determined by pagan beliefs and traditions that were absorbed, and transformed, by Christianity.

As is well known, in classical Antiquity the eagle is not only the bird of victory but — probably in the first place — it is the bird of Apotheosis [87] (and incidentally the only bird in Greek mythology which is of a strictly divine character).[88] A man being elevated to the heavens by means of an eagle, or on eagle's wings, is an antique motif well known from both literary and visual imagery, and probably going back to very ancient times.[89] Such a lifting up by an eagle could be interpreted as the elevation of a ruler, and thus be the manifestation of his political

---

86 Cumont, *Etudes Syriennes*, p. 63 ff., adduces many examples. For the symbolic meaning of this motif, cf. Cabrol-Leclerq, *Dictionnaire d'archéologie chrétienne*, s.v. "Aigle", I. p. 1037.

86a Cf. Martin Ninck, *Wodan und der germanische Schicksalsglaube*, Jena, 1935, p. 160 ff. The following references are taken from this work. For the hero appearing as an eagle, cf. Thule, *Altnordische Dichtung und Prosa*, I, p. 73. For the giant Hrälsweg, cf. Ninck, p. 84. For attacking the face, see Thule, XV, p. 315.

87 Cumont, "L'Aigle funéraire", *passim*.

88 Pauly-Wissowa, *Real-Encyclopädie der klassischen Altertumswissenschaft*, p. 373, s.v. "Adler"; Keller, *Tiere des klassischen Altertums*, p. 238; Wittkower, p. 307.

89 Cf. Cumont. *Etudes Syriennes*, pp. 35, 83.

or military glory ,but it could also be understood as the soul's elevation to heaven. With the latter meaning the eagle appears as the symbol of the soul,[90] and is frequently represented on sarcophagi, stelae, and other funerary monuments.[91]

In Christian imagery the classical Apotheosis becomes an Ascension, an achieving of immortality by salvation. The eagle lifting up the soul to heaven thus becomes an image of salvation. In this sense the Middle Ages understood *Exodus* 19 : 4 "You have seen what I did to the Egyptians, and how I bore you on eagles' wings and brought you to myself".[92] It is therefore perhaps not surprising that one finds the eagle linked with other symbols of redemption, rejuvenation, and eternal life. Thus the eagle is frequently connected with the baptismal font, the source of rejuvenation, this connection being based on Psalm 103 : 4–5 (...who redeems your life from the pit, / who crowns you with the steadfast love and mercy, / who satisfies you with good as long as you live / so that your youth is renewed like the eagle's"), and the well known stories told in the Physiologus.[93] This association is found not only in literary formulations, but also in visual expression. Here it may be sufficient to mention only one artistic representation, a twelfth century liturgic rotula in Kremsmünster. Three eagles are represented in one of the rotula's compartments, one flying towards the sun, another into the clouds, and the third dipping his head into the rejuvenating water of the font. An in-

90 That the Apotheosis could also mean a Christian Ascension is, of course, well known. For an extensive discussion of an early example, cf. Guillaume de Jerphanion, *Le Calice d'Antioche* (Orientalia Christiana, VII), 1926.
    For the eagle as a bird of the soul, cf. Cumont, p. 35 ff., and also Newbold in *American Journal of Archeology*, XXIX (1925), p. 361 ff. Weicker, *Der Seelenvogel in der alten Literatur und Kunst* was not available to me while writing this paper.
91 Many examples of stelae are discussed by Cumont, p. 38 ff. See also R. Dussaud, *Notes de Mythologie Syrienne*, Paris, 1903, p. 23 ff. For eagles on sarcophagi, cf. Cumont, p. 50, note 3. See the famous sarcophagus in S. Lorenzo fuori Le Mura in Rome (third century). Cumont has shown (*Syria*, X [1929], p. 217 ff.) that it belongs to a group of motifs illustrating Dionysiac enthusiasm at the prospect of eternal happiness in heaven. And see Wittkower, p. 311, — an extensive discussion of Coptic monuments, which may have been the source of many images in the west, cf. Jerphanion, Le Calice d'Antioche, pp. 139–145.
92 Cf. also the verse of Deuteronomy 32 : 11 which was so frequently quoted in the Middle Ages: "Like an eagle that stirs up its nest, that flutters over its young, spreading out its wings . . ."
93 For the eagle in the *Physiologus*, cf. the now easily available *The Bestiary*: *A Book of Beasts*, Translated from the Latin by T. H. White, New York, 1960, p. 105 ff.

scription reads: "Hic aquile gestus Jehsu typus est manifestus".[94]

Throughout the Middle Ages the eagle is endowed with miraculous and divine qualities. The buoyancy of wings in particular indicates the superterrestrial.[95]

Seen in this context it is, of course, not surprising that the eagle represents heavenly figures, such as the archangel Michael.[96] To the medieval mind, many passages in Scripture seemed to allude to the eagle. Thus, to give but one example, the verses of Psalm 91 : 1 :

> He who dwells in the shelter of the Most High,
> who abides in the shadow of the Almighty,

was interpreted as referring to the soul of a believer lifted up to heaven by an eagle.[97] The eagle therefore symbolizes the protection offered by the church to the faithful.[98]

In the present context, however, it is most important that the eagle was sometimes understood as a symbolic personification of Christ himself. Scripture seemed to be full of this suggestion. Again we shall limit ourselves to one example only. Jeremiah 49 : 22 reads:

> Behold, one shall mount up and fly swiftly like an
> eagle, and spread his wings against Bozrah, and the
> heart of the warriors of Edom shall be in that day like
> the heart of a woman in her pangs.

The eagle of this verse was interpreted as pointing to Christ.[99] Another verse of Scripture was similarly interpreted. Proverbs 30 : 18–19 :

> Three things are too wonderful for me;

94 See Hubert Schrade, "Zur Ikonographie des Himmelfahrt Christi", *Vorträge der Bibliothek Warburg* 1928–1929, Leipzig–Berlin, 1930, p. 162; Heider, *Mitteilungen der Kaiser-Königlichen Central-Kommission* XI, 1861, p. 65 ff., and pl. 2.

95 In a text as early and as influential as Dionysius Areopagita, *Celestial Hierarchy*, XV, 3, most of these "superterrestrial" qualities are already formulated.

96 For the eagle as a "figura" of St. Michael, cf. Picinelli, *Mundus Symbolicus*, Cologne, 1687, p. 265, still a mine for the iconographer.

97 Beautifully expressed by the sixteenth century saint, S. Thomas Villanovanus, as quoted by Picinelli, p. 265, § 124: "Spera in Deo, & ipse te velut Aquila in altissimo collocabit nido, . . ."

98 One should also not forget that on the basis of Psalm 103 : 5 and of Isaiah 40 : 31, the eagle can represent the community of the chosen with God. Cf. T. Scheider, art. "Adler", *Reallexikon für Antike und Christentum,* I, col. 92, and E. Kantorowicz, "The Archer in the Ruthwell Cross," *Art Bulletin,* XLII (1960), p. 59.

99 Cf. Debidour, *Le Bestiaire Sculpté,* p. 291.

Four I do not understand :
the way of an eagle in the sky . . .

was understood as indicating Christ's Ascension, as already shown by the Church Fathers.[100] The eagle overcoming, and devouring, the snake was also understood as a simile for Christ overcoming Satan.[101]

Not only Scripture verses were interpreted as suggesting a special link of the eagle and Christ, but artistic images received a similar meaning. Thus the eagle that is a symbol of St. John is frequently understood as signifying Christ, "the true eagle",[102] A ninth century manuscript bears, close to St. John's eagle, a *titulus* reading : "Hac ave Johannes Domini signat Deitatem".[103] The inscription besides St. John's eagle in the Uta-Codex is not less clear : it reads : "In Christo completa est visio aquilae ascendendo." [104] This symbolism continued to exert its influence for a considerable period. Sometimes the eagle appears as an abbreviation of Christ's ascension.[105] Even in the late Middle Ages it appears as the favourite bird on lamps, a clear indication of its divine nature.[106]

We need not go on collecting examples. It is fairly certain that in certain contexts at least the eagle may stand for Christ. The question that thus arises is whether this is the case in the sculpture under discussion? Does the Acre group represent Christ overcoming Satan, or perhaps even the Antichrist, in the guise of an eagle overcoming a lion, or rather the cut-off head of a lion? Do we have before us another version of the *Beau Dieu,* namely, according to Psalm 91 : 13, Christ as the "true eagle" treading on the lion?

While such an explanation cannot be proved it should not be altogether excluded. It at least does justice to the expressive characters of the two beasts and their relationship.

100 Some material collected by Picinelli, p. 266, & 128.

101 Cf. Pseudo-Ambrose's sermon quoted above, note 14.

102 See Kraus, *Real-Enzyklopädie der christlichen Altertümer,* I, p. 20 ff.; Molsdorf, *Christliche Symbolik der mittelalterlichen Kunst,* Leipzig, 1926, p. 81 ff. In this context one might also mention the motif of the eagle with spread-out wings as a *Figura crucis* especially in early Christian times. Cf. H. Rahner, "Antenna Crucis", *Zeitschrift für Katholische Theologie,* 75 (1953), p. 169.

103 Cf. *Topographie der historischen und Kunstdenkmäler Böhmens*: Die *Bibliothek des Metropolitankapitels* (Podlaha), Prague, 1904, p. 20 (not available to me at this moment); and see also Schrade, p. 162.

104 G. Swarzenski, *Die Regensburger Buchmalerei,* Leipzig, 1901, pl. 14.

105 Schrade, p. 162, believes that the eagle appearing in the *Noli me tangere* scene of the Hildesheim Bronze Doors should be understood as a symbol of Christ's Ascension (which is not represented on the doors).

106 Cf. Schrade, p. 162, note.

V

We have discussed some of the principal meanings that might have been attached to our group in medieval secular and religious iconography; these meanings, it must be admitted, are of a rather broad validity, and are present in almost all phases of medieval culture. Can we not, then, place our group in a more limited, more concrete historical context?

The likelihood of such a definite situation, it should be said immediately, is very remote. As I remarked at the beginning of this paper, there is no external evidence whatsoever to help establish the origin of our work, and the fact that it is largely unfinished, of course, severely limits its possible ascription to a more clearly outlined group or school even on stylistic grounds alone. Nevertheless, in looking at our sculpture one cannot help feeling that it may have had some connection with a specific, and major figure of medieval history, the Emperor Frederick. Needless to say, there is no reason that would absolutely compel us to link our sculpture with Frederick's court; it is only an intrinsic affinity between the work in Acre, its style, theme, and expressive quality, and the cultural tendencies that were characteristic of Frederick's court, that suggest such a connection.

The heraldic character of our work agrees strikingly with certain tendencies typical of the cultural atmosphere in Frederick's court. The eagle as a royal bird played a major role in his political and military symbolic imagery, and, probably patterned after Roman models, was a constant feature in his military emblems. At least once his standard was described as an eagle holding a dragon in his claws. In 1229 the people of Brindisi, seeing the eagle standard, recognized the Emperor returning from the Holy Land; an eagle standard was displayed on the occasion of all his major military operations.[107] In the course of time the eagle of the imperial emblem became Frederick's personal symbol, and the emperor himself was metaphorically described as an eagle. Thus his court rhetorician, Petrus de Vinea, compared Frederick to that great eagle of which the prophet speaks: "Hic est, de quo Ezechielis verba (XVII : 3) provclamant: 'Aquila grandis magnarum alarum, longo membrorum ductu, plena plumis varietate multiplici' ".[108] We also know that many

---

107 For the eagle standard seen in Brindisi, cf. Muratori, *Rer. Ital. Script.*, XII, p. 1162. For this, and other sources, cf. Deér, p. 121.

108 Cf. Huillard-Breholles, *Vie et correspondance de Pierre de la Vigne*, Paris, 1864, p. 427. Cf. Deér, p. 122.

of Frederick's contemporaries believed that he was the apocalyptic eagle who chases everything in front of him.[109]

It is tempting to think, although the idea unfortunately cannot be proved, that our work may have had some relation to Frederick.[110] The period in which our sculpture was created, i.e. the early thirteenth century, makes such a relationship at least possible. The sculpture's style points, as I have tried to show, to Southern Italy, that is, to the central realm of Frederick's kingdom. It seems at least possible that when Frederick went to the Holy Land, where he in fact spent most of his time in Acre, Sicilian and South Italian artists went with him, and perhaps one of them carved our sculpture. But while all this necessarily remains hypothetical speculation one can say, I think, that in expression and meaning our work has some relation to the ideas current in Frederick's court.

109   Cf. Kantorowicz, *Kaiser Friedrich II,* p. 620 of volume I, and p. 247 of volume II.

110   We may also note Frederick's interest in birds, especially in conection with hunting, as amply attested in his monumental work *De arte venandi cum avibus.* It is true that this work deals with falcons and not with eagles, and it does not discuss lion-hunting. Nevertheless it has some interest for our purpose since it proves Frederick's interest in rapacious birds, especially hawks, as well as in other forms of hunting. Cf. Charles Homes Haskins, "The *De arte venandi cum avibus* of Frederick II", *Studies in the History of Medieval Science,* 1927, pp. 299–326.
Frederick had undertaken to write a special book on hawks (cf. Haskins, p. 308, note 35), and Albertus Magnus cites the *experta Frederici imperatoris* on the care of hawks (cf. Haskins, p. 307). Frederick seems to have believed that the East possessed a special wisdom in these matters. — Although falconry was an art long established in the west, he collected oriental treatises on hunting, falconry and hawking, and had falconers from the East brought to his castles in Sicily. He also imported birds from the East, and the emissaries of Michael Comnenus considered a couple of hawks a present worthy of the Emperor. (cf. Haskins, p. 324). It has been shown that Frederick's *De arte* was written late in his life, but the collecting of materials for the treatise occupied him for thirty years (cf. Haskins, p. 310) and he himself says that he had the work in mind for about thirty years and finally completed it upon the urgent request of Manfred, to whom it is dedicated (cf. preface to *De Arte . . .,* reprinted in Haskins, p. 312 ff.). This means that the Acre period, at least partly coincided with the preparation of the book, and our sculpture may perhaps reflect something of the Emperor's interest in predatory birds and hunting.

CARO, MUNDUS ET DEMONIA
dans les premières oeuvres de Bosch

par
MOSHÉ LAZAR

> "L'Enfer? mais je m'y trouve! C'est cette cité monstrueuse, c'est l'existence quotidienne; et les damnés? mes contemporains hideux et moi, dans leur troupe infâme."
>
> Michel de Ghelderode *

Faut-il pour pouvoir expliquer la peinture visionnaire de Bosch avoir irrémédiablement recours à l'arsenal des archétypes jungiens, aux théories freudiennes sur les rêves et la sexualité, aux élucubrations des alchimistes, aux listes des équivalences symboliques? Faut-il, pour pouvoir comprendre sa vision du monde, supposer nécessairement une personnalité pathologique, un peintre au bord de la folie ou membre d'une secte hérétique qui, par crainte, s'exprimerait en hiéroglyphes? Enfin, par sa conception absolument grotesque de la réalité matérielle et spirituelle, Bosch est-il un produit indépendant de toute durée historique et culturelle, de toute technique plastique et formelle, de toute iconographie ancienne et contemporaine? Nous ne pouvons, dans le cadre de cette étude,[1] répondre en détail aux questions que nous posons; celles-ci, cependant, suggèrent que nous entendons analyser la métamorphose grotesque de la vision infernale dans l'oeuvre de Bosch à l'intérieur d'une perspective exégétique à la fois diachronique — du point de vue de la littérature et de l'inconographie médiévales — et synchronique, du point de vue de la civilisation de *l'automne du Moyen-Age*. La biographie spirituelle d'une durée historique, affirmons-nous, peut mieux rendre compte d'une oeuvre qui lui est inhérente et en un sens l'exprime, qu'une théorie psychanalytique ou pathologique de la personnalité. D'autre part, le rapprochement établi entre un phénomène isolé et contemporain d'un côté et l'oeuvre littéraire ou plastique d'un autre côté ne suffit guère non plus à expliquer celle-ci ou même à justifier le rapproche-

---

* Michel de Ghelderode, *Sortilèges et autres Contes Crépusculaires*, Verviers, 1962.

1 Cette étude fait partie d'un essai que nous préparons sur la métamorphose grotesque de la vision infernale dans les peintures de Bosch.

ment; l'existence d'une secte hérétique au temps de Bosch ne prouve pas, comme Fraenger a voulu le démontrer, que le peintre était membre de cette "secte du Libre Esprit" et que son oeuvre illustrait dans un langage chiffré les dogmes du Grand Maître.[2] Pas plus que l'existence du mouvement cathare au XIIe siècle n'est une raison suffisante ou valable pour présenter la lyrique des troubadours comme le message codé d'un pseudo-manichéisme.[3] Il y a certainement plus de rapports entre l'oeuvre de Bosch et un courant de pensée mystique (Erasme, Ruysbroeck, Pic de la Mirandole) auquel Fraenger se rapporte également par moments.[4] Nous pensons qu'une *mentalité*, circonscrite dans une durée historique plus ou moins longue, peut se manifester à travers une série d'expressions philosophiques, littéraires et artistiques qui n'ont pas besoin d'être absolument synchroniques et dont la signification ne réside pas dans la trajectoire biographique de leurs auteurs.

Etant donné que notre étude concerne avant tout la *métamorphose* grotesque de la vision infernale dans les peintures de Bosch, il serait nécessaire pour pouvoir situer celles-ci dans leur contexte exact de prendre en considération tous les éléments qui ont contribué à leur formation. En d'autres termes, il faudrait analyser la gestation de cette vision à travers une multitude de manifestations culturelles de plusieurs siècles, afin de comprendre ses aboutissments et sa métamorphose dans une conception nouvelle et synthétique. Cette vision de la Chair, du Monde et de l'Enfer, est immergée dans plusieurs matrices créatrices : théologique, psychologique, sociologique, folklorique, littéraire, dramatique et artistique. Car Bosch, plutôt que d'être un "*faizeur de dyables*", est le créateur d'un monde grotesque complet, le metteur en scène d'un *teatrum mundi* total, l'arbitre suprême de la "bataille entre Carême et Carnaval" et entre un *Ars Amandi* et un *Ars Moriendi*, plus concerné par une vi-

2 W. Fraenger, *Le Royaume Millénaire de Jérôme Bosch,* Paris, 1966. Cf. p. 22–23 : "A l'Eglise s'oppose la Secte. Nous voyons donc apparaître un type nouveau de peinture religieuse pour hérétiques. Seule une secte, une communauté extra- et anticléricale, pouvait trouver son édification et se raffermir dans sa foi devant de tels rétables...Il y a là une volonté délibérée d'ésotérisme, *cela est bien évident si l'on convient que les oeuvres de Bosch servaient des idées hérétiques*". Fraenger dit fort justement: "*si* l'on convient", mais l'essentiel de son ouvrage considère cette hypothèse comme une certitude et une vérité axiomatique. Cf. aussi, p. 237, cette conclusion aberrante: le Grand Maâître de la Secte propose un programme idéologique détaillé et précis à Bosch, et "la part du peintre semble se réduire à celle d'un simple exécutant, au rôle, secondaire, d'artisan".

3 Cf. par exemple, Denis de Rougemont, *L'Amour et l'Occident,* Paris, 1939; R. Nelli, *L'Erotique des Troubadours,* Paris, 1963.

4 *Op. cit.,* p. 232–33.

sion du Paradis et de l'Enfer dans le "royaume de ce monde" que par
le Paradis et l'Enfer d'un Au-delà. Bosch est un "faizeur de songes" qui,
dans le cadre d'un réalisme mythique et grotesque, imprégné d'ironie et
de satire, représente un *monde à l'envers,* où la symétrie et l'harmonie
n'ont plus leur place. Nous nous limiterons dans cette étude à l'analyse
de la vision infernale dans les premières oeuvres de Bosch, telle qu'elle
émerge sur le fond de la représentation de l'Enfer chez les peintres néerlandais qui l'ont précédé ou qui lui furent contemporains. Ceux-ci et
ceux-là, contrairement à Bosch dans ses premières oeuvres, n'ont pensé
la vision infernale que dans le cadre traditionnel du Jugement Dernier
et non pas à l'intérieur d'une vision totale du royaume de ce monde. Et
même lorsque Bosch traitera le thème de l'Enfer dans le cadre d'un
Jugement Dernier ce ne sera que pour rompre absolument les conceptions médiévales de la vision infernale traditionnelle.

*

*   *

La représentation du Diable et de l'Enfer, spécialement dans le cadre
du *Jugement Dernier,* après de longs tâtonnements dans l'art byzantin
puis dans l'art roman, acquiert une forme plus ou moins fixe à partir
du XIIIe siècle dans la peinture et surtout dans la sculpture monu-
mentale.[5] Dans l'ensemble, peu de changements importants y seront in-
troduits avant la seconde moitié du XVe siècle, époque où la perfection
de la peinture à l'huile dans les Pays-Bas va permettre aux peintres néerlandais une technique de travail révolutionnaire,[6] dont les répercussions
sont manifestes également dans le traitement du *Jugement Dernier.*

L'Enfer du *Jugement Dernier* des frères, ou un des frères, Van
Eyck est l'un des plus impressionnants de cette époque. Le peintre
accorde à son Enfer la moitié d'un panneau; cette division en deux parties, bien que n'étant pas originale, est loin d'être commune parmi les
contemporains de Van Eyck.[7] La partie infernale l'intéresse nettement
autant que le domaine céleste. Le groupe composé du Christ, des anges
et des élus, suit le modèle traditionnel. Immédiatement sous ce groupe,
la terre et la mer rendent leurs morts pour être jugés; ceux-ci, les bras

5   Outre les travaux de Mâle, Réau, cf. W. H. Mülbe, *Die Darstellung des Jüng-
    sten Gerichts an den romanischen und gotischen Kirchenportalen Frankreichs,*
    Leipzig, 1911.
6   E. Panofsky, *Early Netherlandish Painting,* Cambridge, 1954; M. J. Fried-
    länder, *Early Netherlandish Painting, From van Eyck to Brueghel,* Londres,
    1956.
7   Panofsky, *op. cit.,* p. 238.

tendus vers le Christ, implorent sa miséricorde. La terre est arride, fis-
surée, comme après un incendie et un tremblement de terre. En arrière-plan, des bâtiments naufragés ou édifices consumés par le feu semblent compléter cet aspect de la fin du monde. L'entrée de l'Enfer n'est
guère signalée et les damnés semblent être tombés d'une région intermédiaire entre la terre et la mer ou des entrailles du squelette-chauve-
souris qui représente la Mort. Sur les ailes arrondies de la Mort, qui
forment les voûtes de l'Enfer, on lit : *Chaos magnum umbra mortis ite
vos maledicte ignem eternum*; et, ce qui nous frappe dans ce tableau,
c'est justement le chaos terrifiant de damnés et de monstres qui couvre
entièrement le registre inférieur du panneau. Malgré l'absence du feu
dans l'Enfer, les bruns obscurs suggèrent la chaleur qui y règne. Dans
cet Enfer, écrit Baltrušaitis, "la cohue explose comme une déflagration.
Le prodigieux grouillement des corps nus qui roulent les uns sur les
autres précipités la tête en bas, déchirés, écartelés ou dévorés par d'abo-
minables monstres fourmille de vie et de détails exacts".[8] Les damnés
et leur agonie, en effet, sont représentés avec un réalisme impitoyable,
avec une abondance de détails extraordinaire pour le format restreint
du tableau. Comme dans les "danses macabres" de la même époque,
toutes les classes sont représentées (l'évêque, le moine, le roi); sans dif-
férencier entre elles quant au type de tortures, tous les damnés sont
soumis à la voracité des monstres. Ceux-ci sont évoqués avec autant,
sinon plus de détails que les damnés; ils sont zoomorphiques et dif-
férenciés : le serpent à deux têtes; le diable gastrocéphale; le monstre
aux ailes de chauve-souris; le chat féroce avec ailes, cornes et pattes
d'oiseau; la gueule de Léviathan. Il y a des yeux étincelants et mena-
çants qui hypnotisent le spectateur du fond de chaque recoin de cet
Enfer. On sent la fascination du peintre devant un thème qui permet à
la fois le réalisme et le fantastique les plus déchaînés; l'énergie de l'ensemble, la puissance évocatrice des détails, la place accordée au thème,
semblent en témoigner. "This work was done in a hot-blooded exalta-
tion".[9]

L'Enfer du *Jugement Dernier* de Petrus Christus est une imitation servile de celui de Van Eyck, sans la puissance et la fascinante
vitalité de son modèle, "plain to the point of artlessness" selon Panofsky.[10]
L'Enfer est d'une simplicité dérisoire; la gueule de Léviathan et l'espèce
de "bulldog' au bas du tableau n'inspirent ni terreur ni horreur; les

8 Baltrušaitis, *Réveils et Prodiges de l'Art gothique*, Paris, 1960, p. 287.
9 Friedländer, *op. cit.*, p. 13.
10 *Op. cit.*, p. 309.

damnés sont rares, insignifiants, détachés de leur situation et du contexte infernal; les diables supplémentaires, placés dans le registre central, loin d'ajouter au caractère dramatique, nuisent à l'ensemble du tableau. Les Saints sagement assis sur leurs bancs, l'archange terrassant un diable, le feu dans la gueule de Léviathan, une certaine réduction de l'Enfer, — sont autant de caractéristiques qui classent le tableau de Petrus Christus dans la tradition médiévale, et certainement pas parmi ses manifestations les meilleures.

La réduction de la place et de la vision de l'Enfer est encore plus manifeste dans le *Jugement Dernier* de Roger Van Der Weyden qui, dans son poliptyque, accorde à l'Enfer le panneau d'extrême droite, symétriquement opposé au Paradis, dans la meilleure tradition des tympans gothiques. Cependant, la réduction de l'Enfer ici est autrement justifiée que dans le tableau de Petrus Christus, car elle correspond à une conception idéologique et artistique nettement définie. Le royaume céleste, par ses représentants et sa topographie, domine l'ensemble du rétable. Quelques rochers et un feu infernal conventionnels composent l'essentiel de l'Enfer. Van der Weyden, contrairement à Van Eyck, n'est pas fasciné par le royaume de Lucifer. Les damnés, incarnant le *nu idéal* de certains peintres flamands de l'époque,[11] n'ont qu'un nombre réduit de gestes dramatiques pour signifier leur agonie et leur terreur. C'est avec raison que Lassaigne écrit: "The looks of horror of the Damned and their gestures of affright count for little *beside the pain of isolation from the Heavenly Father, eternal exile from felicity*".[12] Ce ne sont pas l'Enfer et les démons qui intéressent Van der Weyden, malgré leurs possibilités dramatiques et plastiques, mais la contrition et le désespoir des âmes, la torture morale, la douleur d'être séparé de l'Epoux et exclu du Banquet de noces, conformément à la parabole de Matthieu sur les Vierges Sages et les Vierges Folles. La structure du tableau et la conception idéologique du sujet, de même que la disposition des personnages, correspondent à un raffinement d'une tradition purement médiévale.[13] Mais nous avons également à considérer ici le tempérament particulier du peintre et le milieu social dans lequel il se forme et pour lequel il peint. "Roger happened to come at the moment when circumstances and the growing wealth of a certain number of individuals involved and imposed the development of a certain kind of paint-

11 Cf. K. Clark, *The Nude,* Londres (1960), 1963, p. 17 ss.
12 J. Lassaigne, *The Century of Van Eyck,* New York, 1957, p. 88; nous soulignons.
13 Cf. Panofsky, *op. cit.,* p. 269.

ing. He could not have broken the way into a new world of art as the Van Eycks did. He was not a *creative exploratory mind*".[14] C'est cette dernière remarque surtout, à notre avis, bien plus que le contexte social, qui explique le traitement du thème de l'Enfer chez Van der Weyden.

L'Enfer d'un *Jugement Dernier* de Thierry Bouts, avec tout ce que ce peintre doit à Van der Weyden, représente un retour à l'affirmation du fantastique et du grotesque. Son Enfer est un peu moins grouillant que celui de Van Eyck, mais par là-même il peut rendre plus plastiquement les divers damnés et démons d'une part, et représenter avec quelque détail la topographie de l'Enfer : sa bouche d'entrée, ses rochers et ses précipices, quelques instruments de torture, les grottes de feu et les lacs, la "lumière noire" et la désolation horrible de ses profondeurs. Les démons anthropomorphiques et zoomorphiques sont relativement nombreux et variés, comportant la plupart des types étudiés par Baltrušaitis; [15] ils ne se rencontrent pas seulement dans l'Enfer, comme chez Van Eyck, mais encore dans l'espace au-dessus de la bouche d'entrée, au milieu des flammes et de la fumée : monstres ailés, insectes, reptiles volants, et autre volaille, survolent le gouffre et amènent leur proie. Par son aspect fantastique, son traitement du diabolique, et par la configuration topographique de l'Enfer, ce tableau de Bouts annonce l'Enfer de Bosch, spécialement celui que l'on voit dans le panneau droit (partie supérieure) du *Char de Foin* (Fig. 3) et dans *La Chute des Damnés* et *l'Enfer* de Venise.

Le traitement de l'Enfer, tel que nous venons de le voir chez Van Eyck et Bouts, mais avec une puissance évocatrice différente nous semble-t-il, revient dans un *Jugement Dernier* de Hans Memling,[16] qui par certains autres détails du tableau d'ensemble s'inscrit dans la lignée de Van der Weyden. Mais comme chez Van Eyck aussi, il y a un véritable *chaos magnum*, une foule de damnés représentés dans des positions corporelles diverses : les uns sont poussés dans l'abîme, les autres entrent par un passage étroit; ils sont d'âges, de classes et de races distinctes. Les diables, en général, sont anthropomorphiques et nantis de membres d'animaux : bec, cornes et pattes pour l'un; ailes de chauve-souris, corne unique et crâne arborescent pour l'autre; cornes, pattes et queue pour un troisième.

14 M. Conway, *The Van Eycks and Their Followers*, Londres, 1921, p. 153; nous soulignons.
15 Cf. *Le Moyen Age fantastique*, Paris, 1955, figures 1, 2, 4, 6, 7, 12, 29, etc.
16 Cf. Conway, *op. cit.*, p. 229. Par contre, G. Bazin, *Memling*, N.Y. 1939, y voit plutôt l'influence de Lochner.

Il ne fait pas de doute que Memling est fasciné par les possibilités fantastiques et grotesques du thème infernal mais, comme chez les autres peintres néerlandais, la part du royaume céleste prédomine : comme si l'accent était mis de préférence sur l'espoir du salut que sur l'horreur de la damnation.

Cependant, tous ces peintres, tout en renouvelant par la technique et le réalisme des détails le sujet du *Jugement Dernier,* continuent à perfectionner et à raffiner un modèle médiéval traditionnel : tant chez Van Eyck ou Petrus Christus où nous rencontrons les trois registres superposés, que chez les autres dans le cadre du triptyque ou du poliptyque. Il faut attendre Bosch pour voir une transformation du cadre écclésiastique, une métamorphose de la vision infernale et une intégration de celle-ci à une conception du monde plus immanente.

*
*   *

Nous avons noté chez les peintres flamands, Van Eyck et Bouts mis à part, une réduction du royaume infernal dans leurs tableaux et une prédominance du royaume céleste, de la grâce et du salut possible. Nous allons assister chez Bosch à une réduction progressive de la présence céleste et de la grâce et, parallèlement, à une amplification croissante de l'Enfer, d'un monde à l'envers, du Mal sous tous ses apscets, pour aboutir à la suppression de toute grâce et de toute miséricorde. Ce n'est plus le Christ qui domine le monde dans les peintures de Bosch : c'est plutôt l'Antéchrist, au moyen de la "grâce diabolique", qui semble avoir conquis les hommes et les objets, la cité et les foyers, le clergé et le culte, la terre et une partie du ciel déjà. Nous assistons non seulement à une conquête progressive des tableaux de Bosch par l'Enfer et ses manifestations grotesques, mais encore le Paradis lui-même n'est guère plus le "Jardin d'Eden" biblique et ecclésiastique; c'est la présence d'un *paradis perdu* dans le dos des exilés, un paradis qui semble un beau fruit mûr dévoré de l'intérieur par le péché originel. Le *Paradis* et le *Jardin des Délices* portent dans leur nom une réalité moins délicieuse et idyllique qu'amère et ironique. Et le Christ trônant en majesté, entouré des intercesseurs, assesseurs et anges trompetteurs, quand il apparaît encore dans le *Jugement Dernier,* n'a plus droit qu'à un espace réduit en haut d'un panneau [17] — comme le Ciel modeste dans une miniature —, à un traitement conventionnel [18] — comme le Christ apocalyptique, avec

17 Voir le panneau central, *Jugement Dernier, Vienne,* et le panneau central du
    Char de Foin où le Christ est seul.
18 Voir le *Jugement Dernier* de la table peinte, Madrid. On remarquera la fusion
    du Christ apocalyptique avec le Christ évangélique, — les instruments de la

la branche de lys et l'épée nue aux lèvres —, ce qui contraste violemment avec l'invention géniale, le réalisme fantastique, la richesse de la couleur et la précision des lignes qui caractérisent l'univers infini en marge de l'Eglise et en dehors du Christ.

A voir les oeuvres conservées de Bosch, on note d'emblée que ce peintre est obsédé par le problème du Mal, métaphysique et concret à la fois, et de là la cristalisation de son activité créatrice autour d'un thème central et quasi-exclusif : celui du *Jugement Dernier* et de la damnation, thème qui comprend les autres : les péchés, les tentations, la corruption, le charlatanisme, le crime. On peut y ajouter : hérésie et, surtout, alchimie — science luciférienne si l'on veut, en ce sens que l'alchimiste rêve d'être égal à Dieu et de posséder le pouvoir de créer un nouveau monde. Bosch est obsédé par la vision du Mal, disions-nous, et il n'est certes pas le seul à l'être autant au XVe siècle; mais contrairement à d'autres, il ne semble pas être obsédé par le problème du salut. Entre le premier qui concerne un monde immanent et réel et le second qui se rattache à un monde transcendant et utopique, Bosch en tant que peintre sinon en tant qu'homme opte pour la représentation picturale du premier. Nous ne mettons pas en question ici la religiosité et la foi de Bosch, et il serait aberrant de vouloir l'imaginer comme un libre-penseur ou un athée, un révolté ou un incroyant,[19] malgré la satire anti-cléricale et le peu d'orthodoxie qui dominent bien des scènes dans ses tableaux. Avec cette conscience du Mal dans le monde, croyait-il à l'existence réelle des diables, à leur présence constante dans la vie, à leurs formes monstrueuses et grotesques? Ou bien, artiste à cheval sur le Moyen-Age et la Renaissance, incarne-t-il les démons dans ces formes si horribles et terrifiantes pour les rendre "horrifiques", pour mieux s'en libérer et en délivrer les hommes? La catharsis au moyen du grotesque peut être un résultat, pensons-nous, et non pas le point de départ ou l'infrastructure idéologique des tableaux. La peinture de Bosch est en dehors de l'art didactique. Mais que signifie en réalité *croire en Dieu* ou *croire au Diable*? N'a-t-on pas affaire là, en fin de compte, à deux "incarnations" anthropomorphiques d'un idéal du Bien et d'une conception du Mal? deux projections dans un absolu de l'espoir et de la terreur, des rêves et des hantises qui habitent le coeur de l'homme? Croire au diable, mis à part le cas des névrosés ou celui des sorciers, n'est-ce pas affirmer tout

passion apparaissant sur les fanions des trompettes des anges.
19   Cf. les travaux de Lucien Febvre, *Amour sacré, Amour profane*, Paris, 1936 (sur Marguerite de Navarre), et *Le problème de l'Incroyance au 16e siècle, La religion de Rabelais*, Paris, 1942.

simplement l'existence du Mal, incarné dans l'esprit et la conduite des hommes, sans être obligé pour cela de reconnaître aux "diables" une réalité corporelle et vivante? Bosch n'est pas seulement obsédé par le Mal à l'intérieur du monde humain, mais il est encore *fasciné en tant que peintre* par une matière qui offre d'immenses possibilités formelles et stylistiques, qui permet une libération totale de l'imagination, un emploi original de la peinture à l'huile, un dépassement de la tradition et des conventions. Bosch est fasciné par l'Enfer et le monde infernal, par les tentations et les péchés, parce que ce sont de beaux sujets à peindre, plus intenses et plus dramatiques, plus vivantes et plus dynamiques, plus variés et plus immédiates, que ceux qui concernent le royaume céleste. On pourrait appliquer à Bosch cette confession significative de Michel de Ghelderode, Flamand comme Bosch, hanté comme lui par le Diable et le grotesque, et inspiré par le peintre dans certains de ses drames :

> "Que le Diable existe, je n'en doute pas; les éducateurs m'ont enfoncé cette croyance dans la tête et, jusqu'à ce jour, aucun rationalisme n'est arrivé à me prouver que cette croyance, ou ce dogme, fût une fable pour enfants. Si je crois au Diable? parbleu! et de manière plus permanente qu'à Dieu et à ses saints! N'a-t-il pas toujours parlé à mon imagination? N'occupe-t-il pas depuis toujours ma cervelle? Ne me galvanise-t-il pas au même titre qu'un héros du théâtre ou du conte?" [20]

Et contrairement à tant de critiques qui ont d'abord analysé Bosch comme un idéologue ou un théologien "défroqué", comme un névrosé sexuel ou un logicien de l'irrationnel, Jean de Boschère a parfaitement raison de nous alerter au fait que Bosch n'est plus un artisan de la peinture mais l'un des grands peintres authentiques de l'histoire de l'art :

> "La première grande révolution, dans les domaines de l'art, date de ces années de la fin du XVe où Jérôme Bosch secoue le poids de la servilité... Les historiens et les critiques des arts qui ignorent la mentalité profonde, la structure et les modes d'élaboration de l'esprit du peintre, errent généralement quand ils établissent des rapports éthiques entre la conception pittoresque de l'image, entre cette réalisation concrète d'une vision de l'imagination et les pensées du peintre sur la vie, la religion, l'organisation sociale de l'art même... Avant toute recherche sur la signification des représentations allégoriques ou symboliques, il est urgent de s'imaginer le plaisir qu'éprouve l'artiste..." [21]

20 Ghelderode, *Sortilèges.*, p. 00
21 Jean de Boschère, *Jérôme Bosch et le Fantastique*, Paris, 1962, pp. 99–101; cf. *supra*, note 2.

A l'opposé des peintres de son siècle qui continuent à raffiner les formes et les thèmes traditionnels ou s'adonnent à la peinture du portrait, Bosch transfigure les thèmes et les motifs bien mûrs déjà en cet "automne du Moyen-Age" et ne se laisse pas distraire de son monde visionnaire par aucune tentation à la mode. Il est de son temps, mais le dévance ; il récolte les fruits des traditions médiévales, mais les métamorphose. Il impose sa vision grotesque du monde dans le domaine de la peinture, comme Rabelais va le faire dans celui du roman. Rabelais, écrit Imbs,[22] fait un *usage* particulier des "matériaux fournis par la tradition. Ceux-ci, Rabelais ne semble en effet pas les prendre entièrement à son compte : ce sont sous sa plume des *moyens pour peindre et faire rire*". Chez Bosch, dirions-nous, c'est moins pour faire rire, que pour peindre et faire réfléchir, pour peindre et alerter la conscience. Ce qui est d'ailleurs vrai également pour Rabelais, pour Erasme et Cervantes.

Dans les nombreuses études consacrées à notre peintre,[23] on trouvera citées certaines sources livresques ou iconographiques qui auraient pu faire partie du bagage intellectuel de Bosch, mais ne sont pas nécessairement, ses sources directes. Ainsi, H. Daniel cite encore le *Malleus Maleficarum* d'Alain de la Roche et le *Roman de la Rose*[24] ; Baldass mentionne l'influence des gravures de cuivre allemandes de son temps ;[25] Combe rappelle van Eyck, les miniaturistes du début du XVe, l'oeuvre des frères de Limbourg, les xylogravures de l'époque[26] ; Linfert souligne certaines correspondances picturales avec Gérard David[27] ; on mentionne aussi Martin Schongauer, le Maître de *Virgo inter Virgines*, et d'autres encore. Mais cet inventaire de parallèles iconographiques n'aide guère à expliquer l'oeuvre de Bosch.

Ce qui nous frappe d'abord chez Bosch, à part sa fascination du monde infernal en tant que peintre et la réduction du royaume céleste, dont

22 P. Imbs, *Le Diable dans l'oeuvre de Rabelaiz, Etudes de vocabulaire,* in "Mélanges Ch. Bruneau", Genève, 1954, p. 260; nous soulignons.
23 Voir, entre autres, Ch. de Tolnay, *H. Bosch*, Bâle, 1937 (éd. rev., Baden-Baden, 1966); L. von Baldass, *H.B.*, Vienne, 1943; J. Combe, *J.B.*, Paris, 1946; H. Daniel, *H.B.*, New York, 1947; C. Linfert, *H.B.*, *The Paintings*, New York, 1959; Cl. A. Wertheim-Aymès, *Die Bildersprache des H.B.*, La Haye, 1961; A. Bosman, *H.B.*, New York, 1963; D. Bax, *Ontcijfering van J.B.*, La Haye, 1949; M. Gauffreteau-Sévy, *J.B.*, Paris, 1965; F.M. Huebner, *Le mystère J.B.*, Bruxelles, 1965; C. D. Cuttler, *Northern Painting, From Pucelle to Breughel,* New-York, 1968, pp. 198–211; et autres déjà cités.
24 *Op. cit.*, p. 13.
25 *Op. cit.*, p. 70.
26 *Op. cit.*, p. 39.
27 *Op. cit.*, p. 6.

nous avons parlé ci-dessus, c'est le changement d'optique absolu qui
s'opère dans ses tableaux : le monde était vu et représenté de l'angle
idéologique de l'Eglise et de la théologie, avec tout ce que cette vue
comporte de sacré, de soumission, de solennel; il est maintenant considéré et concrétisé d'un angle plus humain et séculaire, à travers un
regard critique et ironique, avec un sens de l'humour et du grotesque;
le peintre n'est plus un prisonnier à l'intérieur de son sujet, mais au
contraire l'observe du dehors, à travers un microscope qui grossit à l'extrême les détails et déforme l'image familière. Ce n'est pas une doctrine
qui observe l'humanité et la juge; c'est un homme qui se dépeint lui-
même et qui peint son prochain, ainsi que le monde terrestre dont ils
font partie. Considérer sa peinture comme une illustration de "sermons
moralisés", même originale et géniale, essentiellement didactique par ses
intentions, comme le fait Cuttler, ne semble guère plus acceptable; il
écrit, en effet :

> "Such a style was well suited to its purpose, the transformation into
> paint of moral sermons that constantly reiterate man's folly and its
> inevitable consequence of punishment in Hell. This moral was either
> stated or implied in almost all his work from beginning to end.
> Basically pessimistic, Bosch repeated almost ad infinitum that man's
> salvation can be achieved through the instrumentality of Christ's
> sacrifice and the heroic acts of the saints whose example man must
> emulate".[28]

Cette intention didactique était certes celle des peintres qui ont précédé Bosch; celui-ci dépasse le cadre strictement médiéval, tant par la
composition de ses tableaux que par la signification sous-entendue. Et
l'imitation du Christ et des Saints n'en est assurément pas le noyau
d'inspiration ni le résultat final.

*

*   *

Les premières oeuvres de Bosch qui intéressent directement notre étude
ici sont : 1) Les *Sept Péchés capitaux*; 2) La *Nef des Fols;* 3) Le *Char
de Foin;* 4) La *Tentation de Saint-Antoine.* C'est dans ces tableaux essentiellement que nous trouvons la gestation de la vision infernale de
Bosch, la vision d'un monde à l'envers ou, en d'autres termes, dominé
par la "grâce satanique".

1. — *Les Sept Péchés* (table peinte, Madrid, c. 1475–1480 [Fig. 1]) :
la peinture comprend sept sphères, trois au centre et les autres aux quatre

---

28 *Op. cit.*, p. 198.

coins de la table ; le Christ avec l'auréole crucifère, formant le premier cercle, se trouve placé dans la pupille d'un oeil, et celui-ci est entouré par sept scènes représentant les péchés capitaux ; une inscription dans la pupille dit : *Cave, cave, Deus videt ;*[29] dans les sphères des angles, quatre scènes : a) la Mort, figurée par un homme agonisant entre l'ange et le diable ;[30] b) le Jugement Dernier ; c) le Paradis et ses élus ; d) l'Enfer et le châtiment des sept péchés. L'ensemble des représentations semble sortir directement d'un *Ars Moriendi*, mais la composition et le traitement sont différents ; alternant et harmonisant les intérieurs et les extérieurs dans lesquels il situe les vices, Bosch présente ceux-ci moins comme des allégories que comme des scènes de moeurs réalistes, avec la couleur locale correspondante ; le Jugement Dernier ne comporte que deux registres, celui du Christ apocalyptique trônant en majesté, et celui de la résurrection des morts. Tout en empruntant à la tradition, Bosch se montre plus original dans le traitement de l'Enfer,[31] qui plus précisément est l'Enfer des sept péchés capitaux. Nous avons là une vision synthétique des vices et de leurs tourments qui étaient dispersés dans les illustrations de l'*Ars Moriendi*, mais groupés dans la représentation théâtrale de l'Enfer. La tableau infernal de Bosch est, en effet, composé à la manière d'un lieu scénique et comporte tous les éléments qu'on trouvait disposés autour de la "gueule infernale" sur les tréteaux : tours, lits de torture, chaudron, forgerons, feu, fumée, diables, serpents et crapauds, etc.[32] D'autre part, en disposant tous les éléments à divers niveaux et coupant l'horizon par la prison infernale, la tour et les collines, Bosch présente un paysage élaboré et lui accorde une profondeur qu'on ne connaissait pas jusque-là dans le traitement artistique de l'Enfer. Cette élaboration du paysage,[33] qui permet une mise en scène interne détaillée, un jeu de mouvements et de gestes multiples et variés, une escalation du regard d'un lieu à un autre, semble contenir en une forme miniaturisée les grands paysages infernaux des compositions ultérieures, où l'on pourra déceler une structuration assez similaire de l'espace (Fig. 2).

Considérons d'un peu plus près cette première représentation infernale de Bosch. Il y a un grand nombre de diables, mais ceux qui sont

---

29 Cf. Boschère, *op. cit.*, pp. 62–62, rappelle des xylogravures du 15e siècle représentant un triangle avec un oeil au centre, portant une inscription flamande : "Ici on ne jure point. Dieu nous voit".

30 Voyez une manière identique, selon une tradition médiévale, de représenter la mort du pécheur, dans *Mort de l'Avare,* Washington National Gallery.

31 Cf. Baldass, *op. cit.*, p. 23.

32 Bosch y ajoute même le fleuve infernal au centre.

33 Cf. K. Clark, *Landscape in Art, Boston,* 1961, ch. 2.

préposés à tourmenter les vices sont mis en valeur; ils sont de nature anthropomorphique et zoomorphique. Chaque scène représentant un vice torturé s'accompagne d'une inscription indiquant la nature du péché. Au premier plan, *Superbia* : incarné par un homme et une femme nus qui se voient tendre un miroir par un diable étrange, tandis qu'un paon mord l'homme et un crapaud dévore le pelvis de la femme. A gauche de ce groupe, *Luxuria* : un couple d'amants au lit; tandis qu'un diable aux ailes de chauve-souris s'attaque à la femme, un crocodile ou un crapaud-lézard grimpe sur la couverture. Sur l'autre rive du fleuve infernal, installé sous une tente, se trouve *Gula* : homme ventru assis à table, poussé par un diable à consommer un serpent, un lézard et un crapaud. Derrière cette tente, dans un champ en amont, un groupe de damnés est attaqué par des chiens et représente selon une tradition médiévale *Invidia*. Au centre, une forge infernale : un diable ailé tient *Acidia* au-dessus de l'enclume, tandis qu'un autre (une diablesse?) le martèle avec une massue. A la droite, *Ira,* étendu et peut-être cloué à une planche, se voit la proie d'un lézard immense et d'un diable (avec tête arborescente, nez en trompe et larges oreilles) qui l'attaque d'une épée. Un peu plus bas, c'est la "rôtisserie" et la "cuisine" de l'Enfer : un diable, ressemblant plutôt à un "Fol" grotesque, tient dans une main une grande louche et avec l'autre fait tourner un damné embroché au-dessus d'un gril; un autre démon surveille le chaudron, portant l'inscription *Avaritia*, où cuisent des damnés et des pièces d'argent. A l'horizon, sur la muraille de la prison et à sa porte, sur les tours et les collines, un grand nombre de diables s'agitent au milieu du feu et de la fumée, entre potences et échelles. Nous avons là une véritable "diablerie" théâtrale, synthétique et miniaturisée, avec l'aspect grotesque et carnavalesque qu'on trouve aussi, par exemple, dans ces passages de Rabelais : [34]

> "Sus diables estoient tous capparasonnéz de peaux de loups, de veaulx et de béliers, passementées de testes de mouton, de cornes de boeufz et de grands havetz de cuisine; ceinctz de grosses courraies, esquelles pendoient grosses cymbales de vaches et sonnettes de muletz à bruyt horrificque...
>
> ... C'estoit une effigie monstrueuse, ridicule, hydeuse et terrible aux petitz enfans, ayant les oeilz plus grands que le ventre et la teste plus grosse que tout le reste du corps, avecque amples, larges et horrificques maschouères bien endentelées, tant au-dessus comme au-dessoubs...
>
> ... Bruslez, tenaillez, cizaillez, noyez, pendez, empallez, espaultrez, démembrez exentérez, découppez, fricassez, grislez, transonnez, cruci-

---

34 Nous citons d'après les *Oeuvres Complètes,* éd. Boulenger, "Coll. Pléiade", Paris, 1955. Cf. pp. 576, 700, 684–5.

fiez, bouillez, escarbouillez, escartelez, débezillez, dehinguandez, carbonnadez ces meschans haerétiques décrétalifuges, décrétalicides, pires que homicides, pires que parricides, décrétalictones du diable".

Une telle exubérance dans la fantaisie diabolique, où les mots et les formes en font naître d'autres, ne caractérise pas encore l'Enfer des *Sept Péchés* mais y est déjà virtuellement et, dans le cadre plus ample des tableaux ultérieurs, trouvera un terrain d'éclosion favorable. C'est d'après le modèle de cet *Enfer* miniaturisé et théâtral que Bosch peindra celui du *Char de Foin* (Fig. 3), celui du *Jugement Dernier* de Vienne (Fig 4) surtout, et encore le plus développé de tous, celui du panneau droit du *Jardin des Délices* (Fig. 5).

2. *La Nef des Fols* (Louvre, c. 1500; [Fig. 7]): inspiré probablement de la gravure qui servait de frontispice à certaines éditions du "Narrenschiff" de Brandt (une nef grouillant de sots qui voguent en buvant et en chantant vers *Narragonia* — le royaume de la sottise), ce tableau de Bosch condense dans un espace limité le contenu et la portée d'un thème philosophique prédominant de son temps (l'Eloge de la Folie) et réussit merveilleusement à amalgamer le carnavalesque avec le méditatif, les cris avec le silence, l'agitation des instincts avec le masque figé des visages, les ultimes allégresses mélancoliques d'un esquif qui sombre. C'est dans ces contrastes que naissent l'ironie et le grotesque qui frappent d'emblée notre regard. La barque est trop étroite et trop fragile pour supporter et contenir une telle agitation et cette communauté de sots. La nef est sans pilote ni gouvernail (la palette de boulanger ayant servi de rame plus tôt n'est plus utilisée); un arbre avec plusieurs bouquets de feuillages remplace le mât; des passagers tout occupés à leurs disputes, ripailles et besoins égoïstes, ne semblent guère s'interroger sur le destin de leur navigation; un Fol avec sa marotte, perché sur une branche, domine la scène mais tourne le dos aux passagers déchaînés; et dans la cîme, au milieu d'une auréole de feuilles, une petite tête qu'aucun des passagers n'aperçoit observe la scène: la tête du hibou, symbole de la perspicacité, de la clairvoyance, de la sagesse. Ce sage, tout en étant capable de s'isoler de la déraison, n'est pourtant pas représenté comme un étranger, extérieur au monde dépeint sous lui; il y a continuité entre les deux grands bouquets de feuillages (celui des instinctifs et celui du hibou) mais aussi rupture (la branche brisée au-dessus de l'oriflamme); le Fol lui-même est en dehors du premier bouquet de feuilles et, bien que paraissant entre ciel et terre, fait partie de la même embarcation; ainsi, le Sage et le Fol ont beau faire bande à part, mais ils risquent le même destin que les passagers inconscients. Bien plus qu'un tableau

représentant une galerie de sots, nous avons ici une vision synthétique de la condition humaine, de la vie comme aventure mystérieuse. L'oriflamme se déroule avec le vent vers un horizon dépeuplé. Si dans certains gravures de l'époque on représentait la vie comme une nef dans une mer agitée, voguant entre l'image du Christ et celle de Satan, ces points de repère ont disparu de notre tableau ensemble avec l'intention didactique évidente. L'attention est appelée à se concentrer entièrement sur la contradiction et le paradoxe qui relient la nef surpeuplée et le hibou isolé dans son halo de clarté. Le lien est l'arbre-mât, qui est surtout mât (bois mort) au niveau des passagers de la nef, et arbre (vivant et florissant) au niveau supérieur du Fol et du hibou. La nef allégorique semblerait supporter également l'Arbre de la Connaissance ou l'Arbre de la Vie. Le croissant de lune dans l'oriflamme est-il symbolique? Représente-t-il la folie et la fantaisie, l'illusion et la mélancolie? Il se trouve en tout cas au niveau de la rupture entre ce qui est mât et ce qui est arbre. Mis à part plusieurs traits caractéristiques qu'on retrouve dans les tableaux ultérieurs de Bosch, il faut mettre particulièrement en relief cette *nef-arbre* qui connaît plusieurs variantes dans son oeuvre. Il y a un rapport évident, semble-t-il, entre cette barque arborescente et le dessin de l'Albertine et, à son tour, entre celui-ci et la scène centrale du panneau droit du *Jardin des Délices* (Fig. 6) et enfin, une parenté avec l'arbre surgissant du foin dans le panneau central du *Char de Foin*. Nous retrouvons dans le dessin de l'Albertine : deux troncs d'arbre, posés comme deux jambes sur deux barques, unis par une excroissance ovoïde (tronc vidé-oesophage-oeuf) et une tête d'homme, et dessus cet ensemble : une cruche, un homme qui essaie d'atteindre quelque chose (voyez la cruche et l'homme grimpant sur le mât dans la *Nef des Fols*), un hibou perché au haut de l'arbre dégarni de son feuillage, un fanion avec le croissant de lune symbolique. Il en est de même dans l'Enfer du *Jardin des Délices,* sauf qu'une cornemuse remplace la cruche et une autre le croissant de lune, et l'absence du hibou. Enfin, dans l'arbre du char de foin, arbre garni de feuilles, une cruche et un hibou sont mis en évidence. Le hibou surplombant le croissant de lune et la cruche dans la *Nef des Fols,* le hibou dominant la cruche et le croissant dans le dessin de l'Albertine, le hibou et la cruche du *Char de Foin,* les cornemuses remplaçant la cruche et le croissant dans l'Enfer du *Jardin des Délices* (sans référence à l'existence du hibou), — représenteraient autant de variations sur le thème *sagesse-folie,* le thème *vie-connaissance-dégradation,* selon la place, la présence ou l'absence, et la prédominance de l'un de ces éléments. Citons ici Fraenger qui écrit fort pertinemment :

"Cette cornemuse n'est qu'un néant plein de vanité qui s'enfle et piaille tant que le souffle vivant emplit son sac, mais qui s'effondre lamentablement dès que ce souffle vient à faire défaut ... la cornemuse est l'incarnation de la folie humaine ... le croissant de lune est le symbole habituel de la vie terrestre où croissance et déclin s'équilibrent. Quant à la cruche, elle ne signifie, elle aussi, que l'éternelle alternance de l'emplissage et du vidage. *Cornemuse, cruche et croissant de lune sont tous des symboles de la Vanité*".[35]

Nous pourrions ajouter: *symboles de la vie, symboles de l'homme*. A travers les pages de la Bible et, ensuite, dans la littérature religieuse et séculaire ne trouve-t-on pas des métaphores ou images du genre: *l'homme est comme l'arbre des champs; la vie de l'homme est comme la cruche; le souffle quittant l'homme, celui-ci retourne à la terre;* sans mentionner l'imagerie populaire: *Jean de la lune, lunatique, être cruche, être plein de soi-même, enflé, sec comme un arbre, être de bois*, etc. Chacun des éléments qui composent une scène chez Bosch, même s'ils se trouvent répétés et partiellement regroupés, peut se prêter à des significations multiples, pas nécessairement identiques, d'un tableau à l'autre. Une fois mis en relief le thème dominant et sa structure métaphorique, il faut éviter, nous semble-t-il, de vouloir coller aux symboles qui intègrent la métaphore générale des significations trop exclusives, trop figées et qui se veulent définitives. En tout cas, l'*arbre-barque* métaphorique [36] et les symboles *cruche-croissant de lune-Fol-hibou* qui l'accompagnent dans le tableau *La Nef des Fols*, de même que les variations dans les tableaux discutés ci-dessus, nous empêchent d'accepter l'opinion de tant de critiques qui ne se lassent de répéter les équations suivantes: cornemuse = organe sexuel; tronc d'arbre = alchimiste; cruche = satanisme; échelle = acte sexuel; et autres équivalences précises de ce genre. La référence constante aux symboles sexuels de Freud, à l'alchimie mystique de Jung, permettent sans aucun doute de sexualiser toutes les lignes, toutes les formes et tous les objets dans les peintures de Bosch selon des préceptes et des formules assez faciles. Il reste à démontrer que cette sexualisation est nécessaire et suffisante pour expliquer une oeuvre d'art dont de nombreux éléments formels et iconographiques, dont une quantité de personnages, de scènes et d'objets, dont la technique et l'esthétique débordent non seulement la personnalité intime de l'artiste mais encore le cadre de son temps.

---

35 *Op. cit.*, p. 111; nous soulignons.

36 Nous reviendrons, à une autre occasion, sur la signification de l'arbre-homme dans le panneau droit du *Jardin des Délices*.

3. *Le Char de Foin* (Madrid, c. 1485–1490; [Fig. 3]) : panneau droit) :
bien que notre intérêt porte principalement sur le panneau central et
celui de droite, il nous faut rapidement considérer aussi celui de gauche
qui comporte trois registres : a) la création d'Eve, près de la Fontaine de
Vie; b) la tentation d'Adam et Eve par Satan en forme de serpent, au
milieu; c) Adam et Eve chassés du Paradis par l'ange à l'épée flam-
boyante, au premier plan. Ces trois registres sont dominés par un es-
saim d'oiseaux-insectes qui tombent du ciel — la chute des anges re-
belles — polymorphes et monstrueux, certains choyant près de la Fontaine de Vie dont la forme ne manque pas de grotesque, d'autres s'écra-
sant en cercle autour du couple cédant à la tentation. Un Dieu miniature
surplombe le tout. La chute des anges et la chute du premier couple font
de ce panneau la représentation du *Paradis perdu*.[37] Une fois de plus, il
élabore le paysage, en étageant une série d'épisodes chronologiquement
successifs mais en les reliant par le mouvement et la couleur autant que
par une correspondance thématique : oiseaux-anges-démons, Satan-ser-
pent, archange-exil. Cette vision synoptique et synthétique du Paradis,
comme par ailleurs de l'Enfer, ne caractérise pas les prédécesseurs de
Bosch ni ses contemporains.

Le panneau central, composé de trois registres et d'un Christ minuscule perdu dans les nuages, peut être considéré et interprété comme une
variation géniale de la *Nef des Fols*. Au lieu d'avoir une *navigatio*, nous
avons une *peregrinatio* à travers le Royaume de *Narragonia*; au lieu d'un
groupe restreint de passagers embarqués vers leur perte, toutes les couches
de l'humanité mènent la danse autour du char de foin, qu'ils dévorent
avec voracité et qui à son tour, non seulement les dévore au cours de
la pérégrination sur terre, mais encore les emporte inévitablement vers la
gueule vorace de l'Enfer. L'arbre, la cruche et le hibou de la *Nef des
Fols* qui, dans le tableau précédent, surmontaient une embarcation fragile, se retrouvent également ici sur une meule de foin mobile et chan-
celante qui, brin après brin, décroît et s'affaisse. En diagonale de la
cruche, le démon de l'amour érotique (diablotin aux ailes grotesques,
Cupidon ridicule avec le nez-trompette diabolique); et en diagonale du

---

37   Le parallèle entre cette représentation du Paradis et celle du *Jardin des Déli-
     ces* est fort intéressant. Notons ici que Fraenger (*op. cit.*, pp. 77–82) considère
     le premier comme étant sous le signe de la "loi mosaïque", le "décalogue de
     Jéhovah"; le second, sous le signe "évangélique", la "loi d'amour du Christ";
     et afin de montrer qu'il y a une évolution spirituelle et optimiste du second
     au premier, il considère le *Char de Foin* postérieur au *Jardin des Délices* (voir
     p. 78), alors qu'il semble généralement admis que le premier est de 1485–
     1490, et le second de 1510–1515.

hibou, un ange de l'amour divin (resplendissant avec ses ailes de papillon); celui-ci, le regard tourné vers le Christ, implore la miséricorde et la protection divine pour les deux couples d'innocents à ses côtés, qui s'adonnent à l'amour et à la musique, sans se rendre compte qu'ils sont assis sur du foin, c'est-à-dire, sur une réalité éphémère et évanescente; celui-là, s'accompagnant d'un battement de pied et d'un regard oblique, joue le contrepoint de l'invocation angélique et interfère brutalement dans l'harmonie du chant et du luth du couple central. Le démon et l'ange sont disposés aux côtés des couples comme leurs semblables dans les gravures illustrant l'homme devant sa mort prochaine; mais personne, sauf une tête curieuse qui surgit derrière le feuillage, ne semble leur prêter attention.

Le char de foin, au centre du panneau, irradie par sa richesse métaphorique tout ce qui l'entoure. Sa signification essentielle : *Vanité des vanités, tout est vanité et poursuite de vent*! C'est une *danse vivante* qui préfigure une *danse macabre* prochaine. C'est le "grand théâtre du monde" ou, si l'on veut un autre titre de pièce de Calderón, "le grand marché du monde". Les scènes diverses qui se déroulent autour du char de foin détaillent sur un registre narratif et dramatique les séquences de la comédie humaine. Il est possible que la présence de personnages orientaux autour du char (avec turbans et barbes) ait éveillé l'attention de Sigüenza, [38] au début du XVIIe siècle, à voir dans le *Char de Foin* une illustration d'un passage d'Isaïe (XI, 6–8), et celle de Fraenger [39] qui le considère comme "une puissante paraphrase du prophète Isaïe" mais d'un passage différent (ch. VIII, 3–4) où on lit :

"Je m'étais approché de la prophétesse; elle conçut, et elle enfanta un fils. L'Eternel me dit : Donne-lui pour nom Maher-Schalal-Baz. Car avant que l'enfant sache dire : Mon père! ma mère! on emportera devant le roi d'Assyrie les richesses de Damas et le butin de Samarie".

Fraenger identifie le personnage en blanc dans le groupe de gauche avec le prophète Isaïe qui "met en garde la cohorte des Juifs qui s'approchent, contre les vanités de la chair et le châtiment divin qui les attend", et la nonne assise par terre, un nourrisson dans les bras, avec "la sombre prophétesse dont parle la Bible". Et Fraenger ajoute : "Bosch dénonce ainsi, avec une rigueur non moins impitoyable que celle de l'Ancien Testament, l'ascétisme hypocrite. Par la prophétesse biblique, c'est toute la corruption morale des couvents qui est stigmatisée." Il ne fait pas de

38 Cf. Cuttler, *op. cit.*, p. 203.
39 Voyez l'interprétation ésotérique de Fraenger, *op. cit.*, pp. 19–20, 29–30.

doute que dans le tableau existe un motif anti-clérical fort développé, mais est-il nouveau dans la civilisation médiévale ? Est-il plus virulent que dans des textes satiriques avant Bosch et de son temps ? D'autre part, prêter à ce tableau de Bosch des intentions typologiques du genre le plus scolastique, comme le fait Fraenger, ne nous paraît guère acceptable. Son exégèse, qui voit dans diverses scènes de ce tableau, des gloses picturales complexes et érudites, n'est ni suffisante ni nécessaire pour saisir pleinement la signification totale de cette peinture métaphorique. Pour représenter le thème déjà abordé dans la *Nef des Fols,* mais d'une manière plus détaillée et plus immédiate aussi, Bosch n'a même pas recours à une métaphore ou à une allégorie complexe de sa propre invention. La sagesse populaire et le folklore universel connaissent d'innombrables proverbes et dictons pour exprimer d'une manière concise les oppositions stabilité-fragilité, éternel-éphémère, ce qui donne vie peut aussi donner mort, du genre : *bâtir sur le sable, tant va la cruche sur l'eau qu'elle se casse, on ne peut manger le gâteau et qu'il reste entier,* ou bien ce dicton hébreu, *celui qui engraisse sa chair, multiplie les vers.* On voit comment de tels proverbes ou dictons peuvent devenir les noyaux métaphoriques d'une illustration picturale. Aussi, Tolnay nous semble avoir raison et, après lui, Combe, Cuttler et d'autres, quand il considère le proverbe flamand *"Le monde est une meule de foin, chacun en prend ce qu'il en peut saisir"* comme point de départ possible de l'allégorie picturale de Bosch. Un grand nombre d'épisodes des registres central et inférieur, en effet, illustrent le proverbe tout en lui donnant des dimensions et une signification métaphysique qu'il ne pouvait contenir. Il y a entre le proverbe flamand et la peinture de Bosch cette même différence de profondeur visionnaire qu'entre une gravure de l'*Ars Moriendi* et une oeuvre de notre peintre sur un thème identique. Tout le monde participe au pillage de la meule de foin, pauvres et riches, jeunes et vieillards, hommes et femmes ; toutes les classes sociales suivent ou poussent le char, en avant, vers la Mort et l'Enfer : pape, empereur, roi, nobles, bourgeois et tous ceux que le peintre laisse deviner derrière eux. Au registre inférieur, des nonnes s'affairent à remplir un grand sac de foin pour un moine ventripotent, oisif et buveur ; le lieu où se trouvent ces nonnes et le moine ressemble à une galerie souterraine, à une grotte sous le signe de Satan ; en effet, un diable-jongleur, avec une cornemuse à la main, s'y trouve également et paraît vouloir éviter une nonne qui lui offre du foin ou son corps. Tout près, un arracheur de dents, charlatan sans nul doute, s'occupe d'une jeune fille sous l'enseigne du Sacré-Coeur cependant qu'une botte de foin dépasse de sa poche. Il y a des rixes, des assassinats, des gens écrasés sous les roues du char, mais peronne n'y prête attention. Pendant ce temps, d'autres attaquent le foin frénétiquement et il semble que peu s'en faut encore pour que les couples, l'ange, le démon, la cruche, l'arbre et le hibou, tous perchés dessus la meule, ne viennent à s'effondrer entre les roues d'un char pillé et dégarni. Cependant que la société des hommes pousse le char, un attelage de diables anthropomorphiques et zoomorphiques tire avec force de son côté pour arriver plus vite en Enfer. Les diables qui tirent ont des têtes ou le corps de divers animaux : poisson, rat, cerf, porc-épic, ours; leur chef, le charretier, semble un squelette de mort.

Il y a un enjambement direct du panneau central dans celui de droite, au moyen des premiers pêcheurs qui arrivent en Enfer, accompagnés des diables qui les avaient inspirés durant leur vie sur terre. L'Enfer de ce panneau n'est pas sans ressemblance avec celui qu'on a vu dans les *Sept Péchés* et, dans une certaine mesure, en est un développement : mise en scène théâtrale, niveaux et étages bien disposés et reliés entre eux par des mouvements ascentionnels (diables en action, échelle, potences); *Ira, Superbia, Luxuria, Avaritia* et *Gula* se détachent au premier plan, formant la tête du cortège; les flammes et la fumée derrière la forteresse à l'horizon. Il y a cependant deux différences notables : a) les diables et les instruments ne sont plus traditionnels; c'est au contraire une véritable mascarade, une galerie carnavalesque de créatures composites : du panneau gauche (insectes et oiseaux polymorphes) en passant par la partie centrale (têtes de cerf, rat, poisson, etc.) et aboutissant dans le panneau de droite (toutes les créatures précédentes, mais ressemblant parfois à des hommes travestis pour le carnaval, et un chien ou loup avec queue arborescente); on a déjà ici le fantastique et le grotesque des enfers ultérieurs; b) l'Enfer ne semble pas achevé, car l'on voit des créatures humaines et diaboliques affairées à construire un grand édifice : tour de prison? purgatoire? ou, probablement, le *puits* de l'Enfer. Cette *collaboration entre hommes et diables* constitue sans aucun doute un des thèmes principaux du triptyque : depuis le péché originel (panneau de gauche), l'humanité court à sa perdition (panneau central) et agrandit le royaume infernal (panneau de droite). C'est l'homme qui construit son propre enfer, activement et jour après jour. Cuttler [40] écrit fort justement que le triptyque présente une métamorphose qui se déroule sous nos yeux : "A metamorphosis of the human into the demonic takes place before our eyes in the figures pulling the wagon toward the Hell scene … where man's misdeeds build a mighty tower in Hell". Mais c'est le traitement grotesque de la vision infernale et de

40 *Op. cit.,* p. 202.

la comédie humaine qui nous paraît présenter le plus grand intérêt, car c'est la première manifestation véritable du génie particulier de Bosch.

4. *La Tentation de Saint Antoine* (Lisbonne, c. 1495–1510 [Fig. 8] : panneau central) : le thème du Saint tenté par le Diable et ses représentants terrestres constitue un des courants les plus anciens et les plus riches de la tradition chrétienne, tant littéraire que plastique. La tentation de Jésus par Satan et la victoire du Christ furent un exemple idéal pour les anachorètes dans leur solitude au désert. Il n'est pas sans intérêt de rappeler ici que le *Physiologus* allégorique fut probablement composé au IIe siècle par un anachorète, car la tentation du Diable (capable de prendre diverses formes animales) en est le thème dominant et inspirateur. Le Diable, mais aussi et surtout la Chair et le Monde. *La Tentation de Bouddha* est probablement le plus ancien prototype des "tentations" chrétiennes en général et de la "tentation de Saint Antoine" en particulier, comme Baltrušaitis l'a clairement montré et illustré [41] : l'attaque de Mâra, à l'aide d'une armée de diables et de créatures "diabolisées", contre le Bouddha qui est sur le point de devenir le sage parfait et le sauveur du monde, est une légende qui a connu une grande fortune dans la littérature et l'iconographie d'Extrême-Orient qui, passant par l'Egypte copte, arrivèrent en Occident. "Toutes les *Tentations* extrême-orientales s'inspirent, de près ou de loin, de cette vision et c'est encore son déploiement qui se reflète dans les dernières figurations de Saint Antoine", écrit Baltrušaitis, et fait également remarquer que c'est avec le développement du fantastique à "l'automne du moyen-âge" que commence une véritable métamorphose dans la représentation iconographique de la *tentation de Saint-Antoine* :

> "Le renouveau des *Tentations* au XVe siècle commence ainsi par un emprunt et par une confusion et c'est en multipliant les fantaisies et les monstruosités des provenances les plus diverses que la vision prendra son prodigieux essor, chez Bosch, Mandyn, Huys, met de Blès, Breughel et les artistes de leur lignée. *La représentation du saint rompt avec la tradition hagiographique. Le solitaire n'est qu'un prétexte, un centre d'attraction ou se récréent toutes les fantasmagories et les hallucinations du monde. Jamais l'anachorète n'avait subi pareilles attaques".* [42]

---

41 *Op. cit.*, pp. 229–234. Cf. aussi, A. Chastel, *La Tentation de S.A.*, "Gazette des Beaux-Arts", 1936, p. 17 ss; Cl. Roger-Marx, *Les Tentations de S.A.*, "La Renaissance", mars-avril 1936.

42 *Ibid.*, p. 233; nous soulignons.

Cuttler [43] pense que saint Antoine a été élevé par Bosch "to a position comparable to that of Chirst", et que notre peintre est le premier à combiner les deux significations que comporte la notion de tentation : "*tentatio* in its meaning of a trial, that is, the temptation of the flesh in form of worldly goods and sexual inducements — always rejected; and tentation in its meaning of an attack". Qu'il ait été le premier à le faire dans l'iconographie occidentale est fort possible, mais les représentations orientales de la Tentation de Bouddha en fournissent déjà le modèle. Sans entrer dans une discussion détaillée de ce problème, il est intéressant pour notre sujet de comparer l'illustration de l'attaque de Mâra contre Bouddha, datant du Xe siècle et se basant sur un récit dont nous reparlerons, une gravure de Schongauer (influencée par l'*Alphabet fantastique* de Maître E.S. et son traitement de la lettre T) et l'oeuvre de Bosch, spécialement le panneau central et la partie supérieure du panneau de gauche (Fig. 8), qui représente saint Antoine emporté dans les airs par les démons. Dans le premier exemple, nous pouvons noter une grande variété de démons anthropomorphiques et zoomorphiques, d'animaux diabolisés, de créatures grotesques, de tentateurs variés (certains blancs, d'autres noirs) et même, à l'extrême droite, un démon qui ressemble étrangement au Lucifer de l'art byzantin en Occident : enveloppé de serpents, avalant un homme, et soutenant sur un plateau enflammé un squelette agressif. Voici, par ailleurs, les détails intéressants que contient le *Lalita-Vistara*, la légende bouddhique relatant l'assaut de Mâra [44] : les attaquants ont la faculté de changer leurs formes et leurs visages, ont "des ventres, des pieds et des mains difformes", corps flamboyants, oreilles pendantes; "d'autres avaient *le ventre comme une cruche* ..."; les monstres infernaux font naître des "nuages noirs, produisant une nuit noire, faisant du bruit"; ils tirent des flèches, lancent des pierres; le *diable envoie ses filles* "qui cherchent à le troubler par les trente-deux tours de la magie féminine, *se dévoilant et se voilant, montrant leurs seins*, faisant sonner les anneaux de leurs jambes, *découvrant leurs cuisses*", mais le Bienheureux résiste à l'attaque du Diable et de ses tentations, et "Bodhisattva devient Bouddha". C'est bien ce que nous voyons aussi dans le triptyque de Bosch. La gravure de Schongauer présente également une agression physique, violente et grotesque, contre saint Antoine : les démons sont zoomorphiques et composites mais ont des bras d'homme (pour frapper, tirer, déchirer, griffer); il y en a avec corps d'insectes, de poisson, d'oiseau, et avec têtes

---

43 *Op. cit.*, p. 204.
44 Baltrušaitis, *op. cit.*, pp. 230–31. Cf. l'illustration orientale correspondante reproduite par Baltrušaitis.

de vautour, de dragon ou d'éléphant; ce qui est plus important encore, le saint est *emporté dans les airs,* comme on le voit également chez Bosch.

Dans le triptyque de Bosch, il y a autour du Saint une véritable mise en scène d'un monde totalement vicié, corrompu par la "grâce satanique". Il n'y a dans le triptyque nul objet,[45] nulle personne, nul animal qui ne manifeste activement ou ne témoigne par sa seule forme des intentions maléfiques. Il n'y a aucune île d'innocence, de pureté, de compassion si ce n'est la présence discrète du Christ (face à son image sur la Croix) au fond de l'édifice en ruine. Nous avons ici le même esprit qui règne dans le *Physiologus* et les *Bestiaires médiévaux*: le diable est partout et en toute chose. Aussi pouvons-nous considérer le triptyque comme illustrant le combat suprême de saint Antoine contre le "satanos energumenos". Dans le panneau de gauche, une minuscule église surmonte un poisson diabolique; des moines corrompus font partie du monde diabolisé; dans le panneau central, le grand édifice en ruine pourrait être celui du Temple, la grande colonne montrant dans ses reliefs des scènes bibliques (la danse autour du Veau d'Or, les deux espions portant la grappe de raisins gigantesque) et un registre représentant le culte du singe. Entre un Temple en ruine et une Eglise abandonnée, saint Antoine est vraiment seul dans le désert peuplé de créatures maléfiques.

Dans le panneau de gauche, la nef naufragée sur un monstre dans le ciel et attaquée par un requin peut provenir des *Bestiaire* où la baleine est décrite comme diabolique (elle fait semblant d'être une île et, quand un bateau se pose sur son dos, elle le renverse et dévore ses passagers); l'homme accroupi, dont les pieds sont enracinés dans la terre et dont le dos est le toit d'une chaumière, représente avec un réalisme obscène l'image de la luxure (la femme à la fenêtre indiquant que cette chaumière est une maison de prostitution);[46] dans le panneau de droite, on trouve plusieurs personnages associés avec gloutonnerie: l'image la plus saisissante de celle-ci est cette forme humaine et grotesque représentant une tête métamorphosée en gros ventre (un Baubô), avec un poignard le transperçant; un autre personnage ventru chevauche un poisson dans le ciel; une femme nue, un personnage renversé soutenant la table et une épée en main (serait-ce *Ira?*), un enfant-vieillard et un jongleur complètent ce panneau.

---

45 Dans la *Tentation* du Prado et dans celle de Kansas City, la menace des objets quotidiens est plus évidente.

46 Cuttler, *op. cit.,* p. 205, voit ici une image que Bosch reprend dans l'*Enfant Prodigue* de Rotterdam.

Dans le panneau central, cependant, la parodie, le carnavalesque et
le grotesque sont pleinement développés autour du Saint qui ne peut
tourner son regard que vers le seul espace libre, celui des spectateurs,
pour échapper aux visions qui le hantent bien plus qu'aux tentations
qui ici ne sont pas nombreuses (la courtisane à ses côtés avec une robe
en queue d'animal; les belles, qui accueillent un jongleur à tête de porc-
épic, surmontée d'un hibou, et traînant un chien aux habits de bouffon);
derrière le jongleur, un autre musicien ambulant, unijambiste et nanti
d'une queue, suivi de tout un cortège de créatures qui semblent des hommes habillés avec des peaux d'animaux comme ceux qui précèdent le
convoi des pécheurs dans le *Char de Foin*. A droite du Saint, une tête
à jambes ("grylle"), le regard fixé en direction de l'hermite et une coupe
de vin (miraculeusement tenue par on ne sait quellle main!), combin-
ent le réalisme le plus exact avec le fantastique pour composer un personnage intrigant: qui est-il? A part le visage du Saint, c'est le seul
visage vraiment *humain* qui appelle notre sympathie. Baltrušaitis [47] écrit:
"Un dialogue semble s'engager. Toute la vision se déploie autour de
cette conversation muette du grylle et du moine. Il a été question de voir
dans cette figure un auto-portrait de Bosch.[48] Par l'attitude, l'anatomie,
les traits, elle est très proche du monstre gravé sur le faux cachet antique de Raoul Aubry, jugeur de Lille, vers 1320".
L'idée d'un auto-portrait n'est pas à exclure, mais tenant une coupe
de vin face à la courtisane qui, elle aussi, propose à boire, et cette scène
se passant à l'avant-plan du Chirst, pourrait induire à penser que, située
dans une ambiance générale de parodie (voir au premier plan, deux
moines à tête animale se faisant face, l'un jouant la harpe et l'autre,
vêtu d'un chasuble, psalmodiant), la scène illustre une messe noire ou
une parodie de l'eucharistie (voir aussi le nègre portant sur un plateau
un crapaud qui soutient soit un oeuf, soit une hostie) ou tout simplement
une parodie dans le genre des *clerici vagantes* (et le nombre de jongleurs
et de fols ici pourraient le confirmer): *carnaval* souriant à *carême* et
lui disant: *In vino veritas!* A droite de la colonnade, un autre groupe
grotesque semble également être une parodie: un personnage composite
(tête végétale, un bras, une aile) chevauche une jarre métamorphosée
en la partie postérieure d'un cheval; une femme, mi-arbre sec en forme
de bonnet de fol, mi-sirène vers le bas, chevauche un rat gigantesque
et, avec des doigts arborescents, caresse un nourrisson en langes; et
derrière ces créatures fantastiques, trois autres personnages dépeints dans

47 Baltrušaitis, *op. cit.*, p. 45, et voir la fig. 22 s'y rapportant.
48 Cf. M. Brion, *Bosch*, Paris, 1938, p. 40.

le meilleur style réaliste! Cuttler écrit au sujet de ce groupe : la scène
suggère "the compositional type of a Flight into Egypt combined with
an Adoration of the Magi, both themes conceived as antitypes, which
are understandable in relation to the prevailing belief in Antichrist. Parallel events from the life of Christ and Antichrist appear in 15th-cen-
tury manuscripts".[49] Ce point mérite d'être étudié avec plus d'ampleur.
Cuttler, qui consacre à la *Tentation de Saint Antoine* la majeure partie [50] de son étude sur Bosch, découvre dans ce tableau des correspondances entre les Vices et les Planètes d'après les croyances astrologiques
de l'époque, et une correspondance constante entre le Christ et Saint
Antoine d'une part, entre l'Antéchrist et les éléments diaboliques d'autre
part. Ses conclusions, qui nous semblent acceptables, sont ainsi formu-
lées :

> "The cosmic character of this conception of the temptation of St.
> Anthony is overwhelming; air, earth, fire, weather, wet and dry, heat
> and cold — everything in the heavens and on earth was Bosch's con-
> cern in this grand pictorial *summa* of all the beliefs and fears of
> medieval man, to which astrology and the theme of the Seven
> Deadly Sins, allied with the theme of Antichrist, contributed the
> chief elements. The synthesis was carried further : the planets were
> related to specific sins, Saturn with Sloth, Lune with Envy, Mars
> with Wrath, Mercury with Avarice, Venus with Lust, Jupiter with
> Gluttony, and Sol with Pride."

Cependant en ce qui concerne ces correspondances astrologiques dans
le tableau de Bosch nous avons nos doutes, malgré l'érudition remarqua-
ble que Cuttler met en oeuvre pour le prouver; la source iconographique isolée [51] qui lui sert de témoin et de base pour ses comparaisons
nous paraît trop rare pour avoir servi comme modèle direct d'inspiration
à Bosch.
    Si les divers panneaux du *Char de Foin* étaient parfaitement soudés
entre eux thématiquement, dans la *Tentation de Saint Antoine* la sou-
dure thématique et formelle des trois panneaux atteint une rare perfection. Les poissons et les embarcations dans le ciel, les collines et les
édifices à l'horizon, l'emplacement du saint par rapport aux multiples
épisodes de la tentation, la rivière et les formes circulaires ou ovales, se
correspondent comme autant d'échos à travers les trois panneaux. Les
sept péchés capitaux et leurs dérivés se trouvent éparpillés dans le

---

49 Cuttler, *op. cit.*, p. 208.
50 *Ibid.*, pp. 204–209.
51 Un traité illustré d'astrologie florentin, datant peut-être de 1460, qui n'est con-
    nu que d'après des copies postérieures.

triptyque et représentés au moyen de personnages qui ne dérivent pas des vices allégoriques médiévaux, du moins pas directement, et témoignent d'une nouvelle étape dans la création de Bosch. Il suffit de considérer les vices dans les *Sept Péchés* de la table peinte pour voir pleinement ici une métamorphose totale. Et même là où des vices conservent certains de leurs attributs traditionnels, Bosch amplifie autour d'eux tout un groupe de personnages dans un style réaliste et grotesque au point de les rendre moins évidents et moins "didactiques". Au lieu de personnifications allégoriques nous avons des personnages bizarres. On verra cette nouvelle manière de concevoir et de disposer les vices dans l'Enfer du *Jardin des Délices*. D'autre part, le grand nombre de formes animales et végétales extraordinaires; les nombreuses combinaisons entre hommes et animaux, entre animaux et objets; la multiplicité d'épisodes élaborés avec une grande variété de métaphores et de symboles; le dosage équilibré entre l'insolite et le familier, entre le réalisme et le fantastique; tous ces éléments intégrés dans une vision synthétique affirment une maîtrise intellectuelle et artistique qui ne peut se comparer qu'à celle que Bosch manifestera dans le triptyque du *Jardin des Délices*.

ARCHITECTURAL DESIGN AS CONCEIVED
BY THE SCHOOL OF URBINO (1460-1512)

Nurith Cahansky

Paintings of the School of Urbino and of artists within its sphere of influence emphasise the creation of architectural settings with the aim of giving a concrete representation of the ideal of "good building".

The subject warrants discussion because it is unique in fifteenth century painting in Italy. R. Wittkower [1] and L. H. Heydenreich [2] have devoted much time and thought to it and have shed considerable light on the problems of "painted architecture", and "projected architecture". In his article "Brunelleschi and 'Proportion in Perspective'" [3] Wittkower comes to the conclusion: "The concept of painting reality as if it were real, is no less unreal or "unrealistic" than that of building in three dimensions and looking upon the result as if it were painted. That fifteenth-century painters thought it necessary to make plans of their architectural settings as if they were to be built, would seem paradoxical if they had regarded space constructed and space painted as different in essence". [4]

In attempting to follow up Wittkower's argument on the further implications, this article proposes to demonstrate that painted, concrete or "realistic" architecture is one of the main characteristics of the Urbinian school, and that this form of painting was able to develop fully at the court of the Duke of Urbino because of the special conditions prevailing there.

The court of Duke Federigo da Montefeltro of Urbino became prominent as a humanistic centre in the 1460's. [5] The Duke surrounded

1 R. Wittkower: "Brunelleschi and 'Proportion in Perspective'", *Journal of the Warburg and Courtauld Institutes*, v. 16, 1953, pp. 275–291; R. Wittkower and B. A. R. Carter: "The Perspective of Piero della Francesca's 'Flagellation'", *ibid.*, pp. 293–302.

2 Ludwig H. Heydenreich: "Strukturprinzipien der Florentiner Frührenaissance-architektur: 'Prospectiva Aedificandi'", International Congress of the History of Art, 20th Congress, 1961, *Studies in Western Art*, Princeton, 1963, v. 2, pp. 108–122. Heydenreich, in contrast to Wittkower, points out the special qualifications of the "Prospectiva Aedificandi".

3 R. Wittkower, *op. cit.*

4 R. Wittkower, *op. cit.*, p. 290.

5 Federigo da Montefeltro, Duke of Urbino, ruler of the town from 1444.

himself with scholars, artists, and men of letters who actually lived at the court, while at the same time he maintained close contact with scholars such as Landino and Ficino, in other parts of Italy.[6] The creators of "the school of Urbino" lived in the Duke's palace, in physical and daily contact with the leading scholars of the time.[6a] The central impulse for their art came from one principal source, the Duke of Urbino, making it comparable to the art of Julius the Second.[7]

As at the court of this important Renaissance Pope of the first decades of the 16th century, artists at the court of Urbino not only worked for the Duke as individuals, but expressed the formal and spiritual ideals crystallised at the court in this period. Their work was consciously aimed at immortalising their ruler.

This characteristic distinguished the art of the court of Urbino from the art of other 15th century courts in Italy such as Ferrara or Mantua. At Ferrara, artists worked not as a team, but individually for the Duke. Pisanello was called to perpetuate the Lionello d'Este profile in tempera and bronze. Rogier van der Weyden stopped in Ferrara in 1450, leaving behind a famous triptych (and much knowledge concerning the Flemish manner of oil painting). But the Dukes of the Este dynasty did not guide the arts towards expressing the conscious ideals of their particular civilisation. Similarly, Alberti's buildings in Mantua did not create a school of architects there; they were an isolated episode in the development of the city, as were Giulio Romano's works seventy years later.

Since art at the court of Urbino bore the character of artistic teamwork, dependent on the ruler, and did not need to vie with older traditions, it could find expression in a pure and unadulterated form reflecting new schools of intellectual thought. This process differs again from the crystallization of the new art in Florence, Milan or Venice, where elements of the old style which belonged to the local traditions always came to be part of, or a detail of, the new system.

It seems to us that at the court of Urbino, as also at the court of Julius the Second, architecture was regarded not only as an art, but as a central

6   According to his biographers, e.g. Giovanni Santi, and Vespasiano. ʝ*Renaissance princes, Popes, and prelates: the Vespasiano memoirs . . .*, Harper Torchbooks, 1963.)

6a Vespasiano, *op. cit.*, p. 106: "As to the ruling of his own palace, it was just the same as that of a religious society . . ."

7   This term—"The art of Julius the Second"—with reference to the art of 1500–1514 in Rome, is used e.g., by C. Frommel. Many scholars see in Urbino art the source of the High Renaissance: e.g., T. Hofmann: *Die Bauten des Herzogs Federiga di Montefeltro als erstwerke der Hochrenaissance.* Leipzig, 1905.

humanistic discipline, because for these rulers and artists architecture represented a monumentalised part of their conscious civilisation to be handed over to posterity. This concept was preached by Alberti in his architectural treatise : "But why need I mention not only how much Benefit and Delight, but how much Glory to Architecture has brought to Nations, which have cultivated it both at home and abroad ? . . . And what potent or wise Prince can be named, that among his chief Projects for eternising his Name and Posterity did not make use of Architecture." [8] Alberti regards architecture, contrary to painting, as a social humanistic discipline, an expression of the ability of mankind to create a continuous and orderly civilisation. His aesthetic theory and his discussions on the subject of "the good and ideal building" are always expressed with regard to an ideal civilisation.

It was natural, therefore, that Alberti's theories on architecture should find fertile soil in this unique haven of art, Urbino. This paper proposes to show that Alberti's ideas — his consideration of architecture as a central, artistic activity — could come to perfect realisation at the Duke's court. Montefeltro regarded architecture as a central humanistic discipline; artists [9] at his court were closely committed to these same ideas; and on this basis the special character of Urbinian art was defined.

This supposition that architecture was regarded not only as an art but also as a humanistic discipline, and as a monumentalised part of a specific civilisation, to be handed over as a heritage, is based on the fact that the Duke had his own palace constructed along the lines of Alberti's conceptions, and on the fact that Vespasiano,[10] in his biography of the Duke, actually describes his ingenuity in the faculty of architecture. Vespasiano devotes considerable attention to the Duke's capabilities and knowledge in the science of architecture, and these qualities are, in Vespasiano's estimation, an essential part of the education of a "learned prince". Vespasiano begins his description of the Duke as a man of letters with his training in philosophy and theology and, on the same level as these subjects, he includes architecture. Only later, he mentions the Duke's interest in painting and sculpture.[11] "As to architecture it may be said that no one of his age, high or low, knew it so

8   Alberti, Leone Battista: *Ten Books on Architecture,* edited by J. Rykwert, London, Tiranti, 1955, p. x.

9   With special reference to Piero della Francesca and Luciano Laurana.

10   Vespasiano, *op. cit.,* p. 100.

11   The major part of Vespasiano's biography is devoted to a description of the Duke's victories on the battlefield.

thoroughly. We may see in the buildings he constructed, the grand style and the due measurement and proportion, especially in his palace, which has no superior amongst the buildings of the time, none so well considered, or so full of fine things. Though he had his architects about him, he always first realised the design and then explained the proportions and all else; indeed, to hear him discourse thereanent, it would seem that his chief talent lay in this art; so well he knew how to expound and carry out its principles." [12]

It is significant to note that the Duke's attitude, and his dedication to architecture, as described by Vespasiano, is almost identical with Alberti's description of the virtues of the ideal architect.

According to Vespasiano, the Duke "first realised the design". This corresponds to Alberti's preliminary remark that "the whole art of Building consists in Design, and in the Structure. The whole Force and Rule of the Design, consists in a right and exact adapting and joining together the lines and angles which compose and form the Face of the Building." [13] Vespasiano states that the Duke first realised the design, although he had his architects about him. This again corresponds to Alberti's proposition "we shall call the Design a firm and graceful preordering of the Lines and Angles conceived in the Mind and contrived by an Ingenious Artist". [14] From these points it can be observed that Vespasiano's description of the Duke forms a parallel with Alberti's "ideal architect" as well as with Alberti's description of the "learned prince". [15]

The architectural arrangements [16] and the sequence of the living units in the Ducal palace realise the ideas of Alberti [17] (Fig. 1). The palace is situated on the uppermost slopes of the Apennine mountains, overlooking the valley below. According to Alberti, this architectural domination of nature is the ideal setting for solitude and meditation. The façade, on the city side, presents the palace to the world in all its purity and economy of design. The inner courtyard of the palace of Urbino (Fig. 2) can be regarded as the perfect realisation of Laurana's architectural design.

12 Vespasiano, *op. cit.,* pp. 100–101.
13 Alberti, *op. cit., Book* 1, Chapter 1, p. 1.
14 Alberti, *op. cit.,* Book 1, Chapter 1, p. 2.
15 Ideal Architect, *cf.* Alberti, *op. cit.,* preface.
16 Luciano Laurana is known as ducal architect and constructor of the ducal palace. Giovanni Santi calls him "L'architecto a tucti gli altri sopra" (quoted in F. Kimball: "Luciano Laurana and the 'High Renaissance' ", *Art Bulletin,* v. 10, 1927, pp. 125–150).
17 Alberti, *op. cit.,* Book 5, Chaps., 14, 15; description of the "country house" which comes close to the organisation of the ducal palace in Urbino.

The courtyard was constructed, it seems, on the basis of the design which was drawn in accordance with the laws of perspective. The spectator, having first walked through a vaulted passageway, is supposed to stand in the entrance to the courtyard, and, from this viewpoint, to experience the development of the whole prospect.

From the courtyard a wide staircase leads to the Sala del Trono. This is the official reception room of the palace, and it has a barrel-vaulted ceiling which is the key point of the architectural construction of the room, once again following the theories of Alberti.[18]

The Duke's private apartments lead directly into his private chapels, the Capella del Perdono (Fig. 3) and the Cappella delle Muse, and to his study, where he was accustomed to receive the scholars of his court.[19] The chapels of the "Perdono" and of the "Muses" bear witness to the Duke's strong ties with the Christian religion and with the philosophy of the ancient world.

The palace of Urbino may serve as a fine example of Alberti's conception and as an illustration of his description of the "house of the gentleman".[20] The inner units portray the way of life of the Duke and his entourage, and the official sections such as the inner court realise the architect's aesthetic conception.

The fact that the leading artists of the court, Piero della Francesca, the painter, and Luciano Laurana, the architect, had an intimate knowledge of Alberti's theories on architecture is well known and authenticated.[21] Following the ideas of Alberti, these artists regarded the process of the architect's creation of a design before the erection of the building as the essence of his activity. Not only did they pursue Alberti's ideas on architectural design as a process of creation, but they also expressed their adherence to Alberti's ideas by faithfully carrying out his architectural descriptions of "good building". The value of the architectural design is thus defined by Alberti:

18 Alberti frequently says, especially in Book 7, that the vaulting and cover are the "fountainhead" of a construction. S. Andrea in Mantua by Alberti, where the barrel-vault is the starting point of the construction, may serve as an example.
19 Vespasiano, op. cit., p. 109: "The Duke would remain for a time to see if anyone had ought to say, and if not he would go with the leading nobles and gentlemen in to his closet and talk freely with them."
20 Alberti, op. cit., Book 5, Chapters 14, 15, 16.
21 Many scholars have shown that Piero della Francesca's De Prospectiva Pigendi was written under Alberti's influence: e.g., H. Focillon: Piero della Francesca, Paris, 1952; for Luciano Laurano's close ties with Alberti, see F. Kimball, op. cit.

"I must not omit to observe that the making of curious, polished Models, with the Delicacy of Painting, is not required from an Architect, that only designs to shew the real Thing itself; but it is rather the Part of a vain Architect, that makes it his Business by charming the Eye and striking the Fancy of the Beholder, to divert him from a rigorous Examination of the Parts which he ought to make, and to draw him into an Admiration of himself . . . Between the Design of the Painter and that of the Architect, there is this Difference, that the Painter by the Exactness of his Shades, Lines, and Angles, endeavours to make the Parts seem to rise from the Canvas, whereas the Architect, without any regard to the Shades, makes his Reliefs from the Design of his Platform, as one that would have his Work valued, not by the apparent Perspective, but by the real Compartments founded upon Reason".[22]

The architectural design, as conceived by Alberti, differs from the design of the painter in that it realises an abstract idea, born of the architect's knowledge and talent, so that a harmonious work, independent of Nature, is created. Contrary to the painter, the architect neither imitates Nature nor corrects it, and the design therefore has an absolute value. The importance of the design also lies in the fact that it must lend itself to practical implementation and not only be pleasing to the eye.

We may assume that to artists at the court of Urbino, architectural design as defined by Alberti was capable of expressing the difference between the work of learned artists such as themselves, (who had a preconceived idea in mind before actual work began), and the work of ordinary craftsmen. We believe, then, that artists at the court, architects as well as painters, employed the principles of Albertian architectural design because they were thus provided with the conceptual framework in which to act both as constructors and as architects. We would like to suggest that painters in Urbino, because of the special conception of the architect developed in that city, worked like architects, making plans and architectural designs for the architectural settings in their works. It was possible for them to have a starting point in common with the architects, as architectural designs were presented in perspective up to the time of the "ultima maniera" of Bramante. This means that here were painters and architects who — according to Alberti — were required to work with the same knowledge and conceptual approach, and to create within the laws of a perspectival presentation. This has been

22 Alberti, *op. cit.,* Book 2, Chapter 1, p. 22

shown by Lotz[23] and Saalmann.[24] Saalmann, in opposition to Lotz, believes that Alberti was the first to ask for an architectural design not presented in perspective.[25]

We are inclined to believe that in his definition of the architectural design, Alberti intends to say that the presentation of perspective in the drawing of the architectural design is not the main task of the architect, but he himself did not yet consider a different system of working. This can be inferred from his drawing for the façade of S. Francesco in Rimini. As we can see from a medal by Matteo de' Pasti[26] which is based on a drawing by Alberti, such a drawing must have been done in perspective, because only by this method could the different surfaces of the façade and the predominance of the dome have been shown.

The following examples show that the painters of Urbino worked with the same type of plan and architectural design as their colleagues the architects, basing themselves on Alberti's practical and theoretical work, and that their vocabulary of forms also remained true to that of Alberti. Human figures were introduced into the framework of the architectural design apparently as a secondary component only.

The panels of Urbino and Baltimore,[27] the so-called "architectural perspective",[28] provide the best illustrations of this thesis. The problem of the attribution of these panels is an old one and cannot be discussed here.[29] For the purpose of this paper it may be assumed that these paintings are a product of the school of Urbino, and, as such, it may be demonstrated that they realise the architectural design theory of Alberti.

23   W. Lotz: "Das Raumbild in der Italienischen Architektur-zeichnung der Renaissance" in *Mit. der Flor. Institute*, 1956.

24   H. Saalman: "Early Renaissance architectural theory and practice in Antonio Filarete's *Trattato di Architettura*", Art Bulletin, v. 41, 1959, pp. 89–106.

25   H. Saalman, *op. cit.*, p. 105.

26   R. Wittkower, *Architectural Principles in the Age of Humanism*, London, Tiranti, 1962, p. 39 (4).

27   Galleria Nazionale delle Marche, Urbino; Walters Art Gallery, Baltimore. Both panels were originally in the ducal palace of Urbino.

28   F. Kimball, *op. cit.*, attributes them to Laurana.

29   Attribution of the Panels: Focillon attributes them to the circle of Piero. In the older literature, e.g., Schubring and Witting, the panels were attributed to Piero. In the first edition of *Central Italian Painters,* Berenson attributes the panels to Piero, but not in the second. A recent article by Howard Saalman (*Burlington Magazine,* v. 110, 1968, pp. 376–383) attributes the panels to Cosimo Roselli.

In the Urbino panel the spectator stands before a scene which portrays an ideal city square, surrounded by palaces that can in fact be built. The types of building shown in the painting conform to Alberti's architectural theories. Plans can be drawn for the octagonal central building, and for the rectangular palaces (the buildings seem like elevations on the basis of such groundplans). No story is illustrated in these paintings, and there is almost no representation of the human figure, while the use of colour is only a secondary feature. These special characteristics point to the inference that these paintings might have served as illustrations of Alberti's conception of architectural design and of his prototypes of "good building".

The circular temple in the centre of the Urbino panel rises above a stepped base. The entrance to the temple is through four porticoes, one in the centre front, two in profile at the sides, and the fourth invisible at the back. Columns in three-quarter profile encircle the building. The cupola derives its shape from the cupola in the Baptistry of Florence.[30] This construction demonstrates Alberti's idea of the circular temple.[31] However, in this case, the artist employs incrustation and a vaulting system which are traditionally Florentine and, in fact, Alberti himself, when building in Florence, remained loyal to the architectural traditions of his native city.[32]

The palaces presented in this painting follow Alberti's known practices. The employment of pilasters on all three storeys of a façade is an innovation initially introduced by him in the Palazzo Rucellai. The frontal façade of the church which is situated in the background corresponds to his principles of the division of a façade, as seen in the façade of S. Maria Novella in Florence. This pattern, which is not found elsewhere, was Alberti's solution to the problem of a façade.[33]

The similarity between the second palace on the right of the painting, and the inner courtyard of the palace [34] of Urbino, emphasises the proposition presented here, that this painting served as an "architectural design", a "concetto", and was realised by Laurana according to the theoretical requirements of Alberti.

In the Baltimore panel, the artist not only uses the prototype, accord-

---

30   F. Kimball, *op. cit.*, works out in detail the formal resemblances between this building and Alberti's work, showing it to be a link with the Florentine tradition.

31   Alberti, *op. cit.*, Book 7, Chapters 1, 2.

32   As in the Capella di S. Pancrazio, or in the façade of the S. Maria Novella.

33   This painted façade can be compared with the façade of S. Francesco da Rimini.

34   F. Kimball, *op. cit.*

ing to Alberti's theory, but also introduces types of buildings "alla antica", such as the coliseum. These he inserts in his paintings as examples of "good building", just as Alberti does in his treatise.[35] The fact that the painter copies these buildings points to his qualifications as an architect, as the routine of copying these examples is to be found in many architects' sketch-books.[36]

It is apparent that these panels were executed at the court of Urbino as an "exemplum" of an architectural design, to be used by both painters and architects. These are not abstract designs in perspective but are concrete architectural ideas of the period, as crystallised under the influence of Alberti's practical and theoretical work. For the painter, these architectural ideas presented an absolute and independent way of creation, which enabled him to draw closer to the architect. From this one may conclude that the architectural design is the starting point for both architects and painters in Urbino; that their work differs only in the second stage of creation, and that the difference then lies in their use of their medium.

Piero della Francesca's mature conception of painting reached definite shape while he was working at the court of Urbino,[37] as demonstrated in the "Pala di Brera" [38] (Fig. 4).

This painting is composed on the basis of an architectural design, which serves as a framework for the whole invention. Not only is it constructed according to the laws of perspective, but it also makes use of colour as in an architectural design (with colours). The forms of the design correspond to Alberti's theory and Laurana's practical work. If we accept the proposition that the architectural design in this painting presents a view of the crossing, apse, and the starting point of the transepts, then the Madonna and the Saints are situated at the crossing point before the apse. Piero's imagined construction is almost identical with Laurana's Cappella di Perdono, or to be more exact, with his architectural design for the Cappella, which unfortunately is not documented. Both Piero and Laurana work with the same conception. They

35 Alberti, *op. cit.,* Book 7.
36 E.g., Juliano da S. Gallo's sketch-book — *Il Taquino Senese di Juliano da S. Gallo,* Sienna, 1902.
37 This picture is a product of Piero's later stay at the court of Urbino.
38 Roberto Longhi, *Piero della Francesco,* 1927, dates this work to 1475; Kenneth Clark, *Piero della Francesco,* 1951, gives 1472. Clark has a strangely low opinion of this work, seeing it as a proof of Piero's "loss of pictorial appetite" (p. 48). This perhaps supports our contention that this is a picture of a very high order emphasising Piero's significance as a constructor.

both regard the barrel vaulting adorned with coffers as the initial point of their construction. Both employ geometric incrustations for the divisions of the wall.

In the "Pala de Brera" Piero places the Duke in the position of a spectator, outside the actual setting of the painting, in such a way as to regard the development of the project. In the Capella di Perdono, Laurana works on the same principle. The Duke has no defined place in his little chapel. He is supposed to stand outside in order to look at the completed design.[39] These comparisons between the work of Piero and Laurana illustrate our contention that the architectural design composed in perspective was the basis of the work of both the leading architect and painter in Urbino, and only the diversity of medium, in the second stage of the work, brought about a differentiation between them. This approach found further expression in the later works of the artists of the Urbinian school as, for instance, in the works executed to decorate the study of the Duke.[40]

The continued existence of the Urbinian conception can be seen in the works of the artists schooled under its influence. Perugino the Umbrian employed architectural settings in the composition of most of his works. Most of these architectural settings are imaginary. Even if the details of the architectural construction are correctly indicated, their function is obviously not practical, their principal purpose being to provide formal support for the figures in the painting and thus they are in no way distinguished from trees and other elements employed with the same intention, i.e. of giving support.[41]

Perugino's "Consegna delle Chiavi" (Christ Giving the Keys to St. Peter) in the Sistine Chapel (Fig. 5), is a departure from his workshop routine. This is one of his most significant paintings, and its quality

39 This setting, placing the duke as an exterior observer of the project, may be compared with the setting in Masaccio's Trinity fresco in S. Maria Novella, where the Donors are also situated on a different level, as onlookers. The two works have other aspects in common. In both, the architectural setting is elevated on a plan, and the concrete architectural idea of an architect is the base for both works, that of Brunelleschi on the Trinity fresco and that of Laurana in the Pala di Brera. See H. W. Janson, "Ground Plan and Elevation in Masaccio's Trinity Fresco", *Essays in the History of Art in Honour of R. Wittkower*, London, Phaidon, 1967, pp. 83–88.

40 Also the doors of the Sala degli Angeli, or the Sala degli Arazzi in the ducal palace, believed by F. Kimball, *op. cit.* to be the work of Francesco di Giorgio Martini.

41 E.g., the "Pala di Fano" – Sposalizio della Madonna, in Fano, or the "Madonna with Saints" in the Uffizi.

makes is conspicuous among the other works of the Florentine and Umbrian painters in the Sistine Chapel.

The Urbinian conception, which regards the architectural design as the dominant element and the figures as a secondary element only, is obvious,[42] and the profound influence of the Urbino panels on Perugino is manifest. Perugino makes use of the central building and the triumphal arches as they appear in the Urbino panels; he constructs his painting as an architect would, and he places his figures in the foreground, as if they were outsiders.

An ideal urban scene is presented. The wide square is developed according to the laws of perspective. The chief building is placed in the conventional central position and two triumphal arches frame the square. This presentation is a perfect illustration of Alberti's theory of the ideal square. "But nothing can be a greater Ornament either to Squares or the Meeting of several Streets than Arches at the Entrance of the Streets; an Arch being indeed nothing else but a Gate standing continually open"; and further on: "A very proper Situation for an Arch is where a Street joins into a Square, and especially in the Royal Street by which Name I understand the most eminent in the City. An Arch, like a Bridge, should have no less than three open Passages..." [43]

The concrete architectural design making use of Alberti's prototypes dictates Perugino's process of creation, as was the case with his predecessors in Urbino. His acute awareness of the concrete architectural idea can be seen in the invention of the central building, which makes use of Brunelleschi's Florentine cupola, a model which was predominant at the time as a manifestation of the "new art".

At the court of Urbino, painters still used the Baptistry in Florence as their model. Perugino's division of the wall approaches the construction of Alberti's actual buildings, and here again he differs from the painters in Urbino, who still made use of the method of wall division by incrustation, derived from the Baptistry.

All these facts show that Perugino worked with concrete architectural ideas, absorbing the changes in architectural practice that were being introduced. Such ideas could be expressed only through the medium of the architectural design. These features of Perugino's work place him in a different category from the painters who worked with him on the adornment of the Sistine Chapel.

42 It is known that many of the figures were not drawn by Perugino, but by his assistants, for instance Signorelli. See: R. Hamann: *Die Früh-Renaissance Italienischer Malerei*, Jena, 1909, p. 271.
43 Alberti, *op. cit.*, Book 8, Chapter 6, p. 174.

Perugino considered himself primarily as the constructor of an architectural idea and, as such, he dedicated his efforts towards a solution of the problem of the central building and the city square, just as did the foremost architects of his generation.[44] His main object here is not the presentation of space in perspective or of "genre" scenes. If we compare this particular work of Perugino with the other works that surround it, we can discern that the other painters worked according to Alberti's description of the painter, and not of the architect. They paint their space in perspective, and there are times when they employ architectural forms for this purpose, but their architectural settings are an imaginary combination of fashionable architectural elements.

Their buildings serve the purpose of creating a certain atmosphere or framework for their traditional religious subjects, but they never represent a concrete architectural design.

Ghirlandaio's architectural settings in the frescoes of S. Maria Novella are an obvious example of this tendency. For instance, he invents a barrel-vaulted ceiling that completely lacks any structural support.

Again, the architectural settings of Filippino Lippi never indicate the location of the scene or, for instance, the point of entry to these imaginary constructions.[45]

Bramante of Urbino raised the Urbinian conception to its greatest heights in his creation of the feigned choir in the Church of S. Maria presso S. Satiro in Milan[46] (Fig. 6). The design continues to consider the spectator, allowing him to view the whole prospect from one particular point.[47] The practical architectural realisation of the design is only of

---

44 Two indications lead us to infer that this work by Perugino stands in close relation to architectural projects being undertaken at the time. The inscription on the triumphal arch, "IMENSU(UM) SALAMO / TEMPLUM TU / HOC QUARTE / SACRASTI SIXTE OPIBUS / DISPAR / RELIGIONE / PRIOR /" seems to be used not only in connection with the representation of the handing over of the keys, but also as a symbol for the Temple. Secondly, the inclusion of the portrait of Giovanni de Dolci, chief architect of Sixtus IV, also points to a concrete architectural idea. It seems that the central building in this work can be connected with an existing architectural idea, e.g., the church of S. Maria della Pace, constructed at the same time (See: Urban Architektur. 15. Jh. in Rom. *Jahrbuch Bib. Hertz.* 1962), and perhaps with certain projects of Sixtus IV for Saint Peter's.

45 E.g., frescoes in S. Maria sopra Minerva — lunette; the miracle of the crucifix, Naples; altar piece — "Madonna enthroned with SS. John the Baptist, Victor, Bernard and Zenobius", Uffizzi.

46 O. Förster dates this work to the early 1470's (*Bramante,* Vienna 1956).

47 R. Wittkower, *op. cit.* points to this conception.

secondary importance, the primary purpose being to translate the artistic conception into an architectural design which faithfully follows the
prototypes of Alberti and the Urbino tradition.

The medium used is of secondary importance. Bramante worked with
an architectural design which he was obliged to construct through the
medium of paint, for objective conditions did not permit him the latitude of an architect.

The importance of the architectural design is to be observed also in
the early works of Bramante and Raphael prior [48] to their mature Roman period, for instance, in the Sposalizio of Raphael, and the Tempietto of Bramante. In both cases, the architectural design for this centrally-planned building expresses the architectural ideals of the 1500's.

The architectural idea of the centrally-planned building leads the way
to new organic forms as compared to the ideal building of Alberti, or
of J. da San Gallo, which comprises four porticoes and a multi-ribbed
cupola (as in the panels of Urbino, and the Sistine Chapel Choir and
the Giving the Keys to St. Peter of Perugino). The centrally-planned
buildings of Bramante and Raphael embrace new forms, such as the
hemispheric cupola, and an Exedra. Despite the introduction of these
new forms, the basic architectural design is still clearly discernible in the
perspective.[49]

The Tempietto of Bramante (Fig. 7) is, in fact, the closest material
realisation of the architectural design. To quote N. Pevsner: "The
Tempietto of 1502 is the first monument of the High Renaissance, as
against the early Renaissance, truly a monument i.e., more a sculptural
than a strictly architectural achievement." [50]

In its aspect this construction is a monument, and it should be viewed
as the central point of a complete architectural prospect.

Such a Tempietto has the same architectural reality as the Temple of
Raphael in his "Sposalizio" (Fig. 8). The Raphael temple, which is also
placed at the apex of the prospect, embodies exactly the same idea. As
with all architectural designs of the Urbinian artists, so Raphael's architectural design is a concrete one. This trend can be followed through
the first Stanza della Signatura in the Vatican. In the "School of
Athens", Raphael's architectural setting is based on the same architectu-

48 The period between 1500 to 1504.
49 We know that Bramante's Tempietto was planned as the central portion of a
    surrounding gallery, e.g. Serlio: *Tutte l'opere d'architettura* ... Venice, 1619.
    (Gregg Press reprint, 1964.)
50 N. Pevsner: *An Outline of European Architecture,* London, 7th edition, 1963.
    p. 203.

ral elements as those employed by Bramante for his feigned choir.

In the "School of Athens", Raphael looks upon the barrel-vaulted ceiling adorned with coffers as the starting point of the whole construction, following the description of Alberti, and put into practice previously by the artists of his home-town, Piero and Bramante. This means that Raphael's architectural design is closely related to the architectural ideas developed by Bramante in Milan some time previously.

Were we to continue further along this line of thought, we might well ask whether the architectural setting in the second Stanza d'Eliodoro does not present the celebrated project for the Church of St. Peter by Fra Giocondo.[51]

---

51 T. Hofmann: *Entstehungsgeschichte des St. Peter in Rom,* Zittau 1928. The architectural setting in the expulsion of Heliodorus occupies the same place in the composition as does the architectural setting in the School of Athens. Only the vocabulary of forms changes. "Heliodorus" presents a domed church similar to that in the Fra Giocondo St. Peter project. Today it is clear that in the last decade of the 15th century and the first decades of the 16th century, the type of the Byzantine church, such as San Marco in Venice, served as the ideal of the "good building", and Raphael's acceptance of this ideal can be seen in his Cappella d'Agostino Chigi, in S. Maria del Popolo.

CHAGALL'S JERUSALEM WINDOWS
Iconography and Sources*

By
Ziva Amishai

One of the recurrent problems of the modern art historian is the validity of examining a contemporary painting or sculpture by traditional iconographical methods. Critics maintain that the modern work of art exists in and for itself, and that any attempt to explain it is not only superfluous, but harmful. However, by refusing to undertake analysis by traditional as well as by modern procedures, are we not impeding rather than furthering our understanding of modern art? Are we not simply opposing the asking of the questions "why" and "what does it mean" because they are the hardest to answer? Is there any reason why we should not examine the work within the context of the artist's oeuvre, or study the pictorial and literary sources which influenced the artist and his work? Both the artist and the public should realize that the revelation of such sources does not diminish the importance of the work. All art, even modern art, is based on tradition, and has sources. What matters is whether the artist has used his source in a new way, transforming it into something which is his own, and what qualities in it attracted him. Should the ever-present danger of over-interpretation be enough to make critics renounce the analysis of meaning, especially when dealing with movements such as Surrealism and Expressionism, which stress this element? If the analysis of meaning is undertaken, will not the critic obtain better results by using accepted iconographical methods rather than by relying only on his intuitive perceptions?

The aim of this article is to attempt a traditional analysis of a work by Marc Chagall, whose style has been hailed as revolutionary, while the details of his subject matter have not been sufficiently clarified. The influence of Jewish traditions, folk art and Russian icons has been noted

* This paper is based on a Master's Thesis done at Columbia University in 1962, reworked with added source material in Jerusalem in 1965–66, and brought up to date in 1972. I should like to thank Prof. Meyer Schapiro for originally sponsoring my research into this subject and for helping me with it in many different ways.

in general stylistic terms, but their iconographical influences have rarely been seriously studied.

Chagall's own attitude to an iconographical analysis of his work is ambiguous. Although his book, *My Life,* is almost an index for the sources of his motifs, he wrote in it:

> It's all one to me if people are pleased and relieved to discover in these innocent adventures of my relatives the enigma of my pictures. How little that interests me! My dear fellow citizens, help your-selves.[1]

Later he stated:

> A painter should never come between the work of art and the spectator. An intermediary may explain the artist's work without any harm to it. But the artist's explanation of it can only limit it.[2]

Normally he confines himself to general statements on his work, stressing its sources "not only in the external world, but also in the inner world of dream and imagination".[3] He emphasizes the need of an element of surprise or shock, of a new "psychic dimension" to create a "world where everything and anything is possible".[4] He explains that the figures who appear in his pictures standing on their heads are not solely play-ful, but are used "to underline another reality by means of contrast".[5]

However, in defending himself against critics who see only anecdotes and symbolism in his work, he has occasionally overstressed its formal side:

> For me a picture is a plane surface covered with representations of objects, beasts, birds or humans in a certain order in which anecdotal, illustrational logic has no importance. The visual effectiveness of the painted composition comes first... In the large cow's head in *Moi et le Village,* I made a small cow and woman milking visible through its muzzle because I needed that sort of form, there, for my compo-sition. Whatever else may have grown out of these compositional ar-rangements is secondary.[6]

1 Marc Chagall, *My Life,* New York, 1960, p. 13. This book must be used with great care, as it was written after the pictures it describes were painted.
2 Quoted by James J. Sweeney, "Art Chronicle I: An Interview with Marc Chagall", *Partisan Review,* No. 1, Winter 1944, p. 88.
3 R. B. Heywood, *The Works of the Mind,* Chicago, 1947, p. 33.
4 *Ibid.,* p. 27; E. Roditi, *Dialogues on Art,* London, 1960, p. 26; M. Chagall, "Marc Chagall über sich selbst", *Bildende Kunst,* 1 jahrg., no. 8, 1947, p. 12.
5 J. Hodin, *The Dilemma of Being Modern,* London, 1956, p. 44.
6 Sweeney, pp. 89–90. As Chagall indicates, the first two lines derive from Maurice Denis' famous and more formalistic dictum: "It must be remembered that any painting, before being a war horse, a nude woman, or some anecdote,

This does not, however, eliminate the element of meaning. One may need a given shape for a given place, but many objects have that shape. The choice of the object is still Chagall's. At the same time, this statement does throw light on the interaction of form and content in Chagall's work while the painting is being created. For Chagall, the meaning of a work grows as he works on it. While at first only one idea may be expressed, his various formal problems and thought associations while painting will cause the finished work to be more complex and to contain many different levels of meaning. Chagall himself has described this process:

> An animal can assume sometimes the aspect of some object. Another object may recall a bouquet of flowers; a bouquet of flowers transforms itself into a house ... You see a tree, but you can make a fish, an ass, a lamp, if only the fish resembles the tree.[7]

Thus to understand Chagall's meaning fully, one must follow his thought associations during the development of the work, starting from his sources, and tracing, through his sketches, the stream of consciousness which unites formal and iconographical elements into a finished work.

Before turning to a detailed study of the Jerusalem windows, which will be conducted in this spirit, it will be worthwhile to cast a quick glance at the iconographical treatment of Chagall's previous religious works. Whereas his early paintings of Jewish themes were basically genre interpretations of life in the shtetl, Chagall had treated Christian religious themes based on Russian icons almost from the beginning. His additions to his sources give us an insight into his aims at this time. It is important that the child in the *Holy Family* (1910, Mp. 75)[8] is bearded, while the crucified Christ of *Golgotha* (1912, Mp. 175) is a child; that the medallion containing the Christ child in the *Maria Blachernitissa* icon has been lowered to the area of the womb in *Russia* (1912–13, Mp. 196). What interested Chagall was the possibility of creating a new and "irrational" reality by making surprising changes in old motifs. However, there is a mind at work behind the "irrational" fantasy. For instance, the substitution of a pig for the infant St. John's lamb in the *Holy Family* is an understandable comment by a Jewish painter on a

is essentially a flat surface covered with colours arranged in a certain order" (Denis, *Théories, 1890–1910,* Paris, 1912, p. 1).

7 Quoted by G. Charbonnier, *Le Monologue du Peintre,* Vol. II, Paris, 1960, pp. 46–7.

8 Franz Meyer, *Marc Chagall,* London, 1964, p. 75. Picture references in the text refer to this book unless otherwise stated, and will be listed Mp. for page numbers and Mc. for catalogue numbers.

Christian theme, and the X-ray vision of pregnancy in *Russia* is both logical and traditionally acceptable.

In 1938, disturbed by the German persecution of the Jews, Chagall painted the *White Crucifixion* (Mp. 417), transforming the theme by reassimilating Christ into Judaism by making him the symbol of the Jewish martyr. Chagall continued to paint Crucifixions after the war, developing his own interpretation of the theme. Juxtaposed to a Torah, it became a symbol of the Judaeo-Christian tradition (e.g. *The Crucified and Moses*, 1954–9, Mc. 991), and, more personally, Christ typified the suffering and self-sacrifice involved in artistic creation (e.g. *The Painter Crucified*, 1938–40, Mc. 689).

In 1911–12, Chagall experimented with a few Biblical themes along the lines he had developed in dealing with Christian subjects. However, it is in his portraits of Jews, done on his return to Russia, that the amount of thought behind his imagery emerges most clearly. In the *Jew in Bright Red* (1914–15, Mp. 223), Chagall filled the background with Hebrew letters, to catch "the atmosphere in which the figure is immersed".[9] Analysis shows, however, that the text is a near letter-perfect combination of *Genesis* xii: 1–3, xvii: 24–7, xxv: 19–22, and xxviii: 5, dealing with God's covenant with Abraham, and the movements of Abraham's family between Padan-Aram and the Promised Land, from Abraham's departure for Canaan to Jacob's return to Padan-Aram, ostensibly to marry within the tribe. This text had personal connotations for Chagall, who had gone forth to Paris (the promised land), and had now returned to Vitebsk (Padan-Aram), partly to marry Bella. The care with which Chagall sought for the appropriate passages in his Bible and his exact transcription of them contradicts his supposedly "irrational" and "intuitive" way of working.[10]

Shortly after 1931, Vollard commissioned Chagall to make a series of illustrations for the Bible. The resulting two sets of illustrations (1931–57)[11] cover most of the events and characters in the Bible. Chagall combines archaeological discoveries, Bedouin types and Near East-

---

9   *Ibid.,* p. 221.
10 The same process can be found in the *Jew in Green* (1914, Mp. 231), in which, on the left, Chagall has copied out, down to the hyphen marks, *Numbers* xxx: 2–4 and xxxii: 40, and on the right, portions of prayers with the heading "The Maggid from Slouzk". The pedlar who sat for this picture had claimed to be the Maggid from Slouzk (Chagall, *My Life,* p. 120).
11 The first set containing the earlier drawings, *Marc Chagall: Bible,* was published only in 1956 as *Verve* 33–34. The second set, *Drawings for the Bible,* was published as *Verve* 37–38, 1960.

ern scenery with the characters and backgrounds of the Eastern European shtetl. Whereas his early Bible drawings remain close to the text, with few variations, the later ones include upside-down landscapes and the artist's own interpretation of the Creation, Ecclesiastes and the Song of Songs.

Chagall based his Church commissions for Assy and Metz, as well as the later Dag Hammerskjold window at the United Nations, on these illustrations, adding elements from his secular iconography and his own interpretation of the Crucifixion. They also formed the cornerstone for his 1950 project for a sanctuary in which the "message" of his Bible pictures would be made clear. Although the program was not executed as planned, and the paintings have since been given to the Louvre, Chagall had worked out a detailed iconographical plan which was to show Israel's relationship with God.[12] Here again he added elements from his secular and Christian iconographies to enrich his meaning and to elucidate a personal message on religion in general and Judaism in particular.[13]

In his use of Old Testament themes, Chagall thus gradually freed himself from the text, creating an iconography for the expression of his own philosophy and personal feelings. His exact iconographic plans for the sanctuary again show the markedly unhaphazard and rational method behind his "intuitive"works. In studying his next major religious work, the Jerusalem windows, we can therefore expect that the qualities we have found in his previous works, his carefully thought out "irrational surprises", his free interpretations and his basically rational manner of working out a personal "message" will once again be clear.

—

In June 1959, Chagall was commissioned to design and execute twelve stained-glass windows for the synagogue of the Hebrew University–Hadassah Medical School Centre in Ein Karem, Jerusalem. He was given

12   For details, see Meyer, pp. 563–4 and 613. It is interesting that he worked on these plans at the same time as on the decoration of Assy, which he had promised Père Couturier in 1950 (*Ibid.*, p. 573). It is also significant that he began to plan the chapel during the time Matisse was working on his own chapel in Vence nearby.

13   A later project, the tapestries and mosaics for the Knesset in Jerusalem, show another use of the same method of work. For details, see Z. Amishai, "Chagall and the Knesset", address at the Fifth World Congress of Jewish Studies in Jerusalem, 1969, to be published by the World Union of Jewish Studies.

the measurements, asked to exclude human forms and otherwise left completely free. He stated:

> Israel I think of as an Oriental queen. This synagogue should be the queen's crown, and I would wish my windows to be the jewels of her crown. When I had decided that was what I wanted to offer her . . . the words in the Bible "You will be as a crown" came back to me suddenly, and I knew I would have God's help.[14]

The twelve windows naturally suggested the theme of the Twelve Tribes, traditional in synagogue decoration. This suited Chagall's analogy between the windows and jewels, as the jewels on the High Priest's breastplate had been engraved with the names of the tribes. The insignia of the tribes, usually drawn from the Blessing of Jacob (*Genesis* xlix: 3–28), are described in Midrash Rabbah's commentaries on their banners which are mentioned in *Numbers* ii. To these sources, Chagall added Midrashic legends and other themes in order to create a new set of symbols with a more universal meaning. In fact he stated that he began work before re-reading the pertinent passages in the Old Testament.[15]

Five sketches were made for each window.[16] The first, a black and white study in ink, over a light pencil drawing, gives the main lines and subject matter. On several of these Chagall has scribbled notes in Yiddish. The second sketch, in ink and wash, gives a scheme of light and shade which does not conform to the finished window, or even to the next stage. The third sketch, in watercolour, works out a simple colour composition and establishes the background colour. The fourth gives us an insight into Chagall's working methods. In this collage, oddly shaped patches deriving their colours from the third sketch, are shifted around until a pleasing arrangement is found. The figures are then sketchily superimposed. The fifth sketch, in gouache and collage, is the window in miniature. Chagall retains the colour layout of the fourth sketch,

14 Quoted by Joseph Roddy, "Marc Chagall", *Look,* October 24, 1961, p. 85. This comment should be compared with Henry Adams' description of Chartres as a palace designed for the Queen of Heaven (*Mont-Saint-Michel and Chartres,* Cambridge, 1925, p. 90), and of the Western rose as a jewel the Virgin had placed on the breast of her church (p. 143). He also writes of the Virgin instructing or inspiring the designers as to how she would like the windows to appear. This is particularly interesting as Chagall was strongly influenced by a visit to Chartres in 1952, when he was struck by the glory of the windows (Meyer, p. 577).

15 Roddy, p. 85.

16 They have been beautifully published by J. Leymarie, *Vitraux pour Jérusalem,* Monte Carlo, 1962. They are printed there as sets before the illustration of each window. References to other illustrations in this book will be labelled Lp.

softened and more flowing, interwoven with the earlier linear figural composition. No real correspondence exists any longer between figure and colour, but the result is a beautifully unified whole.[17] The fifth sketch is copied, stroke by stroke, into the windows, which were enriched by Chagall with purely decorative little birds, animals and flowers, painted on lightly in black or etched into the glass. The spectator's reaction to this is as joyous as Chagall's application of these "psychic shocks" must have been: "Oh, look, there's a little upside-down bird hidden in that tree!"

We now turn to an analysis of each window individually.

REUBEN (Fig. 1)

ראובן בכרי אתה כחי וראשית אוני יתר שאת ויתר עז. פחז כמים אל־תותר כי
עלית משכבי אביך אז חללת יצועי עלה.

Reuben, thou art my first-born, My might and the first-fruits of my strength; The excellency of dignity, and the excellency of power. Unstable as water, have not thou the excellency; Because thou wentest up to thy father's bed; Then defiledst thou it — he went up to my couch. (Genesis xlix: 3–4)[18]

Reuben's banner was red, and on it were the *duda'im* (possibly mandrakes) which Reuben picked for his mother, Leah, who exchanged them with Rachel for a night with Jacob (*Genesis* xxx: 14–16). They were thought to influence fertility. The tribe's usual symbol is a red, five-petalled flower, resembling a man.

Chagall chose to accent other elements than those usually depicted. The window's base colour, a light midnight blue, interprets "unstable as water", and indeed the whole window can be read as a materialization of instability. The fish swim in opposite directions, and the central bird turns against the line of flight of the flock. Actually, this flock can be understood as representing the movements of one bird, who first flies one way, then changes direction, and finally turns back again.

In the upper part of the arch, a white sun contains fragments of Jacob's blessing. These fragments provide clues to the window's basic theme, with the words "my first-born" and "the beginning". The source of this window is Chagall's *Creation* illustrations (Figs. 2 and 3), and the great sun which dominates both window and drawings is Chagall's

17 This orderly working procedure is another warning against accepting Chagall's work as a purely spontaneous creation. The development of the final motifs can be followed step by step through many of the sketches. The division of the frames of each window into twelve parts (four tri-partite horizontal rows) echoes the structure of the building as a whole.

18 The translation of the *Soncino Chumash,* London, 1956, is used throughout.

symbol of godhead, a generating source of life and vitality.[19] Comparison of the window and the illustrations show that the same basic blue of the colour plate, and the same layout and figures are used, with few changes. Man-like forms have been eliminated as requested in the commission : the angel in the upper left-hand corner is replaced by the bird, both being winged creatures who fly towards the sun, and Adam and Eve are replaced by fish. The illustrations show all aspects of creation : sun and moon, trees, water and land, fish, birds, animals and man. The window retains all of these, except the moon and man, who is, however, suggested in the distant houses. The differentiation of land, sea and sky hinted at by the waves in the *Creation* is fully developed in the window. The three central birds have shifted position : the bird formerly at the bottom now leads the line, which forms a gentle curve instead of a triangle. Changes have also been made in the bird turning in flight.[20]

In the *Creation* there are four trees; in the window — two. Throughout the sketches, a vestige of the tree missing on the left forms an otherwise mysterious winding line leading into the wing of the lower left-hand bird. The two trees on the right of the *Creation* are blended into one in the window. The green colour of this area in the third sketch has been moved into a hill above it, and it is now dominated by two large red areas full of leaves, flowers and berries. This clearly refers to Reuben's traditional symbol, the red flower of the *duda'im*. But red is also the colour of the apple, the traditional fruit of temptation. In the *Creation* scenes, it is from this tree that Adam and Eve pick fruit, and when Eve does so, the trees seem alive with heads and limbs, as though the Tempter was within them. This compositional analogy connects the illicit bargain of Rachel and Leah concerning the flower as a fertility symbol, to the fruit which led to the Fall of Man.

The lamb at the bottom of the window was added only in the fifth sketch. Chagall would explain that he had wanted a grey echo of the sun, which he had added in the third and fourth sketches, and that the irrational addition of a figure, seemingly at the bottom of the sea, would strengthen its compositional effect. However, a stream of associations led to the choice of this specific figure. The gray spot occurs in an area dealing with the analogy between the *duda'im* and the

19 See for instance the *Creation of Man* (1956–8, Mp. 574).
20 A secondary source for the window is Chagall's *Song of Songs, Verve* 37–38, Pl. 71. Here the sun is in the right upper corner, and three birds fly away from it, one turning in flight. They lack the sweeping curve of the birds in the window and are seen in reverse.

Temptation. The name of Rachel, who bargained for the *duda'im*, means lamb. Chagall turned to the window of Joseph, Rachel's eldest son, for both the lamb's position and the herd of grazing sheep on the hill, added here at the same late stage, but present in *Joseph* from the start. The isolation of the lamb from the herd and its placing at the bottom of the window recall the story wherein Reuben tossed Joseph into a pit to save him from his brothers (*Gen.* xxxvii : 21–22).

SIMEON (Fig. 4)

שמעון ולוי אחים כלי חמס מכרתיהם. בסדם אל־תבא נפשי בקהלם אל־תחד
כבדי כי באפם הרגו איש וברצנם עקרו־שור. ארור אפם כי עז ועברתם כי
קשתה אחלקם ביעקב ואפיצם בישראל.

Simeon and Levi are brethren; weapons of violence their kinship. Let my soul not come into their council; Unto their assembly let my glory not be united; For in their anger they slew men, And in their self-will they houghed oxen. Cursed be their anger, for it was fierce, And their wrath, for it was cruel; I will divide them in Jacob, And scatter them in Israel (*Gen.* xlix : 5–7).

Jacob cursed these sons for having massacred the men of Shechem, in revenge for the rape of Dina, the night after Jacob had made peace with them (*Gen.* xxiv). Rashi explains that "they houghed oxen" indicates that Simeon and Levi were the brothers who tried to kill Joseph, who was likened to an ox (*Gen.* xxxvii : 20 and *Deut.* xxxiii : 17). Simeon's banner was green, and his symbol was usually a castle, representing Shechem.

The window's basic colour is midnight blue, eerily juxtaposed to purples, greens and violent reds. Chagall's clue to the subject matter is the first nine words of Jacob's speech. Simeon's name is inscribed in a blood red circle, while Levi's appears along with the rest of the passage, as though Chagall placed the responsibility for evil on Simeon, while minimizing the participation of Levi, the forefather of the priests. Shechem appears at the bottom of the window, clothed in night.[21] Under the tree on the left, two eyes (Simeon and Levi) watch the town stealthily, ready, no doubt, to pounce. They were added in the fifth sketch to compensate for a change in the brothers' previous symbols, the two birds who escape from the town in the first four sketches. The eery feeling is magnified by the measured tread of the sinister winged horse, or donkey, symbol of Hamor (חמור), father of Shechem, who signed the

---

21 In both his Biblical illustrations and the windows, Chagall usually represents houses in Israel as flat-topped or domed, rather than gabled as in Vitebsk.

treaty with Jacob.[22] In the bottom half of the window, a large purple-
blue orb contains the sun, the moon and the stars. This orb must have
reminded Chagall of one of Joseph's dreams (*Gen.* xxxvii : 9),[23] for in
the last sketch, the lower of the two birds to its right becomes a flying
ox (symbolic of Joseph), who gazes back at his dream while being chased
away because of it.

However, Jacob's curse is not the only source here. Chagall was also
inspired by another Biblical passage, Joel's apocalyptic vision of Judea's
destruction by a swift, efficient enemy, likened to a horse :

כמראה סוסים מראהו וכפרשים כן ירוצון...כגבורים ירצון כאנשי מלחמה יעלו
חומה ואיש בדרכיו ילכון ולא יעבטון ארחותם...בעיר ישקו בחומה ירצון
בבתים יעלו בעד החלונים יבאו כגנב.

The appearance of them is as the appearance of horses; And as
horsemen, so do they run ... They climb the wall like men of war;
And they move on every one in his ways And they entangle not their
paths ... They leap upon the city, They run upon the wall, They
climb up into the houses, They enter in at the windows like a thief
(*Joel* ii : 4, 7, 9).

Thus the ominous horse also symbolizes the dread enemy, and the eyes,
creeping up on the town, those who will enter the houses as thieves.
Joel continues with a description of the coming of the Day of Judg-
ment :

ונתתי מופתים בשמים ובארץ דם ואש ותימרות עשן. השמש יהפך לחשך והירח
לדם לפני בוא יום ה׳ הגדול והנורא...שמש וירח קדרו וכוכבים אספו נגהם.

And I will show wonders in the heavens and in the earth, Blood,
and fire, and pillars of smoke. The sun shall be turned into darkness
And the moon into blood, Before the great and terrible day of the
Lord come ... The sun and moon are become black And the stars
withdraw their shining (*Joel* iii : 3–4, iv : 15).

This passage explains two of the orbs : the red one is the moon turned
to blood, and the dark one that contains the sun, moon and stars is
the universe "become black". The wavy lines close to the horse's wings
are the pillars of smoke. Joel's vision ends with a promise of the End
of Days :

והיה ביום ההוא יטפו ההרים עסיס והגבעות תלכנה חלב...

And it shall come to pass in that day, That the mountains shall

---

22   This may be a reminiscence of the "large green Chagallesque donkey" which
     struck Chagall's fancy at Chartres (Meyer, p. 577).

23   The fact that there are more than eleven stars proves nothing, as Chagall en-
     joys making a seven-branched menorah with five branches, and a five-fingered
     hand with seven fingers.

drop down sweet wine, And the hills shall flow with milk ... (*Joel* iv: 18).

This explains the third sphere of light, decorated with leaves, and the flowering tree nearby.[24]

Why were these passages used here? In working on the window, Chagall must have used symbols which reminded him of Joel's prophecy. These symbols derive from the *Reuben* window and its sources. The large orb not only echoes the concentric circles in *Reuben,* but is itself an accepted symbol for the Creation, found anywhere from Monreale to Burne-Jones,[25] to the Creation sphere from the Sabbath plate in Raskin's *Siddur* (Fig. 5). This last, like the window, contains spheres both inside and outside the main orb, and the sun and moon parallel the positions of Chagall's other two spheres. The horse or donkey derives from the winged animal striding across the sky in Chagall's black and white *Creation* (Fig. 2), a figure which had been eliminated in *Reuben.* The animal in *Simeon* is also winged, similarly placed, and moves in the same direction. Chagall, thinking of Ḥamor, economically adopted into this window a figure left over from the source of the previous one.[26]

The orb containing the sun and moon, and the striding animal were present from the first and were the pictorial elements which reminded Chagall of *Joel,* and caused him to add the two other spheres in the third sketch. In using Joel's prophecy here, Chagall was opposing *Simeon's* window to *Reuben's*: the apocalyptic End of Days versus the Creation. The orb reinforces the connection and opposition between the two: the symbol of Creation becomes the darkened sun, symbol of destruction and of the end.

The combination of green, purple and deep blue contrasted with blood red, creates a tone of mystery, which is heightened by the figures,

---

24   Chagall's illustrations for *Joel* (*Verve* 37–38, pls. 77–79) have practically no connection with these parts of the text and, figure for figure, *Simeon* is a much better illustration of them. The colour plate of *Isaiah* (*Verve* 33–34, between Plates 97–98) with its blackness and large red orb is also closer to *Joel* than to *Isaiah,* or to Chagall's illustrations for *Joel.*

25   It is particularly close to the orb in Burne-Jones' *Fourth Day of Creation,* which also contains a larger and a smaller sphere within it (W. S. Sparrow, *The Old Testament in Art,* London, 1905, Pl. 39).

26   There are two other ties between the *Creation* scenes and the *Simeon* window. The first is in the handling of the tree on the left. The two eyes lurking under it in the window recall the head sticking out of this tree in the black and white *Creation.* The second similarity, which is particularly striking in the first sketch, is the flight of the birds. The right-hand bird has been shifted to the top, while the other two have moved further to the right.

even when their meaning is unknown. Thus Chagall creates a formal aura of tension and catastrophe, evil and cataclysm, which is indeed the theme of his window. On one level, it is the evil of Simeon; on the other, it is the apocalyptic cataclysm of the End of Days.

LEVI (Fig. 6)

Since Jacob cursed Levi with Simeon, Chagall turned to Moses for this tribe's blessing:

וללוי אמר תמיך ואוריך לאיש חסידך אשר נסיתו במסה תריבנו על־מי מריבה. האמר לאביו ולאמו לא ראיתיו ואת־אחיו לא הכיר ואת־בנו לא ידע כי שמרו אמרתך ובריתך ינצרו. יורו משפטיך ליעקב ותורתך לישראל ישימו קטורה באפך וכליל על־מזבחך. ברך ה׳ חילו ופעל ידיו תרצה מחץ מתנים קמיו ומשנאיו מן־יקומון.

And of Levi he said: Thy Thummim and Thy Urim be with Thy holy one, Whom Thou didst prove at Massah, With whom Thou didst strive at the waters of Meribah; Who said of his father, and of his mother: "I have not seen him"; Neither did he acknowledge his brethren, Nor knew he his own children; For they have observed Thy word, And keep Thy covenant. They shall teach Jacob Thine ordinances, And Israel Thy law; They shall put incense before Thee, And whole burnt-offering upon Thine altar. Bless, Lord, his substance, And accept the work of his hands; Smite through the loins of them that rise up against him, And of them that hate him, that they rise not again (*Deut.* xxxiii: 8–11).

This blessing, which lists the good things the tribe had done, gives two views of Levi. They can be seen as warriors of the Lord, who wreaked God's vengeance on Israel after the incident of the golden calf, and who, as the priestly Maccabees, fought for religious and national freedom.[27] On the other hand, they are the teachers and priests of Israel. Levi's traditional symbol is the High Priest's breastplate on a black, white and red ground.

Chagall stresses the tribe's role as teachers and priests and quotes that part of the blessing. The window is dedicated to holiness, as is evidenced by the rich, yellow colour, the colour of light, and the appearance, here alone, of God's name.

The design of the window resembles that of the Tabernacle in the early Bible illustrations (Fig. 7),[28] which had been rendered atypically as a European Ark-cloth. In the window, Chagall has added a second pair of traditional heraldic animals and has reversed the positions of the

27 See Rashi's interpretation of the meaning of verses 9 and 11.
28 See also *Verve* 33–34, Pl. 68. The ease with which Chagall varies the elements on the cloth can be seen in comparing the two illustrations.

Tablets of the Law and the pitcher, which has been developed into a cup of flowers. Around the Tablets of the Law, Chagall set candles and flames whose light is reflected in the curved lines above them. Light and candles are traditional symbols of holiness and ritual: candles are lit on the eves of Sabbaths and holidays to welcome the coming day's holiness, and are used in the Havdalah ceremony to symbolize the Sabbath's end. The holiness of light is shown by the Eternal Light placed before the Ark in synagogues.

Two objects, apparently empty candle-holders, appear beneath the tablets. They resemble the scroll rods of the Torah, and their position suggests that the Tablets of the Law are also a Torah scroll. The combination of Torah and candles recalls the motto:

"כי נר מצוה, תורה — אור"

"For a good deed is a candle, the Torah — light". The tablets also symbolize the High Priest's breastplate. This is seen clearly in the division of this area in all the sketches, and carries over into the window in the multitude of colours and in the checkered effect of the leading.

However, there is another source for *Levi* in a source-book which helps to explain several of the windows: Gutmann's *Hebraica* (Fig. 8),[29] to which Chagall turned in working on the details of the fifth sketch. The source is a Hanukah menorah in which the larger set of heraldic animals is similar to that in the window. The right-hand animal, a crowned lion with a bushy tail, turns his head back, sticking his tongue out. The parallel animal in the fifth sketch, though crownless, has the same gay pose, a tongue sticking out, wide eyes with double lines around them, and the vestige of a mane. The bushy tail suggested the shape of a bird who seems to stand on the animal's back. The left-hand animal is not a lion (although usually the same heraldic animal is used on both sides), and seems to be munching something, an illusion created in the menorah by its position in the photograph, and enlarged upon in the window. The animal in the window is, however, wingless. In the source, these animals have a tree between them. Chagall has changed this to a bowl of flowers, a compromise between the tree and the pitcher from the Tabernacle source.

The candle-holders under the animals in the menorah are an important point in favour of this source. This combination of heraldic animals and light from below exists in a similar relationship in the window. The connection between the tribe of Levi and the Hanukah menorah

---

29 Henri Guttmann, *Hebraica: Documents d'Art Juif*, Paris 193–. For the most obvious use of this source-book, see the *Naphtali* window.

is clear. The menorah symbolizes the miracle of the Maccabees, who were both Levites and warriors of the Lord.

The meaning of the animals and birds is problematic. Landsberger explained the use of such animals in Beit Alpha as the cherubim on the Holy Ark.[30] However, whereas there were only two cherubim on the Ark, Ezekiel saw four creatures with the heads of an eagle, a man, a bull and a lion respectively. These became the Evangelists' symbols and in Christian art they often appear winged and carrying books. Chagall toyed with the idea of using these symbols in the second sketch, where the bull is winged and carries a book. The obvious problem in representing Ezekiel's beasts was the man. Chagall may have solved this by arbitrarily adding another animal instead. At any rate, he returns to the bull-headed bird only in the fifth sketch, by which time the winged bull had appeared in *Simeon*.

The ל of Levi seems to have a head at its tip. This derives from another of Chagall's sources — folk art and mediaeval manuscripts which may also have inspired the almost illegible lettering here. As evidenced by his early works and his Bible illustrations, Chagall can write Hebrew legibly. In the windows and sketches, letters are missing, and some are confused (e.g. ב and כ, ו and י, ד and ר) as if an untutored hand had executed them, and Chagall's hand is far from untutored. However, the same problem of illegibility is often found in Jewish folk art, and Chagall, basing himself on such art, has complemented his simplified animals with simplified lettering.

This window of light and holiness ends the first wall.

JUDAH (Fig. 9)

יהודה אתה יודוך אחיך ידך בערף איביך ישתחוו לך בני אביך. גור אריה יהודה
מטרף בני עלית כרע רבץ כאריה וכלביא מי יקימנו. לא־יסור שבט מיהודה
ומחקק מבין רגליו עד כי יבא שילה ולו יקהת עמים אסרי לגפן עירה ולשרקה
בני אתנו כבס ביין לבשו ובדם־ענבים סותה. חכלילי עינים מיין ולבן־שנים
מחלב.

Judah, thee shall thy brethren praise; Thy hand shall be on the neck of thine enemies; Thy father's sons shall bow down before thee. Judah is a lion's whelp; From the prey, my son, thou art gone up. He stooped down, he couched as a lion, And as a lioness; who shall rouse him up? The sceptre shall not depart from Judah, Nor the ruler's staff from between his feet, As long as men come to Shiloh; And unto him shall the obedience of the peoples be. Binding his foal unto the vine, And his ass's colt unto the choice vine; He

---

30 F. Landsberger, *A History of Jewish Art,* Cincinnati, 1946, p. 152.

washeth his garment in wine, And his vesture in the blood of grapes;
His eyes shall be red with wine, And his teeth white with milk (*Gen.*
xlix : 8–12).

Rashi interprets the mention of Shiloh as the coming of the Messiah, who is himself the Son of David and heir of the Judaean kings.
Judah's flag was azure with a lion as his symbol.

In this window Chagall has kept close to the blessing. The colour
is a deep blood red, interpreting the "blood of grapes" of Judah's numerous vineyards. Chagall quotes the beginning of Jacob's blessing,
stressing the kingly and warrior qualities of the tribe. The last word,
"בעטרֿף, in the back of the neck, amusingly ends up against the neck
(albeit the front) of the crouching lion. This playful, smiling cub is Judah, who was compared to a lion's whelp. He guards a walled city which
rests comfortably behind him. This is Jerusalem, which David, first of
the Judaean kings, captured and made his capital. Chagall recalls the
conglomerate buildings of Jerusalem, and depicts both gabled (Vi-
tebskian) and flat-roofed (Palestinian) houses.

Above, two hands hold a crown bearing Judah's name. The hands,
in this position, symbolize the priestly blessing, although Chagall does
not depict the second and third fingers and the fourth and fifth ones
held together as is usual. His variation on the theme is purposely inexact
(witness the four-fingered hand here). The crown above the priestly
blessing is traditional in Jewish iconography, and is usually explained
and even labelled as the "כתר כהונה, the crown of priesthood.[31] However, here the name Judah is inscribed on the crown, and this juxtaposition becomes a symbol of religious recognition of the kingship of
David's line, and perhaps hints at the future Messiah who will combine religious and secular rule. This interpretation is reinforced by the
rays of light which shoot forth from the hands and illuminate the lion
and city below, as though showering them with the blessing, and compositionally uniting the window's two halves.

A tradition states that God's spirit can be seen between the fingers

31   For examples of the crown above the hands, see *Hebraica*, Pl. XVII, where it
     occurs on a Hanukah lamp, and R. Wischnitzer, *Gestalten und Symbole der
     Jüdischen Kunst,* Berlin, 1935, Abb. 37, where it occurs on a Mizrach-tablet
     cut from paper. For the כתר כהונה, see S. Yudovin and M. Malkin, אידישער
     פאלקס־ארנאמענט (Jewish Folk Ornament), Vitebsk, 1920 (Fig. 10), in which there
     is a folk art example of the priestly blessing where the fingers are placed
     scarcely more traditionally than they are in Chagall's window. I should like to
     thank Dr. Bezalel Narkiss for showing me the importance of this book for
     the understanding of the windows.

of the priestly blessing. Here the letters of His Name (included in Judah's) are seen not through, but directly above, the fingers. The use of only part of Judah's name in most of the sketches may indicate Chagall's awareness of this tradition.

Some of the elements here appear in Chagall's illustration of the *Future Happiness of Jerusalem* (Is.. lxii: 6–11, Fig. 11), which, like the window, portrays the protection of Jerusalem. There the crowned lion stands before Jerusalem's walls. In the window the lion's crown has ascended to the top of the arch (however, he is crowned in the third sketch), human and angelic forms have been eliminated, and the lion crouches to conform to the blessing. The illustration also deals with the coming of the Messiah which is hinted at in Jacob's blessing.

Thus the second wall begins with the protection of Jerusalem, looking back to the early Judean kingdom and forward to Messianic times.

ZEBULUN (Fig. 12)

זבולן לחוף ימים ישכן והוא לחוף אנית וירכתו על־צידון.

Zebulun shall dwell at the shore of the sea, And he shall be a shore for ships, And his flank shall be upon Zidon (*Gen.* xlix : 13).

This tribe's seafaring character is underlined by linking it to the great port, Sidon of Phoenecia. Zebulun's white banner displayed a ship.

Although there is no quotation in the window, the first level of interpretation is clear. The bright red colour is associated with that of the rising or setting sun. Both the colour and the sun appear first in the third sketch.[32] Overhead two fish fly toward each other, echoing the movement of the hands in *Judah*. They are the smiling symbols of Zebulun's fishing industry. In the water, two small fish, swimming in opposite directions, recall those in Reuben; both windows also show one fish nibbling a plant at the lower right. This and the water motif in both windows link these two tribes, whose founders were the first and last sons of Leah.

The tribe's traditional symbol, a ship, is set near a capsized boat, seemingly part of Chagall's whimsical desire to see how the world would look upside down. Present from the start, the capsized boat may originally have developed from reflections of boats in water, e.g. in *Time is a River without Banks* (1939 , Mp. 425). The theme of the capsized and upright boat in combination with the fish had already been developed in works such as *Fishes at Saint-Jean* (1949, Mp. 495). In *Boat*

---

32   The basic orange of the sketches was changed to deep red in the window, probably to reduce its vibrancy in the intense Jerusalem light.

with Two Fishes (1952, Mc 907), two fish fly towards the sun, echoing
the positions of the figures below. These pictures, associated with periods
when Chagall, like Zebulun, lived on the coast, are the sources of his
inspiration here.

The almost unreadable lettering is highly reminiscent of mediaeval
manuscripts. The ל this time has the head of a rooster. The strange red-
green area above the head of the left-hand fish is the result of green
brush-strokes applied over the red background in the fifth sketch.

The main theme of this window is Zebulun's life on the coast. But
this is only a partial explanation. This window is closely tied to that of
Issachar, and will be discussed again below.

ISSACHAR (Fig. 13)

יששכר חמר גרם רבץ בין המשפתים. וירא מנחה כי טוב ואת־הארץ כי נעמה
ויט שכמו לסבל ויהי למס־עבד.

Issachar is a large-boned ass, Couching down between the sheep-
folds. For he saw a resting-place that it was good, And the land that
it was pleasant; And he bowed his shoulder to bear, And became a
servant under taskwork (*Gen.* xlix : 14–15).

Rashi explained that Issachar bowed his shoulder to bear the study
of Torah because this tribe produced great scholars and law-makers.
Issachar's banner was blue-black with a sun and moon on it, symbolizing the tribe's astrologers, but the usual artistic representation is the
donkey mentioned by Jacob.

The window's green colour, the grazing sheep, the town nestling
among the flowers, the plentiful foliage and the trellis running around
the window's arch, indicate the fruitfulness of the land, which Issachar
found pleasant. Chagall's symbol for Issachar is the traditional "couching" donkey,[33] and he inscribes the first line of Jacob's blessing on a
white triangular area between the Tablets of the Law, partly covered by
two hands, which again suggest the priestly blessing. This combination
of motifs illustrates Rashi's interpretation of Issachar as a Torah scholar.
This smiling donkey's burden of flowers is as sweet and light as the Torah, and the bird he carries on his back shows the ease with which he
supports Israel by his learning.

This interpretation is reinforced by the window's main source, Chagall's illustration of the description of the Torah scholar in *Psalms* i
(Fig. 14). As in the window, a bird is set on each side of the Tablets of

---

33 His two eyes, placed one under the other, result from a change made in the
fifth sketch and retained in the window to establish a freedom of touch.

the Law, on one of which is written "Heureux L'homme", the first
words of the psalm:

אשרי האיש אשר לא הלך בעצת רשעים ובדרך חטאים לא עמד ובמושב לצים
לא ישב. כי אם-בתורת ה' חפצו ובתורתו יהגה יומם ולילה. והיה כעץ שתול
על-פלגי מים...

Happy is the man that hath not walked in the counsel of the wicked,
Nor stood in the way of sinners, nor sat in the seat of the scornful.
But his delight is in the law of the Lord, And in His law doth he
meditate day and night. And he shall be like a tree planted by streams
of water... (*Psalms* i : 1–3).

The upper and lower halves of the illustration have been reversed in
the window, and the donkey and birds now look back over their
shoulders instead of straight ahead. This change in the donkey occurred
in the fourth sketch, suggested by the direction of a blue triangle of
paper pasted on in this area. The flowers and leaves which the donkey
supports are the remnants of the tree mentioned in *Psalms,* which had
supported him in the illustration.

The resemblance to the source is most marked in the first sketch
which repeats the donkey, tree, birds and Tablets, but adds the hands
and the triangle. In the next sketches, Chagall tried several variations
on the upper part of the design. In the second sketch, he changed
the trellis border into a geometric decoration, set both heraldic birds on
the left, and placed symbols closely associated with *Simeon* opposite
them : a horse strides across the sky above a white orb containing a
moon. The moon, deriving from the astrological symbols of Issachar's
banner, must have recalled *Simeon's* motifs, and the curve sketched under the right-hand bird in the first sketch formally suggested the horse's
head. The objects disappear in the third and fourth sketches, replaced
by the undefined curving lines from the first sketch, as though Chagall
was not sure what to place around the hands-triangle-Tablets symbol.
A black area is all that remains of the horse in both sketches.

At this point Chagall sought inspiration for this area, and one of the
independent sketches (Lp. 211), done while working on the windows,
seems to bear evidence of renewed experimentation. Here he reinstates
the heraldic birds, basing them on a tombstone illustrated in *Hebraica*
(Pl. XLVIII).[34] The candelabrum between them, four-branched rather
than five-branched as in the tombstone, had also formed a part of his
Heureux l'Homme, where it had been three-branched.

---

34 A similar set of birds, much closer to those in *Hebraica,* appears in another
 independent sketch, along with the initials פ"נ from the tombstone (Fig. 21).

For the final solution, Chagall turned to another source: Yudovin and Malkin's *Jewish Folk Ornament* (Fig. 15), perhaps because of the triangular composition of the central part in both the plate and his sketches for the window. In the fifth sketch, he reversed the positions of the birds, copying the details of the feathers,[35] changed the branches they hold in their mouths to bouquets which seem to grow out of their tails, and hinted at the heavy branches beneath their feet. The upflung wing of the right-hand bird is based on that of the top bird in the second sketch and on the shape of the branch near the right-hand bird in the source. The snake-like quality of the foliage in the source is echoed in the snakes in the window's trellis.

In the fifth sketch a black bird appears at the top of the arch, growing out of the black area in the two previous sketches and replacing the horse of the second sketch. This addition again demonstrates the interrelationship of the development of motifs in adjacent windows. Another black bird, similarly placed, appears in the fifth sketch of the following window, *Dan,* also replacing an animal, and functioning in a more meaningful manner, which will be analyzed below.

However, *Issachar* is more vitally related to his other neighbour, *Zebulun.* Chagall owes his inspiration to the first line of Moses' blessing to the two tribes:

ולזבולן אמר שמח זבולן בצאתך ויששכר באהליך.

And of Zebulun he said: Rejoice, Zebulun, in thy going out; And, Issachar, in thy tents (*Deut.* xxxiii: 18).

Rashi explained that the two tribes had an agreement whereby Zebulun's foreign trade helped support Issachar, who stayed at home, farming and studying Torah. In *Issachar,* one of the hands is green and one is red — the base colours of the two windows. They are joined together in friendly cooperation, superimposed over the triangle of Issachar's tent and the Tablets, thus symbolizing their union dedicated to the study of Torah, which Issachar taught Zebulun in return for the latter's material support. The heraldic birds can be similarly interpreted — one is partially red, with a wing raised, ready to fly (Zebulun), and the other is green and stationary (Issachar). This dualism also appears in *Zebulun,* where the two flying fish, representing the two tribes, parallel the

---

35 The treatment of the feathers is particularly indicative, as it is very rare in Chagall's work, occurring only when the bird is clearly a cock (e.g. *The Red Rooster,* 1940, Mp. 454, and *Cock with Little Clown,* 1958, Mc. 979), which is not the case here.

motions of the hands in *Issachar*.[36] The two windows are also united formally by the heads of most of the animals and birds in *Issachar*, which are directed towards *Zebulun*.

This window, whose main theme is the scholarly aspect of Issachar, ends the second wall, which achieves a visual unity through the similar composition and unified horizon line of its windows. All three set a triangular area into the upper part of the arch, and the two end windows place a reclining animal below a pair of hands, and frame the wall with animals and birds facing inwards towards *Zebulun*. These elements give the wall a unity which transcends the thematic union of *Issachar* and *Zebulun*.

DAN (Fig. 16)

דן ידין עמו כאחד שבטי ישראל. יהי־דן נחש עלי־דרך שפיפן עלי־ארח הנשך
עקבי־סוס ויפל רכבו אחור. לישועתך קויתי ה׳.

Dan shall judge his people, As one of the tribes of Israel. Dan shall be a serpent in the way, A horned snake in the path, That biteth the horse's heels, So that his rider falleth backward. I wait for Thy salvation, O Lord (*Gen.* xlix : 16–18).

Dan's personal banner was sapphire-coloured, and displayed his usual symbol, a serpent. However, the banner of the three-tribe group he led in the desert had an eagle on it.

Chagall quotes the first line of Jacob's blessing, dealing with Dan as a judge. In the centre of the window appears a three-branched candelabrum, whose left arm curves upward, holding a candleless flame, while the right arm, holding a candle, curves up and then down and around, like the arm of the Scales of Justice. This dual symbol, a candelabrum-scale, disperses both physical light and the abstract light of justice. The position of the areas of light reinforces this interpretation: yellow light radiates above the left and middle arms, and beneath the right arm pure white light illuminates the city, which appears to be being weighed in the balance. This is the city of Dan, the northernmost outpost of the tribes, to which the horses below are laying siege. These horses, based on Franz Marc's *Tower of Blue Horses*,[37] are those which Dan's serpent

---

36 A midrash-like moral can be derived from the two boats in *Zebulun*. The upright one has a red base (the commercial aspects of Zebulun), and a partially green sail (the spirit or רוח (ruaḥ) of Issachar) providing the wind (רוח — ruaḥ) that carries the boat along. On the other hand, the capsized boat has a red (commercial) sail which provides neither spirit nor wind. The moral is that if spiritual values are replaced by Zebulun's commercial and practical methods, the results will be disastrous.

37 K. Lankheit, *Franz Marc,* Berlin, 1950, p. 41.

will bite, and the hand holding a sword may refer to the fallen rider.

The snake on the candelabrum is that of Jacob's blessing, but this combination is rare.[38] Snakes twined around temple columns are fairly common in Jewish art, but there is disagreement as to whether they are symbols of good or of evil.[39] In Christian iconography, the snake symbolizing the Brazen Serpent is wound around a cross or T-shaped rod as a prefiguration of Christ, both being symbols of salvation. The three-branched candelabrum-scale here bears a resemblance to a cross, but Chagall, in adapting the symbol to Jewish use, naturally replaces the cross with a Jewish symbol, the menorah.[40]

The actual visual source for this motif is the *Temptation* in Yudovin and Malkin's *Jewish Folk Ornament* (Fig. 17). There a simplified striped snake with his tongue sticking out as in the window,[41] curls up a basically three-branched tree, whose right-hand branch clearly curves downward. The resemblence can be seen in the first sketch, especially in the curve of the right-hand branch and the similarity of the flames to fruit. The hand of Eve in the *Temptation* may have inspired the two hands and a foot coming out of a group of vertical lines at the top of this sketch. The connection of the snake and candelabrum with the snake and tree of the Temptation is reinforced by the horned animal and bird on the left, who are similar to those in Chagall's *Creation*, where Eve picks the fruit (Fig. 3), and to those in his *Temptation*. Chagall has turned the serpent of evil into one of justice, because, as Dan's heraldic sign, it is a symbol of good in the defence of Israel, but also because of his

38 One example of such a combination is the Gloucester Cathedral candlestick (1104–13), with serpents and monsters entwined around it (E. Gombrich, *Story of Art,* London, 1958, p. 126).

39 See Landsberger, pp. 40–41 and Wischnitzer, p. 65.

40 There is a German fifteenth century manuscript tradition for combining a Cross with the Scales of Justice, although in a different fashion. See F. Wormald, "The Crucifix and the Balance", *Journal of the Warburg Institute,* Vol. I, 1937, pp. 276–280. Chagall has juxtaposed the cross and the candelabrum in several works, e.g. the *White Crucifixion* (1938, Mp. 417), in which a six-branched candelabrum is set at the foot of the Cross. In *Obsession* (1943, Mp. 447), *The Painter Crucified* (1938–40, Mc. 689) and *Deposition* (1941, Mc. 698), a three-branched candelabrum is used.

41 The stripes and tongue appear first in the fifth sketch, and are not usual in Chagall's portrayal of snakes. Those in the first four sketches and in the *Temptation* (*Verve* 37–38, colour plate between Pls. 2 and 3), are much more typical. The snake's undulations and part of the idea for its juxtaposition with the candelabrum may derive from the *Vision of Zechariah* (Fig. 26), where a snake appears inexplicably to the left to the candelabrum.

own love of the inversion of symbols. This inversion is similar to that of the Brazen Serpent to which one looked to be cured from snakebite.

The upper part of the window underwent many changes during the sketching process. The two hands and a foot of the first sketch become a fish, a bird and a bird-headed foot, all holding swords, in the second, and, in the third, a red bird and purple and black beasts, very similar to the animals and bird in the same sketch for *Gad*. Although in the third sketch, these two animals seem to be fighting the red bird (who may be the eagle of Dan's second banner), in a manner paralleling the confrontation of the bird and the three horses on either side of the candelabrum below, the situation is changed in the fifth sketch. Here it is the red beast (again similar to that on the bottom left in *Gad's* third sketch), who dominates, holding both the candelabrum-scale and a sword.[42] He seems to be fighting the fish and the crow, who is coming in behind him, paralleling the motion of the horses below, and to be protecting both the town below him and the candelabrum-scale.[43] The red bird points to this fight without participating in it. The beast may symbolize the lion cub of Moses' blessing:

ולדן אמר דן גור אריה יזנק מן הבשן.

> And of Dan he said: Dan is a lion's whelp; That leapeth forth from Bashan (*Deut.* xxxiii: 22).

His importance is still greater in the independent sketch paralleling this window, where he practically replaces the symbol of the candelabrum and the snake (Lp. 195).

To summarize, the main theme of this window is justice and light, and the defence of these values and of Israel.

GAD (Fig. 18)

גד גדוד יגודנו והוא יגד עקב.

> Gad, a troop shall troop upon him; But he shall troop upon their heel (*Gen.* xlix: 19).

Gad's banner was black and white and showed an army camp, usually represented as tents.

Chagall quotes the whole blessing, placing the word "heel" between

---

42 Leymarie has aptly compared the red beast with *Ezekiel* v: 1, where the prophet is commanded to take up a sword and a balance (Leymarie, p. 102).

43 Visually the idea may have derived from the drawing *Christ and the Horses* (c. 1940, Mp. 432), which shows horsemen with swords, closely resembling the four horsemen of the Apocalypse, beside a crucifix, and over a group of agitated figures, while opposite them stands the figure of an erect animal. The group seems to express the catastrophe of World War II.

the two left feet of the purple beast. He shows a troop of vicious monsters attacking a purple animal with red wings who may be Chagall's variation on the lioness mentioned by Moses:

ולגד אמר ברוך מרחיב גד כלביא שכן וטרף זרוע אף־קדקד.

And of Gad he said: Blessed be He that enlargeth Gad; He dwelleth as a lioness, And teareth the arm, yea, the crown of the head (*Deut.* xxxiii : 20).

A crowned bird, whose sword projects into the circle containing Gad's name, soars above the beleaguered animal, symbolizing Gad's eventual victory. Its body is composed of the Shield of David (although the six points are not properly spaced). Before the fourth sketch, the body had been composed of a group of concentric circles, Chagall's symbol of godhead and vitality. The bird thus represents the protecting spirit of God, the Shekhinah, whom the Cabbalists pictured as a bird.[44] On the left, Gad's eventual victory is shown by the formerly besieged animal who, sword in hand, now attacks a walled city. Beneath him a bouquet of flowers testifies to the richness of the land he fought for.

The development of these motifs was slow. In the first sketch, the crowned bird, the animal with a sword at the lower left, and the one entering at the right, are set among plants and snake-like forms. In the second sketch, the curving lines become a snake, similar in its shape and stripes to that in Yudovin's *Temptation,* another interplay of sources between adjacent windows. In the third sketch, animals, birds and people were added below, and in the fourth, the final composition began to evolve and the base colour was chosen (usually this was done in the third sketch). The first lines of the building at the left and the grey patch from which the bird at the right will grow, make their appearence here.

At this point Chagall, having determined on a troop of monsters below, turned in search of them to *Hebraica,* a source which explains most of the changes made in the fifth sketch. He tried out his source material in two independent sketches. In one of these (Fig. 19), only the circular body-shield of the crowned bird remains, with its six-armed spoke-like star, whose centre contains Chagall's Hebrew name. Its source is a table of chapter readings from a thirteenth century Bible (Fig. 20), with variations in the number of lines in the outer and inner rings, and con-

---

44   This is seemingly the explanation for another crowned bird who fills the background of *Eden* (*Verve* 37–38, Pl. 1).

taining a seven-spoked star. At the bottom left of the sketch, Chagall copied almost line for line the beast appearing at the upper left of the Bible-table. In the second drawing (Fig. 21), under his copy of the birds from the same book, Chagall copied more freely the beast from the bottom of another thirteenth century Bible chapter-readings table (Fig. 22). He retained the three-pronged tongue, the long ears, wings, striated tail and position of the legs, but eliminated one of the heads and changed the eyes.[45]

In the fifth sketch, the influence of these sources can now be traced. The spokes of the bird's circular body originate from the first Bible Plate (Fig. 20). The snake-necked animal in the centre derives from the head on the tail of the lower left-hand beast in Figure 22, with the tri-lobe tongue of the beast's main head added. Beside this animal is the original snake form Chagall had drawn, in red. The green beast at the right, although carrying a sword, assumes the silly, playful aspect of the winged beasts on the top of Figure 22. The toothy, winged purple beast in the centre derives from the upper left-hand animal in Figure 20, which accounts for its two left feet. In the source, this foot was raised to accommodate the circle below it. Chagall lowered it, without erasing the original placing, to improve the animal's warlike stance. His three-pronged tongue derives from the beasts in Figure 22. The winged red beast on the lower left derives from the similarly placed animal in Figure 20, and the snakes in the bottom centre come, pretzel-shape, dots and position facing each other, from a calendar table from a thirteenth century Bible in *Hebraica* (Fig. 23). The remaining beasts derive either from similar sources or from Chagall's imagination stimulated by those he had found.

A basic modification occurs between this sketch and the previous ones, in which it had been the soaring bird who was besieged by the animals. The addition of the central winged animal in the fifth sketch and its identification with the winged animal at the left, changes this. The animal forms a link between the bird soaring above and the animal below by means of the red colour which runs through them all, and differentiates between the warring animal and its protector, the bird-like Shekhinah.

Formally as well as iconographically this window is one of strife: the deep red is spilled like blood on the bluish green, which is rent by rays of light. However, this red acts as a focus for the crowded strife-laden

---

45   Similar beasts occur in other medieval Hebrew manuscripts, such as the *Machsor Lipsiae* (Leipzig, 1964, pp. 6, 55, etc.), but the differences merely emphasize the fact that *Hebraica* was the source.

lower area, gathering it into the central Gad animal and rising through
the victorious bird to the circle containing Gad's name.

ASHER (Fig. 24)

מאשר שמנה לחמו והוא יתן מעדני־מלך.

As for Asher, his bread shall be fat, And he shall yield royal dainties
(*Gen.* xlix : 20).

Moses added to this :

ולאשר אמר ברוך מבנים אשר יהי רצוי אחיו וטבל בשמן רגלו.

And of Asher he said, Blessed be Asher above sons; Let him be the
favoured of his brethren, And let him dip his foot in oil. (*Deut.*
xxxiii : 24).

Asher's banner was red with an olive tree on it.

The subject of this olive-coloured window [46] is the uses of the oil in
which Asher abounds, whose source is seen in the olive trees on the
right. This tribe supplied the foods and anointing oil of the kings and
the pure oil for the Temple. Chagall quotes Jacob's blessing and illustrates it in the upper half of the window, where a crowned bird looks
up joyfully and expectantly at the bird carrying an olive branch who is
labelled Asher. Another bird on the right pecks at the flowers and fruits
on its back, which seem to grow out of the trees below. This bird developed out of a tree which appears in the first and fourth sketches, with
which Chagall merged the bird from Yudovin and Malkin's book which
he had already used in *Issachar* (Fig. 15).

The lower part of the window deals with the uses of oil in the Temple
and the ritual aspects of Temple worship. Beside the seven-branched
menorah stands a two-eared jug which holds the sacred oil. This jug
is a humorous interpretation of Moses' blessing, since the feet of the bird
"sitting" in the jar are indeed dipped deeply in oil.[47] The human hand
of the jug holds flowers, and others lie below, representing incense for
the Temple. The menorah standing between a jug and two olive trees
can be found reversed in a thirteenth century Bible (*Hebraica*, Plate
XXV), where it refers to the Tabernacle as the inscription around the
border shows (*Numbers* viii : 4).

The ritual of sacrifice in the Temple is symbolized by a slaughtered

---

46 The colour, as in *Gad,* was not chosen until the fourth sketch.
47 The development of Chagall's motifs from his form associations is clear in the
    bird-headed jug. The first sketch showed a jug with one clay and one human
    arm. The shape of the jug's opening suggested a bird's head, which it becomes,
    by the addition of a few lines resembling an eye, in the second sketch, and
    more clearly in the fifth.

animal lying on its back to the left of the Menorah, and the knife next to the bowl of fruit on its right. The addition of bowls, pitchers and a similar upside-down sacrificed animal to symbols of the Temple appears in a miniature depicting the sanctuary from the fifteenth century Bible of the Duke of Alba, illustrated in *Hebraica* (Fig. 25).

One of the olive tree's legendary qualities is its immortality. New trees grow from the roots of the old one, so that when the old tree withers, part of it lives on in the trees formed from its roots. This eternal quality explains the use of the olive branch for Noah's dove, and its expansion into a symbol of peace, as well as the use of only pure olive oil in the Temple. The dove carrying the olive branch at the top of the window thus has a wider meaning than simply the strict interpretation of Jacob's blessing.

The eternal quality of the olive trees is paralleled by that of the menorah, which the Midrash and the Zohar equate with the Tree of Life. This equation is extended in the Apocrypha to the olive tree as well, and all three become united as "bearers of light" in Messianic themes.[48] Chagall hints at this here by the juxtaposition of the menorah to the two olive trees, one above the other at its right, a combination based on his illustration of the *Vision of Zecharia* (Fig. 26), which deals with symbols of redemption. Thus, although the primary level of meaning here is the secular and religious use of Asher's oil, these symbols are expanded to take on meanings of peace and redemption.

NAPHTALI (Fig. 27)

נפתלי אילה שלחה הנתן אמרי־שפר.

Naphtali is a hind let loose, He giveth goodly words (*Gen.* xlix : 21).

Moses added :

ולנפתלי אמר נפתלי שבע רצון ומלא ברכת ה' ים ודרום ירשה.

And of Naphtali he said : O Naphtali, satisfied with favour, And full with the blessing of the Lord, Possess thou the sea and the south (*Deut.* xxxiii : 23).

Naphtali's banner was wine-red and had a figure of a hind on it. Chagall gives no quotation, but seems to have integrated both blessings.

---

48 Z. Ameisenowa, "The Tree of Life in Jewish Iconography", *Journal of the Warburg Institute,* 1938–9, pp. 326–345, and R. Goodenough, *Jewish Symbols in the Greco-Roman Period,* New York, 1954, vol. IV, pp. 92–93. Rare as this motif is pictorially, it has been used recently by Motherwell in his decorations of the B'nai Brith synagogue in Millburn, New Jersey (*Interiors,* Nov. 1951, p. 14).

He makes Jacob's fleet hind so self-satisfied that he lies down, obliviously smiling up at the bird who is about to pounce on him.

This work is the key to one of Chagall's main source-books for the windows. He has lifted the composition almost completely from *Hebraica* (Fig. 28), and its full development can be seen in the first sketch.[49] This illustration shows two votive tomb plaques in fresco, copied by Jak Messenblum, the upper one from Prague, dated 1893, and the lower one from Mariampol, dated 1894.[50] In the upper plaque a bird clings to a leafy branch. In the window, the slightly modified bird flies freely in space, its foot touching the tree which is an extension of the tomb's branch. In the first sketch, the bird still clung to a branch of this tree. In the window the tree becomes an extension of the bird, so that it will compositionally balance the animal.

The antlered stag on the lower tombstone is another interpretation of *Ayalah*, translated above as hind. The treatment of the antlers there explains the four horns of the animal in the window. The bodies are in exactly the same position, although the legs in the tombstone are thinner. In the first four sketches, the head had been altered from a full face to a profile view. However, in an independent sketch, Chagall copied his source more closely and the head is seen full face (Lp. 205). In the fifth sketch, a compromise is reached: the top of the head is en face, but the muzzle is in profile, so that one's eyes move back and forth, considering the face first one way and then the next. The animal in the tombstone rests against a bank with a small tree on it, which becomes a hill with houses in the window.

The connection between the window and the plate is clear; only the reason behind it is problematic. Chagall saw that the juxtaposed plaques in *Hebraica* could form a unified composition. He used it here because the antlered animal fitted his subject, and possibly because the letters פ״נ on the plaques, meaning "here is buried", reminded him of the first two letters of Naphtali's name, נפ.

But it was not just the formal elements that attracted Chagall here. As in the other windows, the meaning of the source is relevant. These tombstones are symbolic of the European forefathers of the modern Jew, and according to Messenblum "bear witness to the perpetuity of

---

49   The first sketch here is the only one in the series done in wash and is practically identical with the third sketch.

50   To have been published in his "Tombeaux peints qui, dans les cimitières de Prague, de Vilna et de Bessarabie principalement témoignent de la pérennité d'un art spécifiquement juif". Quoted in *Hebraica*, notes to Plates XLIV–XLVIII.

a specifically Jewish art." Chagall here connects modern Judaism not only to the Biblical past and the Messianic future as he had done in the other windows, but also to the immediate past, to the heritage left by European Jewry. This conscious aim, which Chagall expresses in much of his art, explains the direct copying of the motifs from the beginning, rather than the usual adaptive process shown in *Levi, Gad* and *Dan*. The source and the meaning were meant to be apparent to those familiar with Jewish art, and this heritage, more than the blessings, is the theme of the window.

JOSEPH (Fig. 29)

בן פרת יוסף בן פרת עלי־עין בנות צעדה עלי־שור. וימררהו ורבו וישטמהו
בעלי חצים. ותשב באיתן קשתו ויפזו זרעי ידיו מידי אביר יעקב משם רעה
אבן ישראל. מאל אביך ויעזרך ואת שדי ויברכך ברכת שמים מעל ברכת תהום
רבצת תחת ברכת שדים ורחם. ברכת אביך גברו על־ברכת הורי עד־תאות
גבעת עולם תהיין לראש יוסף ולקדקד נזיר אחיו.

Joseph is a fruitful vine, A fruitful vine by a fountain; Its branches run over the wall. The archers have dealt bitterly with him, And shot at him, and hated him; But his bow abode firm, And the arms of his hands were made supple, By the hands of the Mightly One of Jacob, From thence, from the Shepherd, the Stone of Israel, Even by the God of thy father, who shall help thee, And by the Almighty, who shall bless thee, With blessings of heaven above, Blessings of the deep that coucheth beneath, Blessings of the breasts, and of the womb. The blessings of thy father Are mighty beyond the blessings of my progenitors Unto the utmost bound of the everlasting hills; They shall be on the head of Joseph and on the crown of the head of the prince among his brethren (*Gen.* xlix : 22–26).

The tribe was divided in two in the desert and named after Joseph's two sons, Ephraim and Menasseh. Their banners were black with the bullock and the unicorn (or wild ox) on them, symbols deriving from the last line of Moses' blessing (*Deut.* xxxiii : 17). Chagall, in reuniting the tribe under Joseph's name, ignored these symbols.

Although no quotation is given, the various levels of meaning in the window are clear. The crowned bird is Joseph, who holds a bow and arrow, showing his victory over his oppressors, for "his bow abode firm". The crown refers to the Israelite kingship founded by Jeroboam of Ephraim, which broke away from the Judean monarchy. The large tree in which the bird sits is opposed to a smaller tree on the right, pointing out the greater size of the Israelite kingdom compared to that of Judah. The tree is set near a crenellated wall, recalling Joseph's branches which run over the wall. The animals at the right refer to Joseph and his brothers. The grey horned animal at the left is Joseph to whom his brothers bow down.

The basket of fruit underneath the tree may refer to the legend of Joseph's third dream, in which he and his brothers collected fruit, and theirs withered while his remained sound. This is taken to refer to the lesser-known tradition of the Messiah, son of Joseph.[51] The horn or shofar held at the top of the arch recalls the horns of the wild ox mentioned in Moses' blessing (*Deut.* xxxiii, 17), but also refers to the horn blast that will announce the coming of this Messiah. The bird looks up at it as though ready to answer the call.[52]

All these ideas, however, are in a certain sense secondary. The window, which almost approaches a representation of an idyllic landscape, should be understood quite simply as an illustration of Jacob's blessing of fruitfulness. The yellow-gold base colour (not decided on until the fourth sketch) is the wheat. The trees, the basket of fruit and the great quantity of fruit and flowers symbolize the fruitfulness of the earth. The sheep represent both wealth in herds and the fruitfulness of the womb, and the bird is the blessing of the heavens and its creatures. The hills in the background represent the blessings to the "utmost bound of the everlasting hills". These blessings explain the richness of etched plants, little birds and animals covering the window. The hands with the shofar above symbolize the blessing of God on Joseph above all others. The only blessing not shown here is that of the sea.

BENJAMIN (Fig. 30)

בנימין זאב יטרף בבקר יאכל עד ולערב יחלק שלל.

Benjamin is a wolf that raveneth; In the morning he devoureth the prey, And at even he divideth the spoil (*Gen.* xlix : 27).

Benjamin's banner contained the colours of all the other banners and displayed a wolf. In the window, the wolf, who looks rather like an innocent bear cub, stands over his prey.

However, the window is also based on Moses' blessing :

לבנימין אמר ידיד ה׳ ישכן לבטח עליו חפף עליו כל־היום ובין כתפיו ישכן.

And of Benjamin he said : The beloved of the Lord shall dwell in safety by Him; He covereth him all the day, And He dwelleth between his shoulders (*Deut.* xxxiii : 12).

---

51 L. Ginsburg, *Legends of the Bible,* Philadelphia, 1956, vol. II, p. 196.
52 In the independent sketch of the window (Lp. 207), the bird is enlarged, emphasizing its aspect as kingly protector of the realm, answering the shofar's call.

Rashi explained that Moses spoke of Jerusalem, which rests in the hills ("shoulders") of Benjamin, and was protected by God as the site of the Temple. At the lower left, a bright yellow Jerusalem is set on the blue background like the sun in the sky. Its towers, accentuated by the sharp points of the leading, are sharply vertical and angular, reminiscent of a Gothic cathedral. Balancing it on the right is a flowering tree in which two birds nest, as Jerusalem nestles in the hills of Benjamin.[53] The wolf, standing before Jerusalem, protects it as Judah's lion had done in the opposite window. But the animal looks forlorn, for the dead prey at his feet is no monster, but a lamb, an innocent victim who suggests the ultimate destruction of Jerusalem's Temple despite the wolf's attempts to save it.

In the upper zone, a bird flies out of a tree at an animal, echoing the theme of this wall's first window, *Naphtali*. The source for the motif of animals flying around a roseate form is the thirteenth century Bible readings chart from *Hebraica* (Fig. 22), which contains a similar seven-petalled rose, enclosed in a circle and attached to a centre of two concentric circles. The two uppermost animals in both works move towards each other, although Chagall has redistributed the elements of the two winged beasts and produced a bird and an animal.

The use of this form here stems from Chagall's wish to complement the arched windows with a beautiful rose, as in most Gothic cathedrals. He chose Benjamin, the tribe in which Jerusalem is located, to be the focal point of the windows, a culmination of the set, placing in it a rose which becomes that of the ancient Temple as well as that of the modern synagogue.

Benjamin provides another example of the formal interplay between adjacent windows. *Benjamin* is adjacent and at right angels to *Reuben*, and both windows are blue, as was the coloured *Creation* plate on which *Reuben* was based (Fig. 3). This illustration also influenced *Benjamin*, for instance in the motif of the bird flying up out of the tree on the left, or in that of the blue animal facing left above it. Both of these were trans-ferred to the top of the arch above the rose, in a relationship not only dependent on the *Hebraica* source, but recalling the positions of the angels in the *Creation*, who are placed above the sun.[54] The forms and

53 This tree has a purple area in it that takes on the shape of a cup in the window. In the fifth sketch the colour had been amorphous in form. This cup hidden in the tree recalls Joseph's cup hidden in Benjamin's sack of grain (*Gen.* xliv). The two birds sitting in it represent the closeness of the two brothers, Joseph and Benjamin, and repeat the motif of the bird in the tree in Joseph.

54 One window helps to explain the other's details. The dead lamb lying at the

colours of this window also link it with those of *Simeon*, where the
animal and bird at the top of the arch reappear, although in a reversed
relationship. The large rose in *Benjamin* recalls the large orb there,
both having other circles within the large outer one. Chagall's quotation from Jacob's blessing, "In the morning ... and at night", set in
the centre of the rose, also suggests such a connection, implying the sun
and moon of *Simeon's* orb. The last window of the series is thus tied to
the first two windows, and the colouring of these three windows forms
a unique solid blue corner, which automatically leads the eye from *Benjamin* to *Reuben* and *Simeon,* forming an unending series. The set of
windows is thus completed with a window depicting the protection of
Jerusalem, and the rose of its Temple, and one is led to start the whole
series over again with *Reuben* and the *Creation.*

THE SKETCHES

At the beginning of this discussion of the windows, Chagall's working method of five sketches for each window was analyzed. After examining the windows, two problems in this sketch sequence must be
discussed, as they relate not only to Chagall's working methods but to
the way in which the programme of the ensemble was developed.

The first problem concerns the first sketch for each window, and the
Yiddish inscriptions on them. Four of these inscriptions do not seem to
relate to the windows the sketches were made for. The first sketch for
Gad, for instance, is labelled שמעון און (איז ?) זיינע ברידער (Simeon and
(is?) his brother), while the first sketch for *Simeon* reads און האט גערופן
(and called (him?)) and a ד (d) on the left border at this level may be
part of either Gad's or Dan's name. An erased inscription at the bottom right may have been relevant, but it is now completely unclear.
The interpretation of these Yiddish phrases is difficult because they are
often almost indecipherable and are open to various readings. In the
first sketch for *Dan,* for example, the inscription may refer to Issachar's
donkey (ישׁשׂכר איז בייניגער), but the middle letters may as easily be read
as a printed פ ג, the letters appearing on tombstones. In *Asher's* first
sketch, the line is almost surely זבולון וועט וינע ביים, the Yiddish translation of the first line of the blessing of Zebulun. These inscriptions in-

---

base of the window may have suggested the lamb at the base of *Reuben,* while
the fish at the bottom of *Benjamin* (on dry land, while Reuben's lamb is under
water) may derive from the fish at the bottom of *Reuben.* Both the lamb in
Reuben and the fish in *Benjamin* appear only in the fifth sketch, although the
fish is visually suggested by the lines of the ground under the tree in the third
and fourth sketches.

dicate that Chagall remembered the blessings first in Yiddish, rather than in the original Hebrew.

It must be emphasized that little is known of the development of Chagall's ideas for the windows before the "first" sketch. No *pensieros* have been published, and there is no knowledge as to whether Chagall "re-shuffled" the themes he had worked on at the stage of the "first" sketch. This "re-shuffling" seems to be indicated by the "wrong" names that appear on these sketches. This would also fit in with Chagall's claim to have looked up the texts only after doing these sketches. After re-reading the Bible, he seems to have tried to pair off his broader meanings with the blessings, with the tribes' characters, and with an overall programme which will be analyzed below.

The second problem concerns the independent sketches, done while Chagall was working on the windows, but not as part of the supposed sketching process for each window. Leymarie feels that these drawings are merely "an exercise in suppleness",[55] but it has been shown in discussing the windows that they are more important. Some are variations on a single window; others combine motifs from several; still others show related themes not found in the windows at all. Several of the sketches seem to have been made to clarify the artist's ideas as he worked, especially before he executed the finished fifth sketch,[56] while in others he may have been re-inspired by the windows themselves or their sources. The line between these different categories is not always clear. For instance, whereas the delicately nuanced sketch of *Judah* (Lp. 203) appears to be derived from the window, care should be taken in dealing with the variations on the themes of *Joseph* and *Dan* (Lp. 207 and 195), which may be closer to some as yet undiscovered source.

The sketches combining themes from various windows may suggest new meanings. For example, the sketch marked *Zebulun* (Lp. 193) combines the fish and the ships of that window with *Benjamin's* rose and *Issachar's* bird. The rose now has six petals corresponding to the number of points of the Magen David in its centre, which is unclear in the window, and is surrounded by a circle of continuity or eternity — a fish-headed snake biting its tail.

The sketches in which Chagall adds new elements are the most revealing, as they are often clear copies from the source books, e.g. the sketch with the spiked wheel linked with *Gad* (Fig. 19) and the variation on *Issachar* (Lp. 211). Some of the sketches deal wholly with these new

55 Leymarie, p. 185.
56 E.g. *Ibid.*, pp. 199 and 201 (*Gad*), p. 205 (*Naphtali*) and p. 211 (*Issachar*). See discussion above.

elements: the sketch with the initials פ״נ (Fig. 28) derives the letters, the two heraldic birds and the scroll at the left from *Hebraica* (Fig. 31), and the beast at the left from another plate in the same book (Fig. 22). The sketch showing two elongated standing animals holding the Ten Commandments (Lp. 197) derives from *Hebraica*, Pl. XLVI, which shows a tombstone with the initials ה״ה.[57] In only one sketch does Chagall break with the tradition of the windows, mixing groups of people and Moses with the animals and other symbols (Lp. 187).

It is not clear whether this last group of sketches was done before Chagall chose the basic compositions for the windows, or whether they were done independently during or after the work on the windows. The problem as to whether they are mere plays on motifs or have a meaning of their own is outside the scope of this article, where only their influence on the windows and the evidence they can give on Chagall's train of thought have been considered.

THE PROGRAMME OF THE WINDOWS

The ensemble shows planning both in the combination of windows on the flat wall surface, and in the play of colours, shapes and themes across the room. Although no base colour is ever repeated in exactly the same shade, each wall is made up of two similarly coloured windows and a third contrasting one. The four basic colours, blue, red, green and yellow, each dominate one wall and supply the contrast for another. However, one of the windows' basic principles becomes immediately apparent: every rule must have an exception.[58] Blue replaces red as a contrasting window, because the intensity of the latter would dominate a wall even if present in only one window.

While the colours of several windows have thematic value (e.g. Judah's red symbolizes its wine), others were chosen merely to complete the pattern. The two cool walls (composed chiefly of blues and greens) are set opposite each other, as are the warm walls (composed of reds and yellows). The corner windows prepare the eye for the contrasted warmth or coolness of the adjacent wall, for instance Levi's warm yellow leads to *Judah's* red. Similar colours echo diagonally across the room: *Levi's* yellow flashes across to *Naphtali's*, and the blue corner of *Benjamin, Reuben* and *Simeon* is answered by *Dan*.

---

57 These uncommon initials are found in another sketch, Lp. 209.
58 Even in signing the windows, Chagall made one exception: he signed them all in Latin letters, except *Judah*, where his signature is in Hebrew.

Traditional Jewish symbols play a minor role in the windows, but when they are used more than once, they are set in counterpoint on opposite walls. The seven-branched menorah appears in *Asher* and is echoed in the candles in *Levi* (diagonally opposite) and in the three-branched candelabrum in *Dan* (facing *Levi*). The blessing hands motif forms another triangle in space, appearing in *Judah* and *Issachar,* and echoed in the hands of the middle window opposite (*Joseph*). The star of David appears clearly only in *Levi*, but is hinted at on the shield of Gad's crowned bird on the opposite wall. The shofar, jug of oil and the High Priest's breastplate are each seen only once in *Joseph, Asher* and *Levi* respectively. Levi, the priestly tribe, has the greatest number of Jewish symbols in his window. *Judah, Issachar* and *Asher* have two symbols each, while *Gad, Dan* and *Joseph* have only one apiece. The remaining five tribes have no Jewish symbols at all. However, all the windows, except *Gad* and *Joseph,* use some form of the traditional tribal symbols. *Gad's* war-camp tents are replaced by the war itself. *Joseph* is sometimes pictured as a tree, which is present, but his more common bull and unicorn are missing. While each window is labelled with the tribe's name, no Biblical quotation is given in *Zebulun, Naphtali* and *Joseph,* another spatial triangle.

Animals and plants predominate over the Jewish motifs. Animals are present in all except *Zebulun*; birds in all except *Zebulun* and *Judah,* although a tiny bird is etched into *Zebulun's* finished window; and foliage is visible in all the windows. Minor themes are also repeated across the room. Fish appear in one window on each wall: *Reuben, Zebulun, Dan* and *Benjamin. Benjamin's* rose echoes *Reuben's* sun, *Simeon's* orbs and *Gad's* shield. The grazing sheep in *Reuben* and *Issachar* echo those in *Joseph,* another triangle in space. *Simeon, Levi* and *Gad* display winged animals, and *Levi, Gad, Asher* and *Joseph* display crowned birds. There is some human dwelling in all the windows except *Asher* and *Levi*, where their exclusion may denote these windows' closeness to the Temple and holiness, as apart from human affairs.

Each wall has a dominant theme. The first wall shows the creation of life (*Reuben*) separated from Holiness (*Levi*) by evil and an apocalyptic cataclysm preceding the End of Days (*Simeon*). This theme is paralleled on the opposite wall in more material terms. Ultimate Justice (*Dan*) is separated from redemption and peace (*Asher*) by warfare and evil forces, which will be overcome with supernatural aid (*Gad*). On the two remaining walls, the strength of the nation and the protection of Jerusalem (*Judah* and *Benjamin*) are attained through the union of commerce and natural prosperity (*Zebulun* and *Joseph*) with the study of Torah and the heritage from the forefathers (*Issachar* and *Naphtali*). Conversely, prosperity and peaceful study are the results of a strong nation and the protection of Jerusalem.

These parallels are reinforced by similar moods and by objects placed opposite each other. In the first and third walls, the same flying bird with the branch in its beak is shown in *Reuben* and in *Asher,* directly opposite. *Asher's* Tree of Life symbolism with its Messianic connotations fulfills *Reuben's* Creation theme. *Simeon's* dark mystery finds a similar chord in *Gad's* mysterious savagery. In *Gad,* warfare is resolved in the victorious soaring bird, affirming the temporary character of the evil in *Simeon* and its connection with *Joel. Levi* is connected to *Dan* opposite through the motif of candles and lights, and to *Asher,* diagonally across, by the Temple motif. Another diagonal relationship links *Dan* and *Reuben* through the use of the Temptation motif in their sources.[59]

On the other two walls, the protection of Jerusalem by a strong benign animal is portrayed in *Judah* and in *Benjamin,* directly opposite. *Judah's* union of strength and plenty carries across into *Joseph,* where the armed bird protects the fertility around it. Judah's crown with the blessing hands and *Joseph's* crowned bird with the hands holding the shofar suggest the two Messiahs of the houses of David and Joseph. Joseph's motif of abundance and fruitfulness is also seen in *Issachar,* which, however, best parallels *Naphtali* opposite it, with the couchant animal looking back over his shoulder and birds flying above. Each wall is framed with similar motifs: the blessing hands and the couchant animal appear in *Judah* and *Issachar* and the animal-bird relationship is found in *Naphtali* and *Benjamin.* On each wall two of the three windows are connected: Benjamin and Joseph are Rachel's only sons and Zebulun and Issachar are Leah's last two. The Benjamin-Joseph tie is hinted at in the cup hidden in the tree at the lower right in *Benjamin,* and the Zebulun-Issachar inter-relationship is found in both windows (see above).

To sum up, the main themes of the windows are salvation from evil leading to holiness, and the building of a strong nation through an alliance between the spiritual and the material. Chagall expressed Judaism's craving for and faith in salvation through God's triumph over evil — in other words, he portrays its Messianic dreams. But he stresses the material as well as the spiritual means of salvation and national strength, ideas already set forth in the later prophets, who declare that God will save Israel from its enemies on condition that the Israelites

---

59 Even the Yiddish inscriptions on the first sketch affirm this relationship. For instance, Simeon is mentioned in *Gad's* first sketch, and seemingly vice versa.

not only worship Him (spiritual means), but that they must also be just to each other and share their wealth with the poor (secular means).

CHAGALL AND HIS SOURCES

In dealing with the windows, Chagall's sources were stressed, and they must now be examined as a whole. When he was finally commissioned to decorate a synagogue, Chagall turned naturally to the Bible and to the legends and commentaries associated with it, sources he had known since childhood. He also naturally sought for motifs in his own previous contact with the Bible — his illustrations for it.

Chagall is not an Orthodox Jew in the accepted sense of the words. His connections with Judaism have rather been at a national, or one might say, at a nationality or folk level. During his return to Russia (1914–22), he had been connected with the revival of Jewish folk culture and art. His work at the Jewish State Theatre is known. Not so well understood, however, is his contact with the artists who joined him in Vitebsk while he was in charge of its art school. One of them was Lissitzky, who is best known for his connection with the Suprematists which led to his break with Chagall. However in 1917–1919, Lissitzky had been involved in a movement for the rebirth of Jewish folk art, and it was no doubt the Lissitzky of the Jewish movement whom Chagall invited to Vitebsk, an artist who had used Jewish tombstones and ritual object motifs.[60] Chagall was also a close friend and teacher of Yudovin, who published his *Jewish Folk Ornament,* which included tombstones and ritual objects, in Vitebsk in 1920 in Yiddish. With this background, it is highly natural that Chagall, presented with the synagogue commission, would not turn to orthodox Jewish iconography, which would be foreign to him, but rather to his previous connection with Jewish folk art, as exemplified in Yudovin's book or in the later *Hebraica.* However, he did not simply copy, but rather adapted his sources to his own needs and style, putting them together within his own programme and for his own aims.

One of these aims was the creation of something new and original, while remaining within his concept of tradition, corresponding to his attitude towards the State of Israel, which houses the windows. In May 1951, in a letter to Mordechai Narkiss, he stated:

> The young people have taken on their shoulders, and with all their heart, the task of opening a new page of our Jewish life; they sac-

60   As had also Nathan Altman, in B. Aronson, *Sovremannaya Yevreiskaya Grafika,* Berlin, 1924, p. 40, based on the tombstone illustrated in Yudovin and Malkin, Pl. 1.

rificed themselves to break the chains of the ghetto and to lead us to
new Biblical horizons, to a new country and a new heroism. To appear before their eyes is a great responsibility and a great honour.[61]

It is this new page, based on tradition, that he expresses in the windows.

Chagall's themes and ideas are hard to understand at first glance,
and the spectator's enjoyment of the windows is often subjective and
purely formal. But a familiarity with Jewish art and traditions will en-
able the spectator to penetrate more deeply into the work, and to understand its inner meaning and the basic programme of the whole. This is
the strength of Chagall's work as a whole and of the Jerusalem windows
in particular.

61 M. Narkiss, *Chagall, Oeuvres, 1908–51*, Association of Israel Museums, 1951,
    p. 4.

SOME ASPECTS OF THE RELATIONSHIP
OF ARCHITECTURE, PAINTING AND SCULPTURE
IN THE TWENTIETH CENTURY

Abraham Kampf

The great amount of building activity going on today makes it urgently necessary to reconcile the dominant functional approach of modern architecture with an expression of the inner purpose of the building; there is now an increasing desire to humanize the shapes and products of the contemporary style. The question of the relation of architecture and art has thus become prominent, and has acquired practical importance.

The place of the work of art in modern architecture has in the last decade become the subject of frequent debate, controversy and philosophical discourse. It is the intention of this paper to state the major outlines of the problem, to trace its historical roots and to examine the suggested solutions.

The difficulties which present themselves today in any attempt to bring about a collaboration between the architect and the artist tend to make us forget that the years following World War I witnessed an intensely close collaboration between painting, sculpture, and architecture. It was then that certain tendencies of cubist and futurist painters and sculptors and the work of artists grouped around *de Stijl* coincided, influenced and mingled with tendencies of the modern architectural movement. The formula of the plain vertical wall and the flat roof, free of decorative elements, derived from Berlage and Loos, coincided with Mondrian's equally simple formula of rectangular patches of colour framed in horizontal and vertical line and free from figurative elements.

At that time, Hitchcock notes, "many young architects also developed close personal associations with painters and sculptors of their own generation, often coming to accept rather completely their increasingly rigid abstract doctrine as a new gospel for all the arts. At the fringes of advanced experimentation, architecture, painting and sculpture came very close — doubtless too close — together in those years".[1] On the

---

1 Hitchcock, Henry Russell, *Painting toward Architecture,* Duell, Sloan, and Pearce, 1948, p. 23.

surface and in retrospect it seems that these were indeed golden years of common collaboration and work. Masters of architecture were either themselves engaged in painting or surrounded themselves with artists and fully collaborated with them. Le Corbusier was then also an active painter, a cubist who published together with the purist painter Ozenfant the influential magazine *L'Esprit Nouveau*. Oud in Holland collaborated with Van Doesburg and with Mondrian on the magazine *de Stijl*. Both magazines championed the cause of modern architecture and modern art. Collaboration was especially strong in the literary and theoretical field although not confined to it. Van Doesburg did designs of tiled floors and stained glass windows for Oud's houses, and Oud himself designed the Café Unie in Rotterdam in the style of Mondrian. Van Eesteren sometimes collaborated with the isometric colour constructions of Doesburg, and Rietveld built a house in Utrecht which seems to translate the compositions of Doesburg directly into architecture. A similar relation can be observed between some of Dudok's buildings and the abstract sculpture of Vantongerloo. The various futurist manifestoes were the result of intense discussion and collaboration among painters, sculptors and architects.[2] We know of the close collaboration of Kandinsky, Feininger and Klee with Gropius and Mies van der Rohe in the Bauhaus in the twenties. These painters, who were not of a geometric persuasion, worked together with the creators of the International Style who themselves stood at the centre of the contemporary art movement. Perhaps these alliances were not all as firm as they seem. There were some serious disagreements and reservations in the *de Stijl* group which had nothing to do with personal causes. "Over the early deliberations of the members broods the spectre of Berlage's version of *Gesamtkunstwerk*, in which painting and sculpture were to be subservient to architecture",[3] and it took some skilful manoeuvering and compromising to find a formula which would allay the fears of the painters. It was the style of painting of the cubists and its various abstract derivations which articulated the new aesthetic premises of the modern architectural movement. On the small scale of painting one could experiment with new forms, with new shapes, with a new equilibrium, with new designs. The new paintings conditioned the public to accept the principles of the new architecture. The first clients of the architects came from the circles of people who were eagerly following the development of modern art.

2 Carrieri, Raffaele, *Futurism*, Milano, 1963, p. 149.
3 Banham, R., *Theory and Design in the First Machine Age*, London, The Architectural Press, 2nd ed., 1960, p. 149.

Thus among the first works of Le Corbusier we find houses for the painter Ozenfant and the sculptors Miestchanninoff and Lipchitz. Indeed, one might say that the aesthetic features of the new architecture first appeared on the canvases of painters.

Yet in retrospect this collaboration seems to have been only an interlude, an accident of history, a confluence of historical forces. With impressionism, painting had travelled to the logical conclusion of its naturalistic tendencies; new developments in materials and engineering accelerated the search for a new aesthetically appropriate expression in architecture and presented to both fields the need for an analysis of their elements. Within a climate of analysis, of rebellion, charged with promises of a bright though yet undisclosed future, a temporary mutuality was affected. Great things were in the air : "A new epoch has begun ! There exists a new spirit !" Le Corbusier assured his readers in his significant book of 1923, *Vers une architecture*. And in the surge of initial enthusiasm, the founders of the Bauhaus had proclaimed four years previously :

"Together let us conceive and create the new building of the future, which will embrace architecture *and* sculpture *and* painting in one unity and which will rise one day toward heaven from the hands of a million workers ilke the crystal symbol of a new faith." [4]

One could quote many more ringing proclamations announcing a new dawn. Yet Victor Hugo's remark about the Renaissance having been a sunset which all Europe took for a dawn was surely true and applicable as far as the relation of sculptors and painters to the new architecture was concerned. As the new mode of building spread and the modern manner conquered a place for itself within the architectural schools and itself became the establishment, cooperation between architect and artists dwindled and eventually ceased. The gulf between the arts became wider than ever.

As efficiency, rationality, economy and order became the hallmarks of the new architecture, as structural logic and structural clarity became the controlling values of its design, as the new materials, concrete, large expanses of glass, the steel skeleton, the curtain wall and the careful balancing of masses became the major elements of its aesthetic programme, and "form follows function" its battle cry — what place was

4   Bayer, H., W. Gropius, I. Gropius, From the first Proclamation of the Weimar Bauhaus in 1919, *Bauhaus, 1919–1928,* MoMA, N.Y. 1938, p. 18.

left for the artist? The new buildings were devoid of all decorative elements. Those who never understood what Sullivan meant when he
proclaimed "form follows function", or disregarded the lesson of the
master's work, ignored his goals and redoubled their efforts. The building was now conveniently considered as a self-contained work of art in
no need of any logically arising further embellishment. The exterior was
supposedly the logical result of the interior arrangement. The development of abstract art had conditioned architects to conceive of their
work as autonomous units, compositions of volume, surfaces, textures,
line, colour and rhythm, exhibiting a strong affinity with certain abstract
tendencies of modern painting and eschewing any artistic addition. The
historian of the modern architectural movement puts it thus:

"The paintings of Mondrian and Nicholson, the sculptures of Domela or
Gabo, are for the architects exercises in pure form, the principle of
which they hope to apply on a large scale and in terms of real space in the
buildings they build. Their devotion to these arts, in other words, is in
the aesthetic field somewhat like the devotion of technicians in science
to the work of pure mathematicians and theoretical physicists." [5]

The theory which asserted function to be the one, timeless and per-
manent feature of architecture, and made it its overriding premise, contained within itself, if narrowly interpreted, the negation of a relationship between architecture and the other arts. Thus Eric Gill could write
in 1933:

"The sculptor is no longer one of the people the architect calls in. The
only sculptor employed in the building is the architect himself. The
building as a whole is a work of sculpture, and any detail or part is in
itself a piece of sculpture. The steel frame work is precisely the ar-
mature, the stone of concrete is the modelled body." [6]

The notions expressed by Gill and Hitchcock did not exist in isolation;
rather, they were representative of the *Zeitgeist*. The attitudes of self-
sufficiency and austerity were not only conditioned by the aftermath of
World War I and a reaction against adding to buildings ornamentation that had become meaningless in the period preceding the advent

---

5 Hitchcock, *The Place of Painting and Sculpture in Relation to Modern Architecture*, Architects Yearbook, V. 2, London, 1947.
6 Gill, Eric, *Beauty Looks after Herself*, N.Y., 1933, p. 77.

of modern architecture. Nor was it only a matter of new materials, new modes of construction or plain good economy, although the contribution of all these factors ought not to be underestimated. The roots of this attitude are to be found mainly in the new environment of science, in the idea that architecture expresses its time and culture, in the belief in mechanical progress and the adoption of its most advanced products — the machine, the steamship, the airplane and the grain silo — as the outstanding symbols of contemporary civilization and therefore as valid and suitable aesthetic models. As long ago as 1901, F. L. Wright had stated in his famous Hull House address to the Chicago Arts and Crafts Society: "... invincible, triumphant, the machine goes on, gathering force and knitting the material necessities of mankind ever closer into a universal automatic fabric; the engine, the motor, and the battleship, the works of art of the century!" [7]

The problem of the naked wall — totally inconceivable to Ruskin, who had equated architecture with ornament [8] — arises as a consequence of the simplifying power of the machine and the theories of design elaborated in relation to that aspect of it. Sullivan had already toyed with the idea of the abolition of ornament; to be more precise, he intimated that it would be a good thing to drop ornament for a number of years:

"Ornament is mentally a luvury, not a necessity. . . . it would be greatly for our aesthetic good, if we should refrain entirely from the use of ornament for a period of a few years, in order that our thoughts may concentrate acutely upon the production of buildings well formed and comely in the nude." [9]

Yet we know from the work of the master that he laboured tirelessly to create a new kind of ornament, to rejuvenate the concept and to bring it up to date. The remark quoted above was meant as a purgative measure so that "the remains of ornamental detail of previous ages persisting in our architecture might be completely eliminated", [10] as Morrison aptly put it.

7 Wright, Frank, L., *Writings and Buildings,* selected by E. Kaufman and Ben Raeburn, Horizon Press, 1960, p. 59.
8 Ruskin, The Seven Lamps of Architecture, Ch. 1, § 1, Noonday Press, Paperback p. 16.
9 Sullivan, L., *Kindergarden Chats,* N.Y. 1947, p. 187.
10 Morrison, *Louis Sullivan,* MoMA, 1935, p. 254.

"Function", as Sullivan conceived it, included not only the physiological but also the intellectual, emotional and spiritual functions of the
building. Function grows naturally and organically out of the social
and technical factors among which the architect lives and it embraces
the utilitarian problems of the building as well as the aspirations, ideas
and needs of human beings. Architecture so conceived means "the hu-
manization through aesthetic statements of the non-human facts of industrial techniques".[11] Architecture was for Sullivan a compound of
subjective and objective factors, cultural and structural, spiritual and
physiological. At the higher level of building it was necessary "to animate buildings with a subjective significance and value, to make them
visible parts of the social fabric, to infuse into them the true life of the
people, to impart to them the best that is in the people, just as the eye
of the poet, looking below the surface of life, sees the very best that is
in the people".[12] These ideas foundered on the rock of a social structure
Sullivan did not perhaps understand.[13] Those days of the birth of the
sky scraper were already showing ominous signs of the advent of an
aesthetic of the naked building, erected upon the basis of economic self-
interest, and rationalized. In her biography Harriet Monroe records the
following about the building of the Great Northern Hotel in Chicago
in 1891 :

"For this building Mr. [Dwen] Aldis, who controlled the investment,
kept urging upon his architects extreme simplicity, rejecting one or two
of Root's sketches as too ornate. During Root's absence of a fortnight at
the seashore, Mr. Burnham ordered from one of the draftsmen a design
of a straight-up-and-down, uncompromising, unornamented façade.
When Root returned, he was indignant at first over this project of a
brick box. Gradually, however, he threw himself into the spirit of the
thing, and one day he told Mr. Aldis that the heavy sloping lines of an
Egyptian pyramid had gotten into his mind as the basis of this design,
and that he thought that he would "throw the thing up without a single
ornament". At last, with a gesture whose pretence of disgust concealed
a shy experimental interest, he threw on the drawing table of Mr. Dut-
ton, then foreman of the office, "a design", says this gentleman, "shaped
something like a capital I — a perfectly plain building curving out-

11   Condit, Carl, *The Rise of the Skyscarper,* Chicago, U. Press, 1952, p. 45.
12   Sullivan, Louis, *Kindergarden Chats, op. cit.,* p. 194.
13   J. M. Fitch in *American Building, the Forces that shape it,* Boston, 1948,
       points to the role of eastern capital in the choice of the Classical Style for the
       Chicago Exhibit., p. 124.

ward at the base and cornice". This was the germ of the final design, and it provoked much discussion and study in the office." [14]

The cynic could make a case for the view that the concept of the naked wall was born in the smoke-filled room of the greedy real estate developer, yet the idea continues to arise with increasing frequency. In 1889 Crane asserts that "plain materials and surfaces are infinitely preferable to inorganic or inappropriate ornament",[15] and Voysey speaks about "discarding the mass of useless ornaments".[16] Berlage visualised in 1895 the architecture of the coming twentieth century, which was to be the century of Socialism, as an art of pure utility. The importance of Berlage cannot be overrated, since he transmitted to *de Stijl* Groot's idea of Vormharmonie, the experience of the Chicago school and specifically of F. L. Wright, and, through his association with Manfred Semper and his teacher Cuipers, the concepts of Gottfried Semper and Viollet-le-Duc.

"Above all we should show the naked wall in all its sleek beauty ... pillars and columns should have no projecting capitals: The joints should be fused with the flat surface of the wall." [17]

Indeed, the outstanding feature of his most famous building, the Amsterdam Stock Exchange, is the treatment of the walls. The brick is allowed to speak for itself; neither inside nor outside is it covered with stucco. All elements have been fused into the flat surface. Neither tower, nor window, nor capital are allowed to protrude from the wall, but are all level with it.

"The art of the architect consists in the creation of spaces and not of façades. Spaces are terminated by walls and therefore manifest themselves externally as a complex of constructed walls ... The essence of the wall is its flatness, articulated too much it loses its character ... its architecture consists of the decoration of its plane...Protruding elements must be limited to architectural parts, conditioned by construction, such as mullions, window posts, gargoyles, drains and single moldings, etc. From this "Architecture of the Wall" which by itself eliminates any vertical articulation, it therefore follows that eventual supports such as

14   *Condit, op. cit.,* p. 101.
15   Pevsner, N., *Pioneers of Modern Design,* New York, MoMA, 1949, p. 13.
16   *Ibid.*
17   Gideon, S., *Space, Time and Architecture,* Harvard University Press, 1959, p. 234.

piers and columns do not receive projecting capitals and that their
various transitions evolve within the plane of the wall. The decoration
of the surface consists of the windows which are installed wherever necessary in their specific different sizes." [18]

Yet Berlage was not ready to dismiss the work of painters or sculptors from his architecture. While he insisted on the primacy of the wall,
he was very well aware of the capacity of art to animate and enrich the
envelopes of his spaces. Projecting the idea of a wholesome unified collective culture into the twentieth century, he became a pioneer of the
Gesamtkunstwerk ideology. If architects were unable to realize such an
idea because they could not find collaborating artists, they should themselves design all they needed, until such time as unity between the arts
would again be achieved. This conclusion Berlage arrived at from his
experience with the building of the Amsterdam Stock Exchange, where
he apparently ran into some difficulties with the artists he employed.
Whatever ornament he had planned in the Stock Exchange was firmly
integrated into the building and, to achieve a unified style, designed according to a preconceived system of geometric proportions. Thus all ornament such as the designs of the various trade products, tobacco, grapes,
rice, etc., was carved on to the pillars and stylized according to a *Füh-
rungslinie,* a guiding line.

He went even further:
"There are in the building also sculptures and frescoes which were
partially planned according to the same system. Partially, because in today's situation one cannot win over all the artists for this point of view,
since most of them have declared themselves for "free art" and in actu-
ality consider a predetermined *Linienführung* as a trap. But are not
painting and sculpture also ornament? And should this ornament not
also be stylized, in accordance with the same laws which govern the architecture? This, indeed, does not mean depreciation, but a mutual ap-
preciation; yet easel painting, which means "free art", looks upon architecture condescendingly." [19]

And here he touches upon a point which he felt to be one of the principal causes of the poor artistic results which were generally obtained in
modern architectural endeavours.

18 Berlage, H. P., *Grundlagen und Entwicklung der Architektur,* Berlin, 1908,
    p. 69.
19 *Ibid.,* p. 63.

For him it is an axiom that sculpture and painting must support architecture; but what happens in the process of execution? As long as one practised so-called historical style architecture, one could easily find artists who worked in the spirit of the architect; but in modern architecture, since there was no precedent and no tradition, there were no shared expectations and no consent among the parties about the nature of the work.

"The modern architect therefore finds himself in the unpleasant situation of either designing the sculpture and painting himself (regardless of whether he is capable of doing this), in which case he is in a certain sense condemning the artists to forced labour and therefore cannot get their best work, or he abstains from doing so, which would be most welcome to the artist. But under present circumstances the architect can be certain that his architecture will not achieve a unified whole, since the chances are that sculptors and painters will not work in his spirit. The fault is not with the artists but with the art conceptions of an age which has not yet matured." [20]

Berlage is quite convinced that in the architectural style of the future there will be no place for the free "drawing room" sculpture or the easel painting.

How is it, he asks, that most modern murals project in an appalling way from the wall? That neither their colour nor their composition are satisfactory? How is it that they fall out of the wall? He finds that they are always treated like easel paintings, that their composition does not take into consideration the strict lines of architecture and therefore always produces an effect of restlessness. Mural painters, because of their deficient training in the academies, he suggests, are too concerned in their minds with easel painting, and are not able to paint with reference to a fixed space.

The mural painters have not freed themselves from their centuries-old tradition and in spite of the fact that they enclose their paintings in ornamented "frames" (ornament *Umrahmung*) their works remain easel paintings and do not become murals in an architectonic sense. They lack restful forms and a proper harmony of colour. A similar situation, Berlage finds, exists with regard to sculpture. He is very definite about what he means by architectural sculpture, and discovers discrepancy between architecture and sculpture when it comes to performance. The sculptors

20   *Ibid.,* p. 64.

also possess picturesque tendencies from which they are unwilling to free themselves and they are not concerned with adapting to the strict lines of architecture. They rarely know how to work according to scale, and their work is therefore often totally inappropriate to the building, according to Berlage who here echoes older complaints such as those voiced by Viollet-le-Duc two generations before and which one finds even as far back as Vitruvius.[21]

21 Viollet-le-Duc in his discourses on architecture gives us in Lecture 16, "Monumental Sculpture", a most comprehensive account of the problems the architect faces in his collaboration with artists, and of the relation of sculpture to architecture. He sees architecture as always having been a complex and most difficult task, a combination of various arts, demanding a mode of co-ordination which can be mastered only by one presiding intelligence. For him the prime example of integration is Egyptian art.

"Their monuments exhibit a stamp of unity so complete that architecture of any other order, even the most perfect of its kind, seems to want cohesion when compared with that of Egypt." There, he finds painting and sculpture participating intimately in the forms of architecture. There, the arts moved within a certain narrow limit which they were not allowed to transgress. "No man of genius could disturb by his invention the harmony established between the arts in the Egyptian building. Accordingly one cannot say exactly where one of the arts ends and the other starts. They are all subject to a rigorous archaic control."

In what way this unity has been achieved Viollet-le-Duc cannot say.

When we consider how matters are managed, in our own day still more then formerly — when a building has to be erected, one wonders that there is not still more confusion than there actually prevails in the heaps of objects of all kinds which are complimented with the title of public edifices. Sculpture which once bore a sisterly relation to architecture, tends to become more and more estranged from it, and sometimes even hostile to it; it insists on choosing its own place as it would in an exhibition of a museum. What it desires is to be seen and there may be nothing in its neighborhood to distract the spectator. And not only does this sculptor wish to be conspicuous of himself, but he wishes to throw into the shade another who is engaged in a theme side by side with his own. A very desirable competition this, if they were producing works destined to be displayed in a public exhibition, but disastrous when occuring in works intended to compose a united whole.

The problem is a old as the wish for fame and immortality for which artists have striven and often competed. Viollet-Le-Duc does not question the equality of the arts of sculpture and architecture, and he foresees clearly their divorce: ... "It must be acknowledged that ... it has become more and more at variance with its sister art of architecture so that we regard the time as not distant when they must part company." (*Discourses on Architecture,* Grove Press, 1959, V. 2, Ch. 16.)

Vitruvius voices this complaint:

We now have fresco paintings of monstrosities, rather than truthful re-

Similar views about the commanding position of the architect in the creation of buildings and in relation to the art work were expressed by Otto Wagner, Professor at the Architectural Academy of Vienna and a leader of the Viennese Secession:

"To the domain of composition belongs also the strategy of the buildings art. By this is meant the proper collaboration with the sister arts, sculpture and painting. The architect may never in such an event relinquish his commanding baton. Whether he deals with external or internal ornamentation of his work, or with sculptures which adorn his gardens, streets or squares, the architect alone has the right to assume the lead-

presentations of definite things ... Such things do not exist and cannot exist and never have existed. Hence, it is the new taste that has caused bad judges of poor art to prevail over true artistic excellence. For how is it possible that a reed should really support a roof, or a candelabrum a pediment with its ornaments, or that such a slender, flexible thing as a stalk should support a figure perched upon it, or that roots and stalks should produce now flowers and now half length figures? Yet when people see these frauds, they find no fault with them but on the contrary are delighted, and do not care whether any of them can exist or not. Their understanding is darkened by decadent principles, so that it is not capable of giving its approval authoritatively and on the principle of propriety to that which really can exist. The fact is that pictures which are unlike reality ought not to be approved, and even if they are technically fine, this is no reason why they should offhand be judged to be correct, if their subject is lacking in the principles of reality carried out with no violations. ... Would to God that Licymnius could come to life again and reform the present condition of folly and mistaken practices in fresco painting! However it may not be out of place to explain why this false method prevails over the truth. The fact is that the artistic excellence which the ancients endeavoured to attain by working hard and taking pains, is now attempted by the use of colours and the brave show which they make, and expenditure by the employer prevents people from missing the artistic refinements that once lent authority to works.

For example, which of the ancients can be found to have used vermillion otherwise than sparingly, like a drug? But today whole walls are commonly covered with it everywhere. Then too, there is malachite green, purple and Armenian blue. When these colours are laid on, they represent a brilliant appearance to the eye even although they are inartistically applied, and as they are costly, they are made exceptions in contracts, to be furnished by the employer not by the contractor.

Vitruvius, *The Ten Books on Architecture*, Bk. 7, New York, Dover 1960, Ch. V, pp. 211–213.

ing role since everything must be subordinated to the basic conception which the architect has created." [22]

Evidently Wagner does not deny the place of the artist in the architectural design, but with his conception as a whole he sows the seeds of future austerity. He turns Ruskin's premises upside down by proclaiming: *"Etwas unpracktisches kann nicht schoen sein"*. With him the accent is on contemporaneity. The successful architect is the one who correctly assesses the actual needs of mankind. Styles evolve gradually from earlier styles as new materials, new methods of construction, new tasks and points of view demand a change in existing forms. The function of architecture is always the same: to create forms corresponding to a way of life. This is an unchallengeable assumption.

"All modern work, if it is to be fitting for mankind, must correspond to the new materials and to the demands of the present, must mirror our own better self, our democratic consciousness, the sharpness of our thought, our colossal technical and scientific achievements as well as the pervasive practical character of mankind — this is to be taken for granted!" [23]

He stresses again and again the utilitarian nature of modern times. It is something one has to accept regardless of one's personal inclinations.

"A certain practical element with which mankind is saturated today cannot be wished away, and every architect must finally accept the dictum: "Something impractical cannot be beautiful" . . . The simple, practical, — one is almost inclined to say military — in our mode of perception must come to full expression in the created work if it is to be a true mirror of our times." [24]

If the practical is the essence of modern times, and if the function of architecture is to reflect modern times, how long will it be before someone raises the question which has become familiar and common-sensical: How practical is it to have works of art, or ornament, on a building? Especially if it becomes apparent that the inclusion of works of art, taken for granted by Berlage and Wagner, not only in-

22 O. Wagner, *Die Baukunst unserer Zeit*. Vienna, 1895, p. 47.
23 *Ibid.*, p. 43.
24 *Ibid.*, p. 44.

creases the cost but also complicates the building process to such a degree that it indeed becomes very "impractical"? It should be said here that the plain interior of Wagner's Viennese Postal Savings Bank of 1904–1906, was an indication of things to come.[25]

With the art of building becoming, since the beginning of the century, increasingly mechanized and complex, with new materials and methods continually consuming more of the architect's time and attention, was it not convenient and logical to solve the problem by discarding the art work as unessential and unpractical, especially when the theoretical foundation sanctioning the solution of the naked wall was being laid by Loos, Muthesius, and *de Stijl*? In the name of practicality, economic survival, civilization and modernity, the cause of the naked wall was carried into the second and third decade of the twentieth century by the powerful logic and prominent public position of Muthesius, founder of the German *Werkbund,* by the literary gift and biting wit of the Viennese journalist and architect, Adolf Loos, and by the missionary zeal of futurist manifestoes and propaganda.

Loos equated ornament with crime, with the tatooing of Papuans, with the daubing of the savage and the scribbling of children on nursery walls. What is natural to uncivilized people is a crime to civilized man: "I have therefore evolved the following maxim, and pronounce it to the world: the evolution of culture marches with the elimination of ornament from useful objects." [26] His attack on *Art Nouveau* art and architecture was as savage as his buildings were plain and unadorned manifestoes of his artistic credo.

25 Reasons of economy alone would have sufficed to end the short interlude of *Art Nouveau* Architecture with its flair for the decorative.

Art Nouveau architects had to design each element from a stanchion to a door-frame — not to speak of all the furniture and accessories — every time they undertook a new commission. Standardization would have been contrary to the organic ideal of their aesthetic, and a mode that considered the smallest elements of domestic furnishings — silverware, glassware, pottery — capable of highly expressive treatment could hardly consent to deprive larger architectural elements of equal invention in design and equal perfection in execution. Most architects evidently grew rapidly tired of a method of design so inapplicable to much of the actual building they were required to do ... In looking at Art Nouveau architecture it is well to consider the enormous difficulties that its integral production entailed.

H. R. Hitchcock in *Art Nouveau,* ed. P. Selz, New York p. 147.

26 A. Loos, *Ornament und Verbrechen* (1908), in *Sämtliche Schriften* (Wien-München 1962), p. 277.

Muthesius was more interested in political economy than in design and it is perhaps for this reason that his name has fallen into relative obscurity. Yet he is one of those powerful figures who stand behind the foundation of the German *Werkbund,* with its clear programme of modernization of design, and perhaps also behind the tendency of large German industrial organizations to employ independent artists to supervise design and act as consultants for their products. (Thus AEG hired Peter Behrens and the *Stahlwerksverband* employed Bruno Taut in the same year, 1907, when the Werkbund was organized.) Muthesius was attached to the German Embassy in London at the turn of the century, and studied English design and specifically English architecture. Upon his return to Germany he succeeded in making "design", instead of quality, a national issue. Good design assured the margin of survival for German industrial products in the fierce competitive battle with other nations for export markets.

"As a Prussian civil servant who regarded himself as an instrument in the furtherance of German economic policy, he naturally stood for order and discipline, and not for the Bohemian individualism and aestheticism of the loosely organized German *Kunstgewerbe* craftsmen and designers." [27]

To an audience which included the future leaders of architecture, he advocated the necessity of establishing standards for a unified style that would be based on a recognition of the essential features of the rationalized corporate society arising from the changes wrought by the machine. [28]

" ... the re-establishment of an architectonic culture is a basic condition of all the arts ... It is a question of bringing back into our way of life that order and discipline of which good Form is the outward manifestation. In modern social and economic organization there is a sharp tendency to conformity under dominant viewpoints, a strict uniformity of individual elements, a depreciation of the inessential in favour of immediate essentials. And these social and economic tendencies have a

27 R. Banham, *Theory and Design*, p. 69.
28 At the *Werkbund's* Congress in 1911 Muthesius delivered the main address before an audience which included among others Mies Van der Rohe, Bruno Taut, Walter Gropius and Le Corbusier who was then working in Germany. Banham, *Theory and Design*, p. 72.

spiritual affinity with the formal tendencies of our aesthetic movement." [29]

It was the mission and vocation of Germany, which enjoyed a reputation for the most strict and exact organization in business, industry and the military sphere, to restore to the world and our age the lost benefits of an architectonic culture. The model for this design, based on rationality, was the work of the engineer.

"One cannot argue that we are not dealing here with art at all, since the structures of the engineer serve bare needs alone and do not display any artistic forms. One treads on dangerous ground when one assumes that the artistic side of a building is to be sought in the superfluous, the non-essential ... Why should machine parts with their eloquent, static, and expressive forms speak only an artistically mute language?" [30]

The work of the engineer could not be measured by the aesthetic values of the past. New acts create new aesthetic laws and judgement must follow creation, not precede it. And using a bit of Pavlovian psychology he maintained that first likes or dislikes are not decisive since the experiencing of beauty is conditioned by habit.

"Do we not experience even today a sense of the beautiful in the face of a bold soaring iron bridge, a steamer or the unending complexity of a machine? Our consciousness of the beautiful has already to a certain degree adapted itself to them." [31]

However, not only the machine was responsible, but as has been pointed out earlier, the major social forces, the whole culture and civilization were moving toward the plain, simple and unadorned. As the aristocracy gave way to the middle class, so its complex etiquette gave way to the latter's plain practicality. We can clearly see these manifestations in the suits men wear; in their plainness and practicality they echo the image of the engineer's creations. Household furnishings were turning more and more toward *"dem Zweckmässigen, Sachlichen, Sinngemässen"*. Architecture had finally to be affected by these developments.

---

29 Muthesius, as quoted by Banham, *op. cit.*, p. 76.
30 H. Muthesius, *Kunstgewerbe und Architektur* (Jena 1907), p. 32.
31 *Ibid.*, p. 32.

"In the struggle against the unessential ornament, against the superfluous phrase, architecture joins in the articulation of the essential form purposes of our age. One can describe these purposes most clearly in the words which Hamlet's mother directs against the phrase-making Polonius, words which contain in a nutshell the essence of the program of modern tectonic art: More matter with less art." [32]

A decade later the Futurists give us a view from "inside" the man for whom all these new forms have been created, who is himself a product of a new environment and whose sensibilities have been thus affected:

"We have lost the sense of the monumental, heavy and static and we have enriched our sensibilities with *a taste for the light, the practical, the ephemeral and the swift*. We feel that we are no longer the men of the cathedrals, the palaces and the public squares; we are the men of the large hotels, the railway stations, the large highways, the colossal doorways, the covered markets, the luminous galleries, the straight roads, and salutary slum clearance." [33]

The new environment will have the quality of a machine and is not in need of painting or sculpture:

"We must invent and reconstruct the futurist city as if it were throughout an immense, tumultuous, agile, mobile and dynamic shipyard, and the futurist home must resemble a gigantic machine ... The house of cement, glass and iron, without painting and without sculpture, rich only in the congenital beauty of its lines and its outlines, extraordinarily *ugly* in its mechanical simplicity ... *The Decorative must be Abolished* ... Everything must be revolutionized. The roofs must be exploited, the basements must be utilized, the importance of the façades must be reduced, and the problem of good taste must be transplanted from the realm of the little decoration, the little column and the little doorway to the more ample realm of *the large grouping of Masses* and of the *vast* arrangement of plans ..." [34]

And finally the authors proclaim,

---

32 *Ibid.,* p. 33.
33 The Futurist Manifesto on Architecture, quoted from R. Carrieri, *Futurism.*
34 *Ibid.*

"that decoration as somthing superimposed on architecture is an absurdity and that the decorative value of future architecture depends only on the use and original arrangement of rough or nude violently coloured material." [35]

At any rate, what sense would there be in works of art it future houses and cities were destined to last for a briefer time than the life span of man and each generation would build its own city as the Futurists envisioned?

The theoretical framework for the Bauhaus and the functionalists of the twenties and thirties was long in preparation, and the dogmatic quality which characterized these movements had been carefully nourished. The machine was the new pivotal force stamping its imprint mercilessly on every phase of modern life, affecting modes of perception, feeling, thought and action. From the rational approach of Berlage and the cool logic of Wagner, who recognized as stubborn and irreversible facts the force of the machine, and the resulting practical, impersonal and collective attitudes which appeared increasingly to condition modern architecture, to the biting wit of Loos, the Prussian determination of Muthesius, the passionate, fanatical frenzy of the Futurists, the theosophical speculations of *de Stijl* members and the didactic zeal of the Bauhaus school which eagerly and hopefully embraced its promises of a new age — the dynamic force of the machine elicited a unanimous response which adopted to a varying extent its norms of precision, rationality, reiteration, economy and efficiency as aesthetic models. The logic of events seemed relentless. The architectural trend which emerged under the name "International Style" in the early thirties based its aesthetic principles primarily upon the nature of modern materials and structure, and upon the requirements of planning, and depended on the capacity of the designers to utilize the possibilities inherent in these elements. But what about Beauty? Gropius asked a rhetorical question, to answer immediately:

"The New Architecture throws open its walls like curtains to admit a plentitude of fresh air, daylight and sunshine. Instead of anchoring buildings ponderously into the ground with massive foundations, it poises them lightly, yet firmly, upon the face of the earth; and bodies itself forth, not in stylistic imitation or ornamental frippery, but in those simple and sharply modelled designs in which every part merges na-

35   *Ibid.*

turally into the comprehensive volume of the whole. Thus its aesthetic meets our material and psychological requirements alike." [36]

One could, of course, ask *how* the aesthetics of the new architecture was in fact meeting one's psychological needs. In any case, the architect based himself on the Platonic principles of ideal forms:

"For unless we choose to regard the satisfaction of those conditions which can alone animate, and so humanize, a room – spatial harmony, repose, proportion — as an ideal of some higher order, architecture cannot be limited to the fulfilment of its structural function.
... In the progress of our advance from the vagaries of mere architectural caprice to the dictates of structural logic, we have learned to seek concrete expression of the life of our epoch in clear and crisply simplified forms." [37]

According to Gropius, the architect knew better, and was going to tell others what their real aesthetic and psychological needs were.

When World War II scattered the leading architects of the International Style, the masters continued their struggle for their ideas in the new world without the heavy ideological baggage they once carried. The style was fought for on the grounds of economics and logic. On the American scene Hitchcock and Johnson, perhaps weary of a too dogmatic approach, in their book *The International Style* adapted its aesthetic theories to a pragmatic, affluent and experiment-prone environment, rather indifferent to theory, and carefully planted the notion of an eventual rapprochement of the arts. Recognizing the independent development of each of the arts, they advocated their union in the architectural work on the basis of complement and juxtaposition rather than by integration.

"Besides architecural detail, related subordinate works of sculpture and painting have on occasion been successfully used to decorate contemporary buildings without degenerating into mere applied ornament. Mural painting should not break the wall surface unnecessarily. Yet it should remain an independent entity without the addition of borders or panelling to fuse it with the architecture. . . . there is no reason why

36 W. Gropius, *The New Architecture and the Bauhaus*. London, 1935, pp. 43–44.
37 *Ibid.*, p. 44.

painting less abstract should not find its place quite as satisfactorily on the walls of contemporary buildings. It is most important that mural painting should be intrinsically excellent; otherwise a plain wall is better. It need not be related, except in scale and shape, to the wall on which it is placed. Contemporary architecture cannot expect to dictate the evolution of contemporary painting, but it offers fields more considerable than the framed canvas panel." [38]

Apparently taking a cue from Mies Van der Rohe's design of the Barcelona Pavilion where the architect had placed a statue of Kolbe against the pavilion and created an ambience which enlarged the functional point to its limits, — they write:

"Sculpture also ought not to be combined or merged with architecture. It should retain its own character quite separate from that of its background. This was true of the best Greek sculpture and often of that of other periods. It is particularly important today that sculpture should be isolated: for if it is actually applied, its suggestion of solid mass is carried over to the wall surface it decorates. Thus far contemporary architecture has served rather as an admirable background for wholly separate units of painting and sculpture not designed for their specific location. But there is an opportunity here for collaboration which may well in the future lead to brilliant results." [39]

The architects must have visualized some of the difficulties which the principle of juxtaposition was bound to produce when they state:

"The current style sets a high but not impossible standard for decoration: better none at all unless it be good. The principle is aristocratic rather than puritanical. It aims as much at making monstrosities impossible, at which the nineteenth century so signally failed, as at assuring masterpieces, at which the nineteenth century had no very extraordinary success." [40]

Needless to say, the suggestions of the authors were heeded only in the rarest instances.

38 Hitchcock and Johnson: *The International Style: Architecture since 1922*. New York, 1932, p. 73.
39 *Ibid.,* p. 73.
40 *Ibid.,* p. 75.

In the meantime the new architecture, carried on the wings of the Bauhaus programme and its instructional method, spread — perhaps not so much as a result of conscious aesthetic innovation as through the profit-inspired discard of economic irrelevancies, and the successful assimilation and manipulation of new materials. As long as the buildings of the International Style were novelties and their number in each city few, their symbolic poverty was not felt; the logical and ideological equipment of the style seemed fairly intact, if often not altogether convincing. But as an increasing number of schools turned out young architects with the same meagre baggage and the same limited vocabulary, imbued with the vision of the plain wall and the right angle, ignorant of art past or present,[41] and in many cases even hostile to it,[42] these fresh graduates blighted cities with their all too generous amounts of glass. Little remained of the austere nobility which the style had possessed in the hands of its masters. Whatever subjective symbolic value the machine cult had for its masters became diluted and negligible through the similarity of the appearance of laundromats and supermarkets, apartment houses and neighbourhood banks, high schools, libraries and eating establishments "dazzling Christmas packages that have no relation to content",[43] to use Mumford's phrase. The sensible suggestions of Johnson

41 J. E. Burchard mentions the elimination of architectural history from the curriculum of architectural schools ("Alienated Affections in the Arts", *Daedalus*, Winter 1962), and Damaz writes about the curtailing of the artistic education of the architect. (*Art in European Architecture*, Reinhold, N.Y., p. 22).

42 How pervasive this influence has been can perhaps best be seen from a Forum conducted by the editors of *Magazine of Building* in June, 1951. Twelve architects were asked to comment on the question: Are there new opportunities of integrating sculpture and painting with architecture?" Some of the answers were telling:
Jack Hillmer: "Neither painting nor sculpture has a very important place in our life today ... the best way of 'integrating' sculpture with contemporary architecture is to melt them down and make bronze hardware out of them."
A. Q. Jones: "The question probably should have been ...Do you believe that sculpture and painting will cease to exist? ... Seriously, I believe they will."
Willian McMaster: "Architecture, sculpture and painting are entities within themselves and therefore cannot be integrated."
Breger and Salzman: "Integrate painters with paintings, sculptors with sculpture ... and architects can go on from there."
Quoted from Winston Weisman and Seymour Fogel, "Architecture and Modern Art, *College Art Journal*, Summer, 1952. V. 11, no. 4, p. 241.

43 Mumford, H. J., "The case against Modern Architecture," in the *Highway and the City*, Mentor paperback, p. 181.

and Hitchcock were not followed. The symbolic poverty of the style became glaring indeed.

The reaction came in the early fifties. A quest for the subjective and the symbolic, for humanizing elements, asserted itself. Voices made them-selves heard from architects and critics alike. Nowicki attacks the fetish made of materials when he refers to the attempt to enrich the surface of buildings by industrial processes like ribbing, corrugating, mottling and spotting building elements :

"One might say that this architecture became a decoration of function. The period of functional exactitude looked for its inspiration toward the physical function. The psychological one was not considered in its philosophy. The concept of controlled environment resulted and the main purpose of architecture was to control the physical environment to the physical satisfaction of its user." [44]

Mumford in 1951 pleads for a re-establishment of the balance between objective and subjective elements in our culture and for a repair of the damage caused by the over-emphasis on techniques and the ma-chine. The machine can no more adequately symbolize modern civi-lization than can a Greek temple. New advances in the social sciences, new social purposes, new psychological insights and a new emerging view of man require new architectural forms as much as do new tech-nical functions and facilities. Human symbolical expression in archi-tecture affects the health, comfort and pleasure of the user, as much as the physical elements of the building :

"When the whole personality is taken into account, expression or sym-bolism becomes one of the dominant concerns of architecture; and the more complex the functions to be served, the more varied and subtle will the form be. In other words — and this is the second modification — expression itself is one of the primary functions of architecture." [45]

Mumford's views echo significantly those aspects of Sullivan's teach-ings which have largely gone unheeded. How is the building to be hu-manized? How is subjective expression to be achieved? Can architec-ture achieve the symbolic quality Mumford speaks of without getting

44 Nowicki, *Origins and Trends in Modern Architecture,* Magazine of Art, No-
    vember, 1951.
45 Mumford, H. J., *Art and Technics,* Columbia, paperback edition, 1960, p. 154.

rid of its fear of the arts and without calling in the artist? Does not the obsession of modern architecture with pure geometry, with elements unique to itself and its general distrust of the arts, border on the pathological? There is no doubt that the accepted programme of modern architecture was conditioned by the corruption of the architectural arts during the nineteenth century. This development seems historically logical and necessary, but the ideology of this reaction against nineteenth century eclecticism was expressed and defined almost half a century ago. J. M. Fitch, an influential modern critic, addresses himself bluntly to the question when he writes:

"The question todaw is not whether these pioneers of modern architecture were correct in 1920 — clearly they were — but rather what use we intend to make of their explorations. Here we stand in a kind of frozen, tasteful mimicry. If we consider at random some of our most successful American buildings — Lever House, Manufacturers Trust Company, General Motors Technical Center, the new Campus of the Illinois Institute of Technology — we are confronted with compositions with which the cultivated taste cannot quarrel. But we must recognize that no artistic statement, no matter how abstract or elliptical, mars the perfect geometry of their walls. Signs, street numbers, flagpoles are suppressed, even the curtains and blinds are rigidly standardized. These buildings must constitute, short of the pyramids, the most noncommittal body of architecture in history." [46]

Fitch, who was aware of the social and economic forces which squashed the activities of Sullivan and defeated his ideas during the Chicago exhibition, is perhaps not aware that the very same forces may have nothing to say which is worth saying in public.

The belief in a strictly functionalist theory of architecture was apparently already on the wane in the late forties, when the great protagonists of the twenties and thirties recognized and expressed the need to counteract the mechanizing, standardizing trends of modern life they had once helped to create, and started to advocate, by word and deed, the inclusion of the other arts in architecture.

With the same enthusiasm with which they once announced the arrival of a new dawn with the plain unadorned wall, the same men proclaimed in the late forties the need for works of art on these walls. A

46   Fitch, J. M., *Architecture and the Esthetics of Plenty,* Columbia University
     Press, p. 27.

plain, naked wall now became a dead wall since emotion and art were proclaimed by Le Corbusier to be "as necessary as bread and water".[47] In its meeting at Bridgewater the International Congress of Modern Architects resolved "to work for the creation of a physical environment that will satisfy man's emotional and material needs and stimulate his growth".[48]

Two years later, as the Congress convened again at Bergamo, the Dutch architect, A. Van Eyck, proclaimed that "Functionalism" concerns itself only with elementary requirements which are no more than the necessary preliminaries.[49] Walter Gropius had found out after so many years that the work of art could after all have functions other than the provision of design prototypes for industrial mass production, that it had an importance for the life of man and for architecture which it was impossible to assess in plain economic terms. He declared:

"The belief that the sciences are of a greater importance than the arts has impoverished culture ... A correction of our educational system is needed which should give arts as much weight as the sciences." [50]

Later congresses of C.I.A.M. and U.I.A., the International Union of Architects, affirmed the need for collaboration among architects, painters, and sculptors.

"The inclusion of artists in a building (or group of buildings) should be foreseen and provided for from the moment an estimate is drawn up, just as is done with material needs and technical installations." [51]

Yet deep-seated attitudes change only slowly, especially where an effort is required, and where from an economic point of view it is considered a purely irrational act to let the other arts make their contribution. Belluschi, influential as architect and as dean of a great architectural school, still maintains that architecture can achieve a transcendental quality by emphasis on structure and manipulation of space sequences, rather than by sensuous external elements:

"... the architect tends to regard with impatience and as an intruding

47   Damaz, Paul, *Art in European Architecture*, Reinhold, N.Y., 1956, p. 75.
     I am following here the account of Damaz.
48   *Ibid.*, p. 73.
49   *Ibid.*, p. 75.
50   *Ibid.*, p. 75.
51   *Ibid.*, p. 76.

element any work which tries to speak for itself in a place where every part is meant to be a clear, self-sufficient declaration. This is particularly true when we observe that any statement the modern artist makes is meant to be a unique experiment of his personal world which must be herad on its own terms as his 'own message of discontent'." [52]

Only an architect-artist or two men specially atuned to each other could perform the miracle of integration. Otherwise, Belluschi says,

"We must admit that pure, uncompromising Architecture is not at ease with Art, even if thirsting for it, because Art will seldom add; much more often it will detract from the purity of the architectural idea." [53]

It is interesting that Belluschi nowhere says that the inclusion of art work is not desirable. His reason for the exclusion of art work is practical. There is of course some justification for his views and as we have seen his complaints are not new. Neither is it difficult to understand the artist, who, having struggled for the autonomy of his art, is not willing to collaborate unconditionally.

"To create something ornamental but nothing more "he [the painter] is in effect asked to take leave of himself for a period, to depart from his role, said Ben Shahn to a gathering of architects and artists who met to discuss aspects of collaboration." [54]

It is only natural that when artists and architects meet to examine the question of collaboration they should shift the responsibility on to each other.[55] Talbot Hamlin puts it squarely on all concerned:

"The obvious answer to the need for decorative elements to express purpose is the use of creative sculpture or creative mural decoration through

52   Pietro Belluschi in *Views on Art and Architecture,* a conversation arranged by J. E. Burchard, *Daedalus,* Winter 1960. V. 89 no. 1, p. 69.
53   *Ibid.*
54   From the words of the artist at a symposium in the Museum of Modern Art on *"How to combine Architecture, Painting and Sculpture",* Interior, May, 1951. This author once participated in a building committee with the artist Ben Shahn and an architect who had built a major building for a large institution. The topic of the discussion was a proposed mural for the foyer of a new building which had just been completed. The architect insisted that the mural should be abstract. The artist told the architect "if you want an abstract mural, why don't you do it by yourself, for this you don't need me."
55   A statement by Jimmy Ernst can be considered typical:
     "Almost all of the artists of my acquaintance are uninhibited in the opinion that most architects are deliberate in their apparent contempt for paint-

painting or mosaic, and it is precisely here that practitioners in all three branches of the arts — architects, sculptors, and painters — have been most backward. The architect has seldom known how sculpture and painting can best be integrated into a design, and the sculptor and painter have been generally ignorant of both the responsibilities and the opportunities of true collaboration. As a result, in most cases the sculpture and painting associated with modern buildings have been afterthoughts, placed without due architectural consideration and frequently designed as independent units, with an almost total disregard for basic architectural requirements." [56]

The problem Hamlin points to is all too real for those engaged in an architectural project and for the future relation of architecture and art. What is to be done? The question really is not who is to blame, but how cooperation can be achieved under present circumstances. Yet when Hamlin notes the following principles for successful cooperation one wonders if he has really come to grips with the full dimensions of the problem with which he is concerned. He suggests:

"1. All sculpture and mural decoration should be designed with direct reference to the place it will occupy and to the architecture of the building as a whole.
2. Every work of painting, mosaic or sculpture should have a definite reason for being — both functional and aesthetic — and should be so placed as to emphasize its function.
3. A small number of salient works of painting and sculpture is more effective emotionally than a great number of insignificant works.
4. Every work of painting or sculpture must be well lighted in a manner appropriate to its nature.
5. Every work of painting or sculpture must be so placed — with regard to its distance from the eye, and so on, — that it is visually effective." [57]

ing and sculpture; that architects seem to consider it a sign of professional weakness if their work is in need of artistic addenda; that some of them consider the artist a mere mechanic who is to carry out a visual idea for which the architect could not spare the time of execution."
Views On Art And Architecture, a conversation arranged by Burchard, *Daedalus, op. cit.*, p. 70.
56 Hamlin, T., *Forms and Functions of Twentieth Century Architecture*, Columbia University Press, 1952, Vol. 1, pp. 745-6.
57 *Ibid.*, p. 746.

Hamlin sets out ideal conditions for an integration of the arts, which have probably not been met anywhere in the world today. I must admit that I do not understand the meaning of "functional and aesthetic" in point 2. Is the meaning of function there distinct from that of aesthetic? Or is he thinking of an art form like the caryatid which met both functional and aesthetic requirements? Does he mean the psychological appropriateness of the kind of sculpture or painting to be placed? Would not this then be part of the aesthetic element? Is Hamlin not aware that the problem of integration is mainly human, social, psychological and economic, rather than technical?

On the whole, the question no longer is whether or not it is desirable to introduce the work of art into architecture. As the Symposium in the Museum of Modern Art and the resolutions of C.I.A.M.[58] show, there are few who are not in favour of it. The problem has shifted to how it can and should be done. How can it be accomplished when the work of art adds a great deal to the building costs, when it complicates the building process which is in any case always difficult, when the disaffection and alienation between the arts is real, when there are no commonly shared symbols genuinely believed in and when that which has been done so far in an attempt to re-establish a communion between the arts often looks neither reassuring nor promising? Is it indeed a fact that the conditions under which we are working and living today exclude the possibility of a successful integration, as Oscar Niemeyer, who has worked together with painters and sculptors of the highest calibre, seems to suggest? He deems it a problem which is

"impossible to solve completely at this time because its solution would call for a far more advanced stage of human, cultural and social conditions than now exist . . . In our time, work presents itself to the artist as a special imposition that he is obliged to accept, a circumstance that degrades and corrupts him, compelling him to serve those who command life with the brutal force of discrimination and money. It follows that a synthesis of the arts will not depend on a Maecenas, nor will it be as it is today, a distant and unattainable mirage. It will be a natural consequence of comprehension and friendship." [59]

To Niemeyer the problem is a human rather than a technical one. It is for these and other reasons that Huxtable and Damaz, who have re-

58 See page 37.
59 Niemeyer, Oscar, in the Preface to Damaz's book, *Art in Latin American architecture,* New York, Remhold, 1963, p. 13.

cently dealt with these questions, follow up the suggestions which Hitchcock and Johnson made thirty years ago [60] and advocate communion or apposition or confrontation — the terms are all interchangeable — rather than integration or fusion as a new basis for the relationship between architecture and art, assuring maximum individual freedom both to the artist and to the architect. They see architecture and the arts in the twentieth century as having developed independently of each other and pursuing different directions and autonomous goals. There is no way to negate or reverse these developments. Therefore, art and architecture cannot be fused under present circumstances. They must be brought together by confrontation. Art might be chosen to complement the architecture either by matching or by opposing it:

"Architecture has developed along materialistic and practical lines and is now a product of the mind. Art, on the other hand, remains by its very nature a product of the spirit ... It is difficult to see how art and architecture can be integrated to the point of becoming completely fused unless we are speaking of an art lowered to the level of a mass produced building material or of an irrational architecture transformed into an abstract sculpture ... What we must strive for is a communion of the arts, in order that the dynamic colors of the painter and the plastic forms of the sculptor may become an integral part of the architectural composition while retaining their independent and intrinsic aesthetic values. Art can be a valuable complement to architecture for it can create an extension and an intensification of its emotional appeal. The inter-relation between a piece of sculpture and its architectural setting is apparent even to the least sensitive observer. The successful result of such mutual influence depends not only on the quality of the architecture and the sculpture but also on the way they have been combined and, most of all, on their respective and reciprocal qualities." [61]

Full integration has been achieved only in some works by F. L. Wright and by Le Corbusier, who acted as their own artists and designers, or by Gropius, who excercised complete control and mastery over designers whom he trained himself.

A relationship in which the architect calls in artists to do a mural here and a sculpture there, restricting them as to finishing materials

60   Hitchcock and Johnson, *The International Style*, p. 73.
61   Damaz, *Art in Latin American Architecture, op. cit.*, p. 14. See also A. L. Huxtable, "Art in Architecture", 1959. *Craft Horizons*, Vol. 19, No. 1.

within an already determined architectural environment, most often brings to the surface all the conflicts and tensions latent in such a situation. Painters and sculptors resent subordination. The architect cannot do other than conceive of the building as his.

Those who still believe in a true integration or a synthesis of the arts will see in the approach advocated by Damaz and Huxtable only a stopgap measure, not a true solution. They claim, not without justification, that the principle of confrontation is the plan of a museum rather than a true architectural work. It is clear today that there is no magic formula for a relation between the arts which would satisfy all concerned or which would allow for a maximum freedom co-existing with maximum team work.[62]

Architects, sculptors, and painters all invest in their work not only time and effort but also their quest for fame and immortality. While all agree and ask for collaboration, their combined deliberations prove that they do not necessarily mean the same when they say or profess the same. The problem of collaboration is much more complex than it seems at first sight. The bringing together of first rate artists does not insure integration. Sources of true collaboration dwell in the deep wells of social feelings.

Collaboration, if it is to be accomplished, has to be learned all over again with a broad understanding of new developments in each of the arts. Though collaboration does not necessarily mean a sharing of a common world outlook, it means at least a community of shared ideas. It means knowing the nature of each art, and early consultation when plans are still in the formative stage. On the part of the architect it means a familiarity with contemporary art, sound judgement in the field, and particular knowledge of the work of the artists chosen. It requires from the artist a knowledge of the architect's work and the problems he faces, and an attitude of respect towards the unity of the wall, the architectural functions of different parts of the structure, their scale, texture and space. It needs — and on this everyone seems to agree — a friendly spirit and cooperation from the very inception of the work.

62 Jimmy Ernst seems to be an exception:
    "All talk of finding a level on which to 'integrate' the various arts to make them more 'meaningful' is Utopian. Utopia presupposes mediocrity, conformity, and the prohibition of dreams. The obvious solution to any contemplation over the relationship between art and architecture seems to be no planned solution at all."
    Views on Art and Architecture, a conversation arranged by J. Burchard, *op. cit.,* p. 71.

It needs intricate teamwork, checking and double-checking, full coordination and a presiding intelligence. It needs a larger common purpose, such as rarely exists today and can be brought about under present conditions only in nearly ideal circumstances. Yet the leading architects still offer us visions of a synthesis of the arts, presumably under the leadership of the architects:

". . . it is not enough to call in a number of famous artists and hand them out this or that spot in the building to be filled with a work of art. True collaboration must start from scratch, the members of the group stimulating each other, conceiving the idea in mutual exchange as the builders of the old cathedrals who were living at the site devoting their life to the task. Time was not of the essence. They changed and rebuilt until they were convinced that it was good enough." [63]

One wonders if this is not the same dream Gropius had of the Bauhaus, in the twenties; even the images are the same. Yet apparently all that the architect can offer us under present circumstances is the vision, which life so seldom grants, of another bright dawn. Le Corbusier, who ought to know, takes it for granted that the future of architecture belongs to a mystical union between the arts:

"What modern architecture has accomplished up till now is but trifle and trash . . . I believe that we are entering upon an epoch that is infinitely more serious, in which we have no longer the right to "stick something on something", but in which the pure spirit of renovation will be expressed by organisms possessing an interior mathematics, together with fixed and inalienable places where the work of art will radiate in all its power in exact concordance with the potential forces in the architectural work." [64]

(On is tempted to think that Le Corbusier achieved something of this perfect union among the arts in the Chapel of Ronchamp, with its sculptural force, its inclined walls, its symbolic shape, its expressive fenestration, colourful enamelled doors and painted windows, its control of light, the textured walls, its flowing rhythmic space, its appurten-

---

63 Gropius in *Views on Art and Architecture*, a conversation arranged by J. Burchard, *op. cit.*, p. 72.
64 Le Corbusier, *Architecture and the Arts* in *Daedalus*, The Visual Arts Today, Winter, 1960, v. 89, nr. 1, pp. 47, 49.

ances that grow from the floor like a plant and belong. Needless to say that this structure is unique and significantly the product of an architect who was also a sculptor and painter.)

In their rebellion against the state of the architectural art of the nineteenth century, leading architects, painters and sculptors cooperated for a short time in adapting their design to a new technology and in attempting to establish an aesthetic position in tune with the spirit of modern times. The period of active collaboration and common search was, however, brief. Each of the arts in fact proceeded along its own road, in the examination of its own elements and their purification, while acquiring a firm belief in the autonomy and self-sufficiency of its own area.

In the field of architecture this self-sufficiency has been sharply questioned by many of the leaders in the 'forties and 'fifties, when the symbolic poverty of modern structures became glaring and when their shapes increasingly multiplied and echoed the standardizing processes of modern machine civilization. When the adverse effects and far-reaching consequences of standardization became apparent, a re-examination of their position found architects seeking a union with other arts as a means of balancing the dehumanizing elements of modern life. Yet for the re-introduction of the arts a new basis had to be found. When architects, painters and sculptors confronted each other they did so as equals, claiming the independent value of their work, even while affirming the need and desire to cooperate. Collaboration threatened the very idea of self-sufficiency and autonomy to which each of the arts had aspired and had committed itself. Factors of personal and aesthetic preference, of artistic conviction, of cost, supervision, ultimate responsibility, further complicated the process of cooperation until the principle of confrontation emerged as a natural solution. When the architect is also a sculptor and painter, fusion can be achieved as in the Chapel of Ronchamp. Ootherwise the theoretical commitment of collaboration becomes a vision for the distant future, rather than a blueprint for the present.

ILLUSTRATIONS

M. AVI-YONAH

1. The Beth-She'arim sarcophagus: short side.
2. Leda, Rome (copy of statue by Timotheus).
3. Leda, British Museum (by courtesy of the Trustees).
4. Leda, Venice (Photo Alinari).
5. Leda. Detail of sarcophagus from Caesarea, now Israel Museum (Courtesy Department of Antiquities and Museums).
6. Beth-She'arim sarcophagus, long side: Achilles on Scyrus.
7. Beth-She'arim sarcophagus, long side, detail.
8. Borghese sarcophagus, Louvre, Paris (Cliché des Musées nationaux, France).
9. Beth-She'arim sarcophagus: detail of other long side.

O. KURZ

1. Bronze lion-mask from Beit She'an. Israel Museum, Jerusalem.
2. The Holy Sepulchre. Early Christian ivory relief. British Museum, London.
3. Tomb slab of Eutropos. From the catacomb of SS. Marcellino e Pietro, Rome.
4. Bronze lion-mask. From Lake Nemi. Museo Nazionale, Rome.
5. Ivory diptych of Anastasius. A.D. 515. Bibliothèque Nationale, Paris.
6. Miniature from Rashid ad-Din's History of the World. A.D. 1317. Istanbul.
7. Lorenzo Ghiberti: Lion-mask with ring. Baptistery, Florence.
8. Rembrandt: Portrait of Jan Lutma. Etching.
9. Head of a demon from a tomb door. Chinese, Han period. Szechwan Provincial Museum.
10. Ceramic mask of a dragon. Chinese, T'ang period. Fitzwilliam Museum, Cambridge.
11. Wine container with dragon-mask. From a porcelain dish. Chinese, eighteenth century.

L. SLEPTZOFF

1. "Paradiesgärtlein", Städelsches Kunstinstitut, Francfort s/Main.
2. Stefano de Verona, "Madone au Buisson de Roses", Musée de Castelvecchio, Vérone.
3. Reliquaire, SS. Giovanni et Paolo, Venise.
4. "Le Bain de Bethsabée et l'histoire de Suzanne", page d'un Livre d'Heures français exécuté par Pigouchet pour Vostre, 1498. Gravure en cuivre.
5. "La Capture de la Licorne", tapisserie. The Cloisters, Metropolitan Museum, New-York.

6. Jean Colombe, "Le Jardin d'Eden", miniature du Livre d'Heures de Louis de Laval. Bibliothèque Nationale, Paris, Ms lat. 920.

7. Gérard David (attribué à), "Fontaine de Sang", Eglise de la Miséricorde, Porto.

8. Jean Bellegambe, "Fontaine de Sang" (détail). Musée de Lille.

9. "Sources médicinales de Pouzzoles", miniatures de la fin du 14ème siècle, Naples. Coll. particulière.

10. Maître aux Banderoles, "Fontaine de Jouvence", gravure au burin (v. note 46).

11. Hans-Sebald Beham, "Fontaine de Jouvence" (détail), gravure sur bois (v. note 47).

B. NARKISS

1. Cambridge, University Library, T-S. K.5.10, folios 2r and 5v: Leviticus I, 1–2.

2. Cambridge, University Library, T-S. K.5.10, folios 2v and 5r: end of Alphabet and Benediction.

3. Cambridge, University Library, T-S. K.5.1, folios 1v and 4r: dragon carpet-page and Leviticus I, 3–8.

4. Cambridge, University Library, T-S. K.5.1, folios 1r and 4v: geometric carpet-page and Leviticus I, 8–9.

5. Cambridge, University Library, T-S. 16.378, folios 1v and Zr: Title-page, Leviticus I, 10–13, and colophon.

6. Cambridge, University Library, T-S. K.5.13, folios 1r and Zv: Alphabet and Candelabrum.

7. Jerusalem, Jewish National and University Library, MS Heb. 8°2230, folios 33v and 34r: Carpet-page and colophon.

8. Jerusalem, Jewish National and University Library, MS Heb. 8°2230, folios 3v and 4r: beginning of the text.

9. Jerusalem, Jewish National and University Library, MS Heb. 8°2230, folio 3r: Carpet-page.

10. Jerusalem, Jewish National and University Library, MS Heb. 8°2230, folio 18r: closed *Parshiyah* sign.

M. BARASCH

1–4. Eagle, Acre, Municipal Museum.

5. Capital, Jerusalem, El-Aksa.

6. Capital, Jerusalem, Cenaculum.

7. Byzantine Marble Slab, London, British Museum.

8. Eagle, Catania (Sicily), Castel Ursino.

9. Pulpit (detail), ca. 1170, Salerno.

10. Relief with Eagle and Lion, Central Italy, second half of XIIth century, Boston, Museum of Fine Arts.

11. Sonder-Augustalis of Friedrich II, Vienna, Kunsthistorisches Museum.

12. Eagle, Bronze, Private Collection.

13. Eagle, Mosaic, Palermo, Royal Palace, Roger Chamber.

M. LAZAR

1. Hieronymus Bosch. Les Sept Péchés, table peinte, Madrid, Prado.
2. Le Jugement Dernier, détail de fig. 1.
3. Hieronymus Bosch. Le Char de Foin, panneau droit, Madrid, Prado.
4. Hieronymus Bosch. Le Jugement Dernier, panneau droit, Vienne, Akademie der Bildenden Künste.
5. Hieronymus Bosch. Le Jardin des Délices, panneau droit, détail, Madrid, Prado.
6. Hieronymus Bosch. Le Jardin des Délices, panneau droit, détail, Madrid, Prado.
7. Hieronymus Bosch. La Nef des Fols, Paris, Louvre.
8. Hieronymus Bosch. La Tentation de Saint Antoine, panneaux central et gauche, Lisbonne, Museu Nacional.

N. CAHANSKY

1. Urbino, Palazzo Ducale, Grand Courtyard, as it is today.
2. Urbino, Palazzo Ducale, Atrium leading to Grand Courtyard.
3. Urbino, Palazzo Ducale, Cappella del Perdono.
4. Piero della Francesca. Madonna and Child with Saints and Angels adored by Federigo da Montefeltro, Milan, Brera.
5. Perugino. Consignement of the Keys to St. Peter, Rome, Sistine Chapel.
6. Bramante. Milan, Sta Maria Presso S. Satiro, Crossing and Choir.
7. Bramante. Rome, S. Pietro in Montorio, The Tempietto.
8. Raphael. The Marriage of the Virgin, Milan, Brera.

Z. AMISHAI

© Hadassah Medical Relief Association, Inc. 1961

1. Chagall, Reuben.
2. Chagall, Creation (*Verve* 37–38).
3. Chagall, Creation (*Verve* 37–38).
4. Chagall, Simeon.
5. Saul Raskin, *Creation* theme, *Sabbath plate, Siddur Tefiloth Yisrael,* New York, York, 1945, pl. 83.
6. Chagall, Levi.
7. Chagall, Tabernacle (*Verve* 33–34).
8. Menorah (Guttmann, *Hebraica,* pl. XVIII).
9. Chagall, Judah.
10. Tombstone with Keter Kehunah (Yudovin and Malkin, *Jewish Folk Ornament,* pl. 5).
11. Chagall, Future Happiness of Jerusalem (*Verve,* 33–34).
12. Chagall, Zebulun.
13. Chagall, Issachar.

Fig. 1 : The Beth-She'arim sarcophagus : short side.

Fig. 2 : Leda, Rome.   Fig. 3. Leda, British Museum.

Fig. 4: Leda, Venice.

Fig. 5: Leda. Detail of sarcophagus from Caesarea, now Israel Museum.

Fig. 6 : Beth-She'arim sarcophagus, long side : Achilles on Scyrus.

g. 7 : Beth-She'arim sarcophagus, long side, detail.

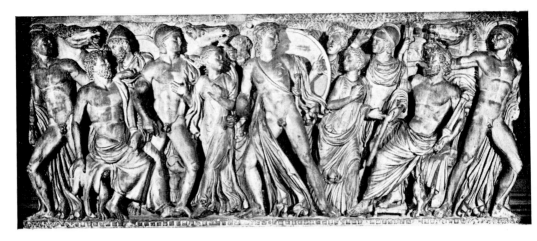

Fig. 8: Borghese sarcophagus, Louvre, Paris.

Fig. 9: Beth-She'arim sarcophagus: detail of other long side.

Fig. 1 : Bronze lion-mask from Beit She'an. Israel Museum,
Jerusalem.

Fig. 3 : Tomb slab of Eutropos. From
the catacomb of SS. Marcellino e
Pietro, Rome.

Fig. 2 : The Holy Sepulchre. Early Christian ivory relief.
British Museum, London.

Fig. 4: Bronze lion-mask. From Lake Nemi. Museo Nazionale, Rome.

Fig. 5: Ivory diptych of Anastasius. A.D. 515. Bibliothèque Nationale, Paris. Detail.

Fig. 6: Miniature from Rashid ad-Din's History of the World. A.D. 1317. Istanbul.

Fig. 7: Lorenzo Ghiberti: Lion-mask with ring. Baptistery, Florence.

Fig. 8 (down left): Rembrandt: Portrait of Jan Lutma. Etching.

Fig. 9 (down right): Head of a demon from a tomb door. Chinese, Han period. Szechwan Provincial Museum.

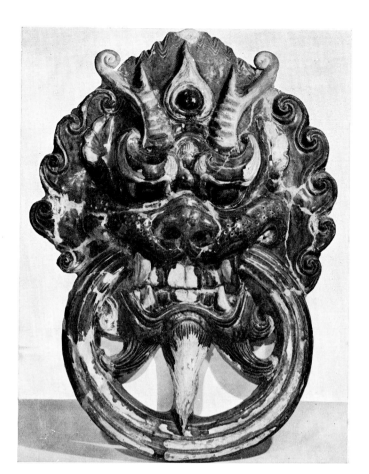

Fig. 10: Ceramic mask of a dragon. Chinese, T'ang period. Fitzwilliam Museum, Cambridge.

Fig. 11: Wine container with dragon-mask. From a porcelain dish. Chinese, eighteenth century.

Fig. 1: "Paradiesgärtlein", Städelsches Kunstinstitut, Francfort s/Main.

Fig. 3: Reliquaire, SS. Giovanni et Paolo, Venise.

Fig. 2: Stefano de Verona, "Madone au Buisson de Roses", Musée de Castelvecchio, Vérone.

Fig. 4: "Le Bain de Bethsabée et l'histoire de Suzanne", page d'un Livre d'Heures français.

Fig. 5 : "La Capture de la Licorne", tapisserie.
The Cloisters, Metropolitan Museum, New-
York.

Fig. 7 : Gérard David (attribué à), "Fontaine de Sang"

Fig. 6 : Jean Colombe, "Le Jardin d'Eden",
miniature du Livre d'Heures de Louis de Laval.

Fig. 8 : Jean Bellegambe, "Fontaine de Sang"
(détail), Musée de Lille.

Fig. 9: "Sources médicinales de Pouzzoles", miniatures de la fin du 14ème siècle, Naples. Coll. particulière.

Fig. 10: Maître aux Banderoles, "Fontaine de Jouvence", gravure au burin (v. note 46).

Fig. 11: Hans-Sebald Beham, "Fontaine de Jouvence" (détail), gravure sur bois (v. note 47).

Fig. 2: Cambridge, University Library, T.-S. K.5.10, folios 2v and 5r: end of Alphabet and Benediction.

Fig. 4: Cambridge, University Library, T.-S. K.5.1, folios 1r and 4v: geometric carpet-page and Leviticus I, 8–9.

Fig. 1: Cambridge, University Library, T.-S. K.5.10, folios 2r and 5v: Leviticus I, 1–2.

Fig. 3: Cambridge, University Library, T.-S. K.5.1, folios 1v and 4r: dragon carpet-page and Leviticus I, 3–8.

BEZALEL NARKISS: ILLUMINATED HEBREW CHILDREN'S BOOKS

Fig. 5: Cambridge, University Library, T-S. 16.378, folios 1v and 2r: Title-page, Leviticus I, 10–13, and colophon.

Fig. 6: Cambridge, University Library, T-S. K.5.13, folios 1r and 2v: Alphabet and Candelabrum.

Fig. 7 : Jerusalem, Jewish National and University Library, MS. Heb. 8°2230, folios 33v and 34r : Carpet-page and colophon.

Fig. 8 : Jerusalem, Jewish National and University Library, MS. Heb. 8°2230, folios 3v and 4r : beginning of the text.

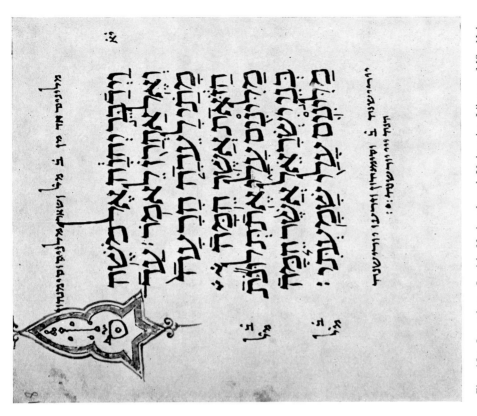

Fig. 10: Jerusalem, Jewish National and University Library, MS. Heb. 8°2230, folio 18r: Closed *Parshiyah* sign.

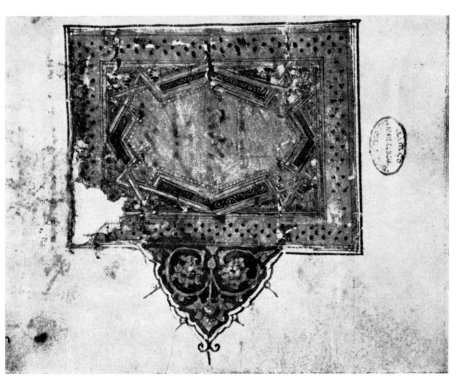

Fig. 9: Jerusalem, Jewish National and University Library, MS. Heb. 8°2230, folio 3r: Carpet-page.

Figs. 1–4: Eagle, Acre, Municipal Museum.

Fig. 5 : Capital, Jerusalem, El-Aksa.

Fig. 6 : Capital, Jerusalem,
    Cenaculum.

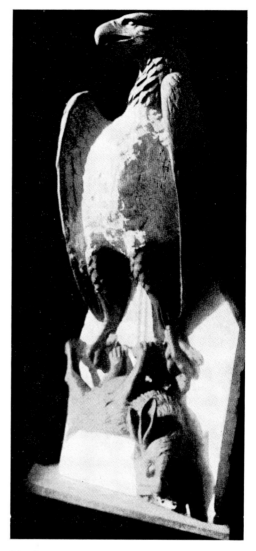

Fig. 8 : Eagle, Catania (Sicily), Castel Ursino.

Fig. 7 : Byzantine Marble Slab, London, British Museum.

Fig. 9: Pulpit (detail), ca. 1170, Salerno.

Fig. 11: Sonder-Augustalis of Friedrich II, Vienna, Kunsthistorisches Museum.

Fig. 10: Relief with Eagle and Lion, Central Italy, second half of XIIth century, Boston, Museum of Fine Arts.

Fig. 13: Eagle, Mosaic, Palermo, Royal Palace, Roger Chamber.

Fig. 12: Eagle, Bronze, Private Collection.

Fig. 1: Hieronymus Bosch. Les Se
Péchés, table peinte, Madrid, Prado.

Fig. 2: Le Jugement Dernier, détail
fig. 1.

Fig. 3 : Hieronymus Bosch. Le Char de Foin, Fig. 4 : Hieronymus Bosch. Le Jugement Dernier, pan-
panneau droit, Madrid, Prado.   neau droit, Vienne, Akademie der Bildenden Künste.

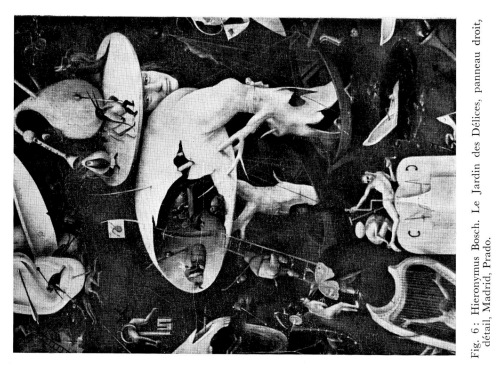

Fig. 6: Hieronymus Bosch. Le Jardin des Délices, panneau droit, détail, Madrid, Prado.

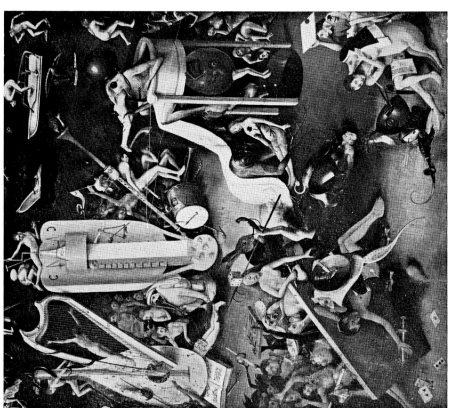

Fig. 5: Hieronymus Bosch. Le Jardin des Délices, panneau droit, détail, Madrid, Prado.

MOSHE LAZAR : CARO, MUNDUS ET DEMONIA

Fig. 7 : Hieronymus Bosch. La Nef des Fols, Paris, Louvre.

Fig. 1: Urbino, Palazzo Ducale, Grand Courtyard, as it is today.

Fig. 2: Urbino, Palazzo Ducale, Atrium leading to Grand Courtyard.

Fig. 3: Urbino, Palazzo Ducale, Capella del
Perdono.

Fig. 4: Piero della Francesca. Madonna and
Child with Saints, Milan, Brera.

Fig. 5 : Perugino. Consignement of the Keys to St. Peter, Rome, Sistine Chapel.

Fig. 6 : Bramante. Milan, Sta Maria Presso S. Satiro, Crossing and Choir.

Fig. 7 : Bramante. Rome, S. Pietro in Montorio, The Tempietto.

Fig. 8 : Raphael. The Marriage of the Virgin Milan, Brera.

Fig. 1: Chagall, Reuben. — Fig. 2: Chagall, Creation (*Verve* 37–38). — Fig. 3: Chagall, Creation (*Verve* 37–38). — Fig. 4: Chagall, Simeon. — Fig. 5: Saul Raskin, *Creation* theme, *Sabbath plate, Siddur Tefiloth Yisrael*, New York, 1945, pl. 83.

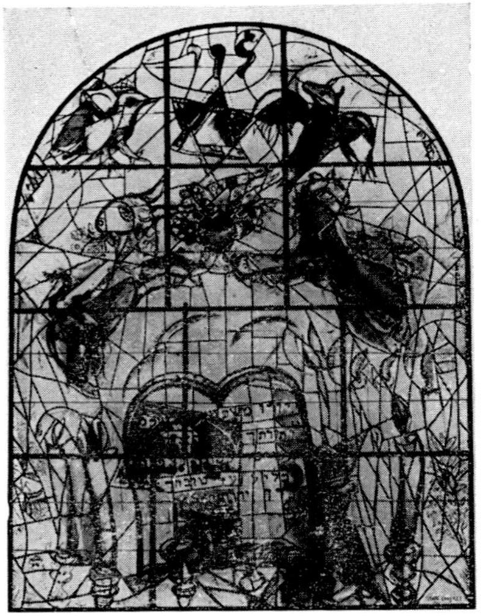

Fig. 6: Chagall, Levi.

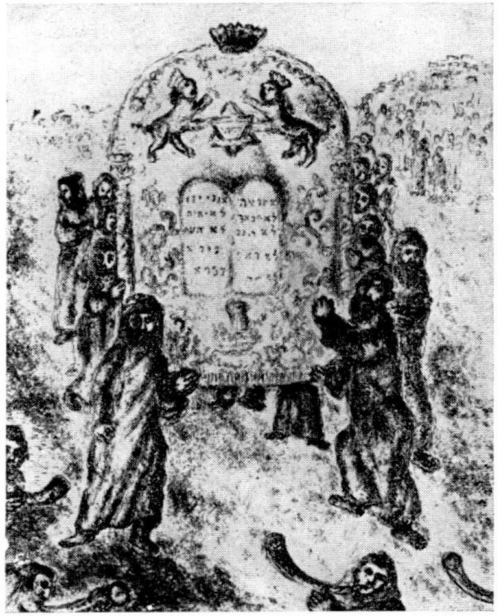

Fig. 7: Chagall, Tabernacle (*Verve* 33–34).

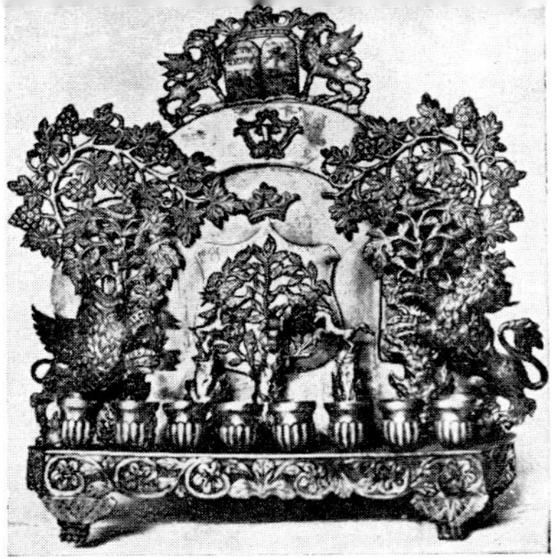

Fig. 8: Menorah (Guttmann, *Hebraica*, pl. XVIII).

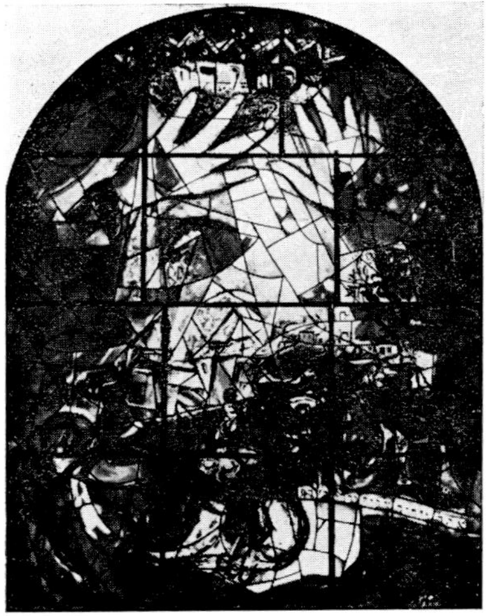

Fig. 9: Chagall, Judah.

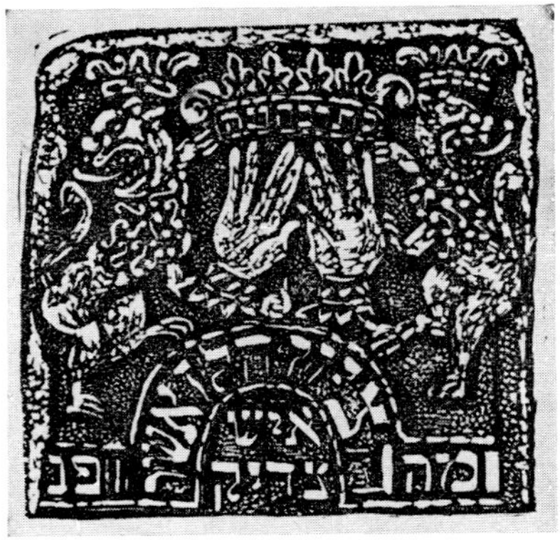

Fig. 10: Tombstone with Keter Kehunah (Yudovin and Malkin, *Jewish Folk Ornament*, pl. 5).

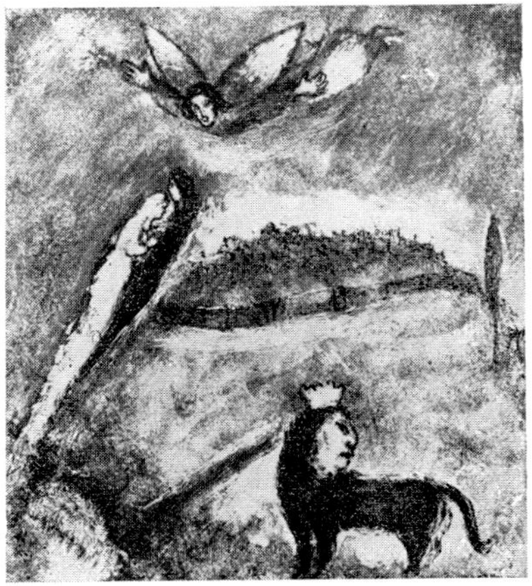

Fig. 11: Chagall, Future Happiness of Jerusalem (*Verve* 33–34).

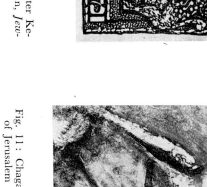

Fig. 12: Chagall, Zebulun.

Fig. 13: Chagall, Issachar.

Fig. 14: Chagall, Heureux l'Homme (*Verve* 37–38).

Fig. 15: Tombstone (Yudovin and Malkin, pl. 16).

Fig. 16 : Chagall, Dan.

Fig. 17 : Temptation (Yudovin and Malkin, pl. 23).

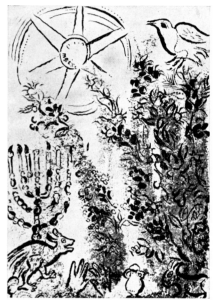

Fig. 19 : Chagall, Sketch connecting Gad
and Asher.

Fig. 18 : Chagall, Gad.

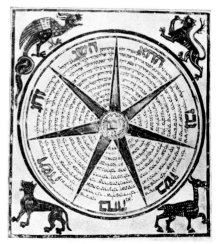

Fig. 20 : Thirteenth century Bible page.

Fig. 21 : Chagall, Sketch connected to Gad.

Fig. 22 : Thirteenth century Bible page

Fig. 23 : Detail of a Table from a thirteenth century Bible.

Fig. 25 : Detail of a page in the Bible of the Duke of Alba.

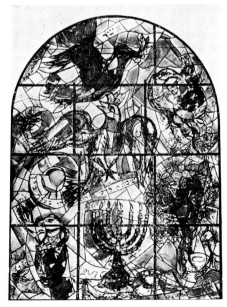

Fig. 24 : Chagall, Asher.

Fig. 26 : Chagall, Zachariah's Candelabrum.

Fig. 27: Chagall, Naphtali.

Fig. 28: Jak Messenblum, Votive Tomb Plaques.

Fig. 29: Chagall, Joseph.

Fig. 30: Chagall, Benjamin.

Fig. 31: Jak Messenblum, Votive Tomb Plaque

SCRIPTA HIEROSOLYMITANA

פרסומי האוניברסיטה העברית